Praise for

THE ELEPHANT AND THE DRAGON

"In *The Elephant and the Dragon,* her fast-paced, readable and revealing book, Robyn Meredith traces the emergence of the two Asian behemoths and looks at the repercussions that their rise will have on the West. . . . She has seen how business works in China and India, and in this multifaceted book she casts a reporter's eye on their convoluted growth, their limitations and their future."
—Chris Nicholson, *International Herald Tribune*

"*The* book to read on the extraordinary economic expansions of India and China, the two most populous nations on earth. Robyn Meredith has produced a well-written and well-researched work chronicling and analyzing the most profound, tectonic shift in economics since the rise of the U.S." —Steve Forbes

"In *The Elephant and the Dragon,* Robyn Meredith, a Hong Kong–based correspondent for *Forbes* magazine, neatly navigates between the boom and the gloom. Her account of India and China today is accessible to the general reader but also brimming with enough data and first-person reporting to get the attention of even those jaded by the recent breathless coverage of Bangalore and Beijing." —Matthew Rees, *Wall Street Journal*

"Meredith upends conventional wisdom in this well-reported book, arguing that the U.S. shouldn't fear these two rising economic powers." —*Publishers Weekly*

"Describes the rise of the two giants in vigorous prose and with a wealth of anecdotes." —Leslie P. Norton, *Barron's*

"One of the best books available about the economic changes underway in both countries. Ms. Meredith brings to the subject deep experience and knowledge of both countries, and a gift for synthesizing a vast array of data in an accessible and lively way, and discerning underlying trends. This [is] a behemoth of a subject, so the book's brevity comes as a pleasant surprise for the reader, and is a tribute to the author's discipline in distilling her arguments. She blends history, vivid anecdotes, personal experience, economic analysis and even occasional bursts of ideological exhortation to produce a work that leaves the reader with a comprehensive understanding of the essence of the transformations in India (the elephant) and China (the dragon)."

—David Plott, *Far Eastern Economic Review*

"In this thought-provoking and well-researched book, the author advises that the U.S. must strengthen its education system, promote innovation, forget about protectionism or unfettered free markets, and focus on creating jobs." —Mary Whaley, *Booklist*

"Airport bookstore shelves groan with new releases comparing India and China, and Ms. Meredith has written the best. She brings insights gathered in countless reporting trips as a regional correspondent for *Forbes* magazine. And unlike most, this tale is a rollicking good read. She gets straight to the point of how the simultaneous emergence of these two giants is affecting how the whole world does business."

—Mary Kissel and Hugo Restall, *Wall Street Journal Asia*

For Norm,
Another China hand. Thank you
for telling me of your adventures!

THE
ELEPHANT AND
THE DRAGON

THE RISE OF INDIA AND CHINA
AND WHAT IT MEANS FOR
ALL OF US

ROBYN MEREDITH

W. W. NORTON & COMPANY
NEW YORK · LONDON

For information about permission to reproduce selections from this book,
write to Permissions, W. W. Norton & Company, Inc.,
500 Fifth Avenue, New York, NY 10110

Manufacturing by Courier Westford
Book design by Chris Welch
Production manager: Julia Druskin

Library of Congress Cataloging-in-Publication Data

Meredith, Robyn.
    The elephant and the dragon : the rise of India and China and what it
means for all of us / Robyn Meredith.—1st ed.
        p. cm.
    Includes bibliographical references and index.
    ISBN 978-0-393-06236-6 (hardcover)
    1. India—Economic conditions—21st century. 2. India—Foreign economic
relations. 3. China—Economic conditions—21st century. 4. China—Foreign
economic relations. 5. United States—Economic conditions—21st century.
6. United States—Foreign economic relations. 7. Globalization. I. Title.
HC435.3.M47 2007
330.951—dc22

                                                            2007009028

ISBN 978-0-393-33193-6 pbk.

W. W. Norton & Company, Inc.
500 Fifth Avenue, New York, N.Y. 10110
www.wwnorton.com

W. W. Norton & Company Ltd.
Castle House, 75/76 Wells Street, W1T 3QT

6 7 8 9 0

For
Christopher

CONTENTS

Introduction: Tectonic Economics 9

CHAPTER 1   Where Mao Meets the Middle Class 15

CHAPTER 2   From the Spinning Wheel to the
Fiber-Optic Wire 38

CHAPTER 3   Made by America in China 58

CHAPTER 4   The Internet's Spice Route 76

CHAPTER 5   The Disassembly Line 97

CHAPTER 6   India's Cultural Revolution 117

CHAPTER 7   Revolution by Dinner Party 138

CHAPTER 8   Geopolitics Mixed with Oil and Water 159

CHAPTER 9   A Catalyst for Competitiveness 188

Afterword 214

Acknowledgments 217

Notes 219

Index 237

TECTONIC ECONOMICS

In June 2003, Prime Minister Atal Bihari Vajpayee of India boarded a plane bound for Beijing. It was to be an historic trip. The last time India's leader had visited Beijing, nearly a decade before, China was a nation of countless bicycles and drab buildings struggling to propel its economy into the twentieth century before the twenty-first arrived. But even as his plane descended, Mr. Vajpayee could see what must have looked like a mirage: thousands of factories surrounding Beijing, almost all built in the previous decade, each offering steady paychecks and, with them, the long-absent dream of a better life. China had gone from the past straight to the future.

He stepped into a new ultramodern airport, only one of China's many. As the prime minister and his delegation drove into Beijing on a smooth new highway, shiny cars zoomed past endless construction sites as the silhouettes of hundreds of cranes loomed over the cityscape. Beijing featured wide boulevards flanked by shimmering new skyscrapers, most built over the preceding ten years as the Chinese economy took off faster than any other in modern history. The view from Mr. Vajpayee's car conveyed what mere statistics could not: China had left India behind.

For decades, the Indian and Chinese economies had plodded along, isolated from and ignored by the rest of the world. Their peoples were poor, with little hope for a better life. But in 1978 China opened its door to the outside world and India did not, and then their fortunes began to change.

By the time the Vajpayee delegation visited China, a quarter century after China began its transformation, hundreds of millions of Chinese had seen their prospects dramatically improve as the Chinese economy blasted off. Foreign companies had poured more than $700 billion into China since 1978—far eclipsing what the United States spent on the Marshall Plan, which helped rebuild post–World War II Europe[1]—and the foreigners had built hundreds of thousands of factories nationwide[2] and hired tens of millions of people. The average Chinese worker now earned nearly five times more than before the reforms began, and millions had bought cell phones, computers, and even cars and apartments.

India, by contrast, seemed stranded in the past. Its airports were decades old and crumbling. There were no new expressways—the nation's potholed, gridlocked streets were lined with squalid shacks. The poor in India's cities lived in slums, bathing and washing dishes in filthy canals that also served as toilets. India had grudgingly begun allowing foreign investment in 1991, thirteen years after China opened its economy, and then followed up with on-again, off-again economic reforms. True, the average Indian was better off than before economic reforms began, but not by nearly as much as the average Chinese.

Twenty-five years after China launched its reforms, the contrast was vast. Chinese incomes had grown to twice the level of Indian wages. Both were still poor nations, but by 2004, 89 percent of Chinese were above the desperate, dollar-a-day poverty line, as compared with just 65 percent of Indians.[3] Foreign companies invested just $15.7 billion in India in the fiscal year ending in March 2007;[4] they invested more than that in China every three months. India's economy was lumbering along, while China's was flying into the future.

How could this be? India had democracy, a vast English-speaking population, an established court system, and plenty of ties to the West. China had authoritarianism, few English-speakers, and no consistent rule of law. Yet Mr. Vajpayee could see it plainly from his car: China had raced ahead of India, and, for the most part, its people were better off for it.

O

THIS IS THE STORY of how India and China are changing their destinies and, with that, changing the world's. As they move from the ranks of developing-world countries toward superpower status, India's slow-but-steady approach contrasts with China's rocketlike rise. In plenty of other ways, India and China are as opposite as Gandhi and Mao. India is democratic, and China is authoritarian. Capitalist India is often antibusiness, and communist China is usually probusiness. Chaotic India is a riot of bright colors, a cacophonous nation with thirty different languages. Even India's nationwide time zone mystifies: it is a half-hour off from those elsewhere in the world, so at noon in New York it is nine-thirty at night in Bombay. China seems more straightforward: the national language is Mandarin Chinese, clocks line up with the rest of the world's, and—no doubt about it—the Communist Party runs the country.

While China's strengths are on display to Mr. Vajpayee and the rest of the world, many of India's are less visible.[5] When China closed its colleges during the Cultural Revolution, India nurtured its universities, educating a generation of doctors, scholars, scientists, and engineers. While China persecuted capitalists, Indian managers gained experience by battling it out in local markets, and its businesses are better run than China's today. India's invisible human infrastructure is the nation's mighty resource now that it has reconnected to the global economy.

The two countries have one thing in common: their transformations—and the way they will transform the globe—are as stunning as any the world has seen since America itself emerged onto the world economic stage. The impact can be seen from the falling prices on Wal-Mart's shelves, the rising prices at local gas stations, the shrinking size of many American paychecks, even in the air we breathe. It can be heard in the voices on the end of tech-support phone calls. It is noticeable from the way freighters float low in the waters of the South China Sea because they are so heavily loaded with goods flowing out of new Chinese factories. Most plainly, it can be seen in the raw numbers: India and China have become the fastest-growing big economies on the planet. They look set to stay that way for decades and are on their way to becoming economic giants within a generation.

Suddenly, both India and China have become a source of employees, co-workers, customers, and competitors. In boardrooms from New York to Tokyo and from London to Frankfurt, executives have now contracted India fever in the same way they caught China fever a decade ago. Business leaders who don't know the difference between a curry and a stir-fry have been checking into freshly built Asian five-star hotels, glamorous but for the fact that the visitors must brush their teeth with bottled water to avoid getting sick. They have been shuttling halfway around the world because the two up-and-coming nations are growing so rapidly that they make the economies in the United States, Europe, and Japan seem as if they are standing still. Suddenly, doing business in India and China has become the only hope for Western companies determined to quickly add new customers—the only way for Western executives to make stockholders happy.

Perhaps the most overwhelming changes are being felt in the newly global job market. As recently as the 1990s, activists worried that globalization would hurt the poor. They have been proved wrong resoundingly when it comes to India and China.[6] Capitalists from corporate America and elsewhere surely did not set out to help Asia's downtrodden, but they did. Call them accidental activists: in the past decade, hundreds of millions of Indians and Chinese have been lifted out of abject poverty as globalization has brought jobs their way— even jobs that pay what in the West would amount to appallingly low wages. Surprising for those concerned about the world's poor, just as it surely would have startled Gandhi, Nehru, Mao, and other twentieth-century politicians who tried to protect the poor from big business, the movement of jobs overseas has pulled hundreds of millions of people out of poverty's quicksand. It turns out that developed nations like the United States, Japan, and the United Kingdom are facing big job losses, while developing countries are winning jobs. Globalization has proved good for the poor even as it puts the American and European middle class under pressure.

This book explores how the ability to connect with those Asian workers with the click of a computer mouse has changed the way the world does business. Millions of jobs are moving across the world to Indian and Chinese workers who are willing to do the same work as Westerners—even specialized, white-collar work—for drastically lower pay. Westerners in many professions are suddenly finding they can no longer expect to be paid ten times more than those in the developing world for the same work. College graduates in India are happy to land a job answering 800-number customer service calls to listen to Americans complain. Meanwhile, tens of millions of young Chinese move from their villages to factory dorms in big cities to make clothes and digital cameras and computers for foreigners. Even highly paid U.S. and European workers now face long-distance competition for jobs: India and China each add more college graduates to their workforces annually than are produced by the United States and Europe combined.[7]

For the American and European middle class, this is the terrifying dark side of globalization. With more than a billion workers suddenly thrown into the world's labor pool, many unlucky Westerners will lose their jobs, and many will see their standards of living fall unless they take action to make themselves better contenders in the worldwide labor market. Farmers were displaced by the Industrial Revolution in the nineteenth century. Sweatshop workers lost their livelihoods to assembly lines in the twentieth, and just a generation ago American factories closed because blue-collar work began moving to Mexico. History is about to repeat itself, sending a spasm through the world's job markets.

O

YET THE RISE of India and China is about much more than jobs moving overseas: it is about a major shift in post–Cold War geopolitics, about quenching a growing thirst for oil, and about massive environmental change. This is tectonic economics: the rise of India and China has caused the entire earth's economic and political landscape to shift before our eyes.

Because the strands of the global economy are now knitted together more than ever, the changes in India and China are shaping the future for the rest of the world—fast, and in some surprising ways. Never before has the global market been so hyperconnected: imagine if the massive trade flowing over the Silk Road were combined with that of the Spice Route and this mix of global commerce were supercharged with modern technology. Today what India and China sell to the West is no longer carried on camels or in galleons, but on cargo flights, in container ships, or over the Internet.

This book strives to help readers make sense of how our world is being shaped by the rise of India and China—the countries whose potential impact over the coming decades is both feared and underestimated. *The Elephant and the Dragon* will show that the rest of the world can adjust to the rise of India and China—and even thrive. But first we must understand the two giant nations that have opened their doors and walked into the twenty-first century.

CHAPTER ONE

WHERE MAO MEETS THE MIDDLE CLASS

Y ou never know where you'll find Jesus. I discovered him in a toy factory in southern China, standing on a shelf of talking toys. This Barbie-doll-sized Jesus, with blue eyes and shoulder-length brown hair, spoke in a gently reassuring electronic voice: "No one can see the kingdom of God unless he is born again." Then another gospel: "For God so loved the world that he gave his one and only son." Mary stood next to him, and beside her was the toy Moses, who rather sternly warned kids not to covet their neighbors' wives.

The Chinese toy factory that made this "Messengers of Faith" line of dolls was nondenominational: Jesus, Mary, and Moses mingled with the Power Rangers, and Mickey Mouse, Barney, Elmo, and Winnie-the-Pooh were nearby. The two thousand workers in the factory turned out millions of toys each year, most of them headed to the United States. When the Qualiman Industrial Company built this factory in Nanhai, China, in 1995, it was surrounded by fields. Now all the farmland for an hour's drive in any direction has morphed into factories, and Qualiman is able to buy most of the parts for its toys within an hour's drive of Nanhai, whether fabric for stuffed animals like Pooh or the electronic innards that allow Barney to sing his "I love you" song. Indeed, in just a decade this single Chinese province—Guangdong, which boasts five thousand other toy factories[1]—has become the center of the $85 billion global toy industry, giving millions of Chinese workers a livelihood that simply did not exist a decade ago.

The metamorphosis from farmland to factories was fast: in 2000, 30 percent of the world's toys came from China. Five years later, a stunning 75 percent of all new toys were made in China. As it goes for toys, so it goes for shoes, car parts, computers, and thousands of other products. The siren song of China's seemingly inexhaustible supply of people willing to work for low wages has lured companies from the other side of the globe, and the nation increasingly dominates manufacturing in industry after industry. For instance, over the last decade, China has become the world's cobbler, exporting one out of every three pairs of shoes in the world.[2] China exported $1.3 billion in auto parts in 2001 but nearly $9 billion just four years later.[3] In 1996, China exported $20 billion worth of computers, cell phones, CD players, and other electronic devices. By 2004, China exported $180 billion, more than any other country.[4] For the nation as a whole, the change is astonishing: China now exports *in a single day* more than it sold abroad *during the entire year* of 1978, when China began opening its economy, and that has returned China to global power and reshaped the lives of workers in China and around the world.[5]

○

WESTERNERS SEE the dramatic changes in the flurry of Chinese-made products landing on American and European store shelves. India's Prime Minister Vajpayee and his delegation saw evidence of a modern China in its cities. But China's breathless sprint toward modernization began in an entirely different part of the nation. The inspiration for revolutionary change in China a quarter century ago came not from Western businessmen trying to make a buck or from Chinese government officials eager to open up to the West but from the very same people around whom the entire Chinese communist experience had been based: the peasants.

In 1978, China's countryside had been impoverished and hungry—sometimes starving—for decades as a result of communist reforms. In the collective farming village of Xiaogang in Anhui Province's hard-hit Fengyang County, annual income had dipped below three dollars per person per year. After Chairman Mao's 1958 Great Leap Forward and the famine that followed, people had eaten their own oxen, pigs, chickens, and dogs to keep from starving; sixty-three acts of cannibalism had been reported in Fengyang County alone during Mao's famine. But while the peasants' lives had improved slightly in the intervening decades, those who had survived the Mao years had little left to risk. Meeting in secret one winter night in 1978, eighteen Xiaogang families pressed their fingers in red ink to seal an illegal—even traitorous—pact that would break China's collective farming rules and contradict the core principles of Mao's communism. With crimson digits and sealed lips, the revolutionaries conspired to divide their collectivized land, with each family responsible for meeting a production quota. The villagers of Xiaogang then scattered to their plots and during the ensuing harvest reaped 153,000 pounds of grain, nearly four times the preceding year's 40,000 pounds.[6]

Today, the Chinese government celebrates Xiaogang as the birthplace of China's rural reforms,[7] the beginning of the nation's historic move from a government-planned economy toward a modern, market economy. Like many of the inspirational stories promoted by the Chinese government, it should be taken with a grain, or even a small handful, of salt.[8] But whether the tale of the Xiaogang peasants' pact is apocryphal or historical fact, or something in between, the crux of the story is true: reforms to China's agrarian policies provided the spark for changes that led to its modern incarnation and rebirth as a world power. China began its economic reforms not by building the factories and skyscrapers visitors marvel at today but by changing the countryside.

It is difficult to make sense of where China is going today without understanding yesterday's China. And not just to grasp the quiet desperation of the peasants of one village but to fathom the slow economic destruction of a nation over a thirty-year period after Mao's move to communism changed the life of every Chinese citizen, and finally to appreciate one man's dogged efforts decades later to reverse that move and bring China into the modern world.

○

IN 1949, CHAIRMAN MAO announced the formation of the People's Republic of China to the world. Much like his counterparts in the USSR, he wasted no time in transforming a nation into his personal vision of an egalitarian communist utopia. But because China was an agrarian nation, Mao's version of communism revolved around peasants, not the factory workers who were the focus of Marxism farther west.

In 1955, Mao collectivized farming. Farmers were no longer allowed to own land or privately to buy and sell what they produced unless they had grown it on small, private plots. In just a few years, production fell by 40 percent in a land that historically had been engaged in a constant struggle to produce enough food. Feeding the entire country, even in a year of good harvests, is difficult because China must feed 22 percent of the world's population with just 10 percent of the world's cultivatable land. By contrast, the United States could feed all of China's 1.3 billion people and still have crops from the fields of the breadbasket states of California, Texas, Nebraska, and Oklahoma to spare.[9]

The food shortages only worsened three years later, in 1958, when Mao's Great Leap Forward program combined rural collectives into communes of about ten thousand people each. Communist Party administrators told farmers which crops to plant, promising that the commune would provide workers with food, medical care, and other necessities. Peasants were required to turn over about a third of the grain grown by the commune to the state as a tax used to feed the cities, with the rest left to feed the compound. But ambitious county officials reported wildly inflated grain production in their regions, competing with each other to please Mao by confirming that his collectivization was a brilliant success.

In one county of Henan Province, officials boasted that harvests had doubled despite a drought. That won the cadres praise, but it raised the grain levy on the imaginary crop beyond the actual harvest. As a result, the commune turned in all its grain to the state and still fell short of meeting its quota. As the commune starved, party officials punished farmers for supposedly hiding grain. The ideology of the fledgling communist state and the stomachs of its people clashed, and the stomachs lost.

Meanwhile, Mao was determined to transform his nation into an industrial power. Peasants were required to hand over all private property—down to bicycles and cooking pots—first for redistribution from rich villages to poor villages, and later to be melted down in backyard furnaces. This nationwide archipelago of backyard furnaces was supposed to take China's steel production beyond Britain's. In some areas, good grain rotted in the fields because so many farmers were told to produce steel instead of taking in the harvest.

Peasants turned into skeletons. The nation's farmers, including the residents of Xiaogang, found themselves going to shocking lengths in order to find food. Communal kitchens were serving only thin gruel, so farmers hunted for frogs or rats to eat. Eventually they ate grass and leaves and even stripped trees of their bark. Some starving families resorted to a practice called *yi zi er shi*:[10] they traded a child for a neighbor's child, then killed and ate the skinny youngster, with the sickening knowledge that their neighbors were devouring their own.[11] Hundreds of thousands of peasants were dying. The bodies of those who starved stayed in fields or along paths when the living lacked the strength to bury them. In some villages, whole families perished. In some counties, whole villages vanished.

Mao's policies created a nationwide famine in which between 30 and 40 million people starved to death between 1959 and 1962. To compound the tragedy, the inflated harvest numbers and resulting heavy grain levies meant that during this famine silos were full, even in hard-hit Xiaogang's Anhui Province. Military granaries were stuffed. While its people starved, China was exporting grain.

Through such extraordinary and tragic means, Mao unquestionably achieved his aim of transforming China with communism: state-owned enterprises made up 77.6 percent of the economy, and collectives owned everything else.[12] No market-based economy remained. Following collectivization, in 1966 Mao introduced the Cultural Revolution, a bloody purge of potential political rivals and those labeled intellectuals or "capitalist roaders." In addition to the massive human toll, books were burned, Chinese art was destroyed, temples and monasteries were smashed, and contact with much of the outside world was severed. The nation's universities closed their doors, a move that would cripple China for decades. For more than ten years, the only education allowed was the study of Communist Party propaganda and of Mao's Little Red Book.

Over the twenty-seven years of Mao's rule, China made itself nearly invisible to the West as an economic force. The nation became a warehouse of political neuroses and an economic disaster. Mao had achieved his goal of egalitarianism for most Chinese—and in doing so, he had doomed China's people to become some of the poorest on the planet.

Mao died in 1976, and after the bitter power struggle that followed, the economic reformer Deng Xiaoping emerged as China's leader. Deng controlled a Communist Party that still clung to Maoism: the chairman's body was, and continues to be, openly displayed in the so-called Mao-soleum in Beijing. Standing in Mao's shadow, Deng, who was not quite five feet tall and came to power at the age of seventy-four, did not look like an agent of change. During Mao's reign, he had been purged twice and even sent to work in a tractor factory. Yet this small man's outsized ideas altered late twentieth-century history.

When Deng took the helm from the man Chinese called "the great helmsman," 80 percent of the Chinese population was still made up of tragically poor peasants living on collective farms, the families of Xiaogang among them. A billion people—one out of every five on the planet—were Chinese peasants. They were better off than they had been in the famine years following the Great Leap Forward, but not by much. The typical Chinese family lived in a mud-walled, straw-roofed house with dirt floors, perhaps raising chickens or a pig in the yard and growing vegetables or extra grain in a tiny private garden. The collectives still told peasants how many hours to work, what to plant, and when to harvest and, in return, gave them grain to eat. At the end of each year, the collective paid taxes to the central government and then paid each worker his or her share of the collective's proceeds. The average annual payout was $16 per worker. The worse-off, and there were plenty of them, gave up and migrated to the cities to seek better opportunities—as beggars. These were the options the families of Xiaogang faced that winter night in 1978 when they dipped their fingers in red ink and made a promise.

Not nearly as dramatic as their secret pact but just as verboten under Mao's communism, the agrarian reform that Deng instigated shuffled China's planned economy towards a market economy.[13] Like Mao before him, Deng began his reforms in the countryside. Land from the collectives was distributed to each household, and farmers began to be paid at the year's end on the basis of how much they grew on their land, rather than being paid for working for the collective. They were permitted to choose which crops to grow. Later, farmers were allowed to keep whatever extra crops they could grow after meeting their grain quota, and eventually farmers paid taxes rather than turning over their quota to the collective. Prices were still set by the government, but between 1978 and 1981 the government raised farm prices by 25 percent, triggering a bonanza for peasants allowed to grow and sell extra food. Later, Deng dismantled the state monopoly on purchasing and selling agricultural products and lifted price limits on most farm products, so farmers could charge what they chose for the food they sold. Farmers felt flush: between 1978 and 1984, rural Chinese saw their incomes rise by 15 percent a year on the average. They still lived on less than a dollar a day, but it was a vast improvement over the four cents a day they had somehow scraped by on before.[14]

With all the changes and new economic freedoms, peasants prospered, and finally had more money and more choice over their livelihoods. Some farmers grew more food, and some simply got out of farming. Small-scale shops, brickyards, and food-processing plants sprang up in rural China as peasants were allowed to leave the fields. Twenty-five years after reform began, there were 22 million of these small businesses—the kind that would have been illegal under Mao—ranging from roadside food stands to factories making auto parts. These pockets of rediscovered capitalism employed 135 million workers, most of whom had previously earned a living by working the nearby fields and who were better off for the change.[15] Some of the little companies served new markets created by the extra spending money: as a result of Deng's decollectivization, four out of every five rural families repaired or improved their homes. Mud-walled huts gave way to brick-walled houses, some with electricity. "The rural reforms triggered the largest housing boom in history," said David Zweig, director of the Center on China's Transnational Relations at Hong Kong University of Science and Technology. These internal reforms bettered the lives of hundreds of millions of Chinese, but they were largely invisible to the outside. Soon, China would begin to reconnect its economy to the rest of the world.

○

WHEN DENG XIAOPING took the helm, he knew China had to modernize, but hardly any Chinese citizens, or leaders, had even seen a modern city, much less possessed the expertise to build one. Deng therefore looked outside China's borders for lessons. In November of 1978, he visited Bangkok, Kuala Lumpur, and Singapore. Deng arrived in Singapore wearing a beige Mao suit, and as he stepped down from his Boeing 707, Singapore's prime minister, Lee Kuan Yew, greeted him personally. It wasn't the last of his considerations: although Singaporean rules barred smoking in air-conditioned rooms, the prime minister made an exception for Deng and had an ashtray put in all their meeting rooms. But Deng did not smoke, because he knew his Singaporean host was allergic to tobacco. The two men held three days of talks, and as Deng toured Singapore, he found a modern, technologically advanced nation suitable as a model for China's development. "That journey was an eye-opener for him," said Mr. Lee decades later, "a turning point."[16] It was indeed, both for Deng and for China. The ethnically Chinese city-state of Singapore was, and remains, famous worldwide for its stable, one-party rule and its lack of freedoms—the sale of chewing gum was not allowed until recently—as well as its remarkably rapid transformation from a developing country to a modern, capitalist one. The government heavily planned Singapore's economic development, building modern infrastructure and attracting foreign investment. Probusiness policies made the city an export powerhouse and quickly raised the standard of living of its people.

China's attitude adjustment was radical and immediate. The Singaporean prime minister saw Deng off at the airport, and after the visit, China's official newspaper, *People's Daily*, stopped referring to Singapore's leaders as "lackeys of the U.S.-British imperialists" and instead touted the city's achievements in building affordable housing. During the 1980s, Mr. Lee met Deng three times in Beijing. In 1992, when Deng was trying to jumpstart reforms, he sent no fewer than four hundred separate Chinese delegations—mayors, party secretaries, and other officials—to Singapore in a single year to marvel at what China could become if it modernized.[17]

Always a pragmatist, Deng sought to advance China through modest, deliberate steps, not with the abrupt, revolutionary nationwide change later tried by Gorbachev in the Soviet Union. After starting with agricultural reforms, Deng experimented with industrial reforms. He formed "special economic zones," limited areas where China suspended its usual antibusiness laws in favor of low taxes and streamlined business rules for factories making goods that would be sold overseas. Deng created the special zones to reintroduce China to the very force Mao had tried to eradicate: capitalism.

Foreign companies faced huge hurdles doing business in most of China but were encouraged to build factories in the zones and to hire thousands of Chinese workers to produce goods for the outside world. Early special economic zones were set up in Fujian Province, across the strait from Taiwan, and in Guangdong Province, near Hong Kong, where opportunistic Taiwanese and Hong Kong companies were eager to build factories that could be staffed by low-wage Chinese workers. Many of these companies were owned by families forced to flee China when Mao came to power. In 1984, Deng expanded his successful experiment, and China set up additional special economic zones in fourteen cities along the Chinese coast.

But the foreign owners of factories in communist China, even those whose families had fled under Mao, were in for a surprise. One of the early investors in mainland China was Edwin Chan of Hong Kong. His company churns out belts for Polo, Banana Republic, and Coach, among others. In 1989, he opened a factory in Dongguan, China, a two-hour drive from Hong Kong. He paid his workers $1.20

a day to make belts and wallets. A decade had passed since China began its reforms, but the villagers who worked in his new factory still had no idea what a finished belt was supposed to look like. They had never seen wallets, much less possessed anything to put inside them. Initially, workers had no idea that if the boss left the room, they were expected to keep working.[18] At factory after factory, the foreign owners were stunned by the time-consuming training the Chinese workers required in order to unlearn the habits they had internalized while working for the communist state.

Nonetheless, wages were irresistibly low by outside standards, and scores of factories were built in the special economic zones, first by the Chinese diaspora in Hong Kong, Taiwan, and Singapore and later by Americans, Europeans, Japanese, and Koreans. Meanwhile, other provinces experimented by giving state-owned companies the autonomy to choose which products to make. Deng Xiaoping kept up his push for gradual reforms. In the spring of 1992, when he was eighty-eight, the grandfatherly Deng toured several southern Chinese cities. This well-publicized tour helped reenergize China's reforms, as Deng encouraged his countrymen to dare to *xiahai*, or "jump into the sea of business." Mainland Chinese, who had been wary of embracing the capitalism so long portrayed as an evil, started companies in waves. Employees of overstaffed state-owned enterprises began to moonlight at privately owned companies or to open small businesses.

All the while, government officials faced the constant tension of dismantling communism while publicly claiming to be faithful to it. Deng said China was experimenting to find out what worked best through "crossing the river by feeling the stones," a Chinese expression meaning to take things step-by-step. Once Deng's experimental special economic zones thrived, China sought to entice more foreign companies to build factories so that they would hire thousands more Chinese workers. The government paved farmland into vast industrial parks designed to house the factories. It offered tax breaks and other incentives, and laid down phone lines and IT infrastructure. The central government pegged local officials' promotions to the number of jobs created, so the cadres dutifully displaced residents from historic villages if a company wanted to plow their homes under to build a factory.

Gradually, government officials became the "capitalist roaders" they had previously persecuted, even as they called China's new approach "socialism with Chinese characteristics." But however you choose to describe it, the transformation from communism toward a market-oriented economy was remarkable for its lack of political turmoil and bloodshed. No wall fell, no war was fought, yet China's tiptoeing away from communism was as momentous as any revolution. The economic revolution was silent, a howl in a soundproof chamber. Rising prosperity for one billion people, plus one of the biggest global business boom times, was gradually and voluntarily unleashed from within by Communist Party cadres, not triggered by a political revolt.

Deng may have betrayed Mao's memory, but he did so to preserve the party that Mao had brought to power. China's Communist leaders knew they had to accomplish a dual objective: to modernize China and to make its people more prosperous after the nation's decades of stagnation. The leaders calculated that they needed to engineer economic growth of 8 percent a year or risk protests that could lead to an overthrow of the party. In order to keep power, the party leaders had to create a perpetual dragon economy—and so they did. Above all, the Communist Party leaders prized political stability, and they were willing to reverse the very essence of party doctrine and accept capitalism to achieve it.

O

WHILE CHINESE LEADERS looking to the outside found inspiration in the Singapore model, they were at the same time horrified by the fate of their former ally the USSR. Seven years after China quietly began its economic reforms, Gorbachev followed suit with his own. His approach was radically different, though, because he called for revolutionary, not evolutionary, economic change as well as freedom of expression, an extra step the Chinese had always carefully avoided. The result, of course, was the end of the Cold War, the collapse of communism in Eastern Europe, and the disintegration of the Soviet

Union in 1991. Chinese leaders, obsessed with maintaining political control and stability, were terrified that China too would break apart.

Indeed, in 1989, when freedom was unfurling in Europe's eastern bloc, social unrest finally erupted in China. Whereas the events taking place in Eastern Europe led to democracy, the demonstrations in China ended in carnage. After weeks of prodemocracy protests led by students in Beijing's Tiananmen Square spread across the country, the Chinese government declared martial law on May 20. When China's leaders, including Deng, sent the army to Beijing to quash the protest, perhaps a million Beijingers poured into the streets to support the students. Old ladies scolded fresh-faced soldiers, and neighbors united to put roadblocks in the path of the Army's trucks and tanks. Then, as a late Saturday night gave way to the early Sunday morning hours of June 4, the Chinese soldiers began to shoot their countrymen. Students who refused to leave Tiananmen Square were killed, some run over by tanks, some shot in the back. Thousands died. After the square was emptied and a tank had destroyed the students' "Goddess of Democracy" statue, the army patrolled Beijing to keep order.[19]

One of the most moving scenes from that tragic confrontation came in broad daylight. The day after the massacre, as a column of tanks rumbled down the Avenue of Eternal Peace along Tiananmen Square, a slight man wearing a simple white shirt and dark slacks stepped in front of a tank. He stood still. The tank paused inches away from him. Television cameras rolled and onlookers were riveted. The tank turned, as if to go around this Chinese Everyman. The lone man moved to block it, daring the tank's driver to run over him. Again, the tank hesitated. Someone ran to pull the lone man—called simply "the tank man" by the Chinese Diaspora—out of the way. But his act of bravery and defiance is remembered almost everywhere worldwide.

China stunned its own people, and the world, when it violently repressed the peaceful protest. As China crushed a political revolution in the public square, Deng and his cadres pressed their economic revolution forward. Democracy remained out of the question, but for Deng and other Communist Party leaders, it was worth killing thousands of Chinese in order to continue the nation's march toward capitalism. China's government established a Singapore-style quid pro quo with the Chinese people: the Communist Party would allow economic freedom, but not political freedom.

Even today, a giant painting of Mao can still be seen from Tiananmen Square, a deterrent against democracy from beyond the grave. Nearly twenty years after the Tiananmen massacre and thirty years after Mao's death, Chinese are still allowed to carry only money, not voter's identity cards, in their new wallets.

○

POLITICAL REPRESSION wasn't the only remnant of the Chinese communist system. Even under the reform regime of Deng, Chinese technocrats continued to plan the nation's economic development using the same no-nonsense five-year plans they had relied on under Mao. Having reformed China's countryside and then some of its cities with special economic zones, Deng embarked on a much broader modernization effort. Because China's bureaucrats were accustomed to a planned economy—one in which the state controlled pricing and production levels—Deng used the five-year plans to map out the move to capitalism. Five-year plans were a technique Mao borrowed from the Soviet Union, but they are still in use in China today.

Deng Xiaoping stuck with Mao's planning technique but combined it with Singapore's development approach, starting with the basic building blocks of infrastructure. Beginning in the 1980s, China built new coal mines to feed its increasing need for electricity. During the 1990s, it raced to increase its natural gas and oil output. The nation constructed a new, modern power grid, nearly quadrupling the capacity of its generators over the period between 1990 and 2003.[20] There are still brownouts and power shortages, but without the increases China would not have been prepared to power the new factories and office buildings that the economic development effort was intended to create. To stay competitive, the new factories needed not just power but efficient ways to transport goods, whether across China or across the world. Without the well-planned infrastructure buildup, the nation's economy would have remained tethered to low levels of growth. To attract more jobs, Chinese officials knew the nation needed modern highways, ports, railroads, and airports. The centrally planned modernization effort continues today: China is building nuclear power plants vigorously, and plans to triple the amount of power generated by 2020.

Cargo ports have been built—including what is expected to become the world's largest port, near Shanghai—and more are planned, with railroads coming next. On the rails, there are bottlenecks and a massively inadequate cargo capacity to move grain, coal, factory goods, and other freight. China's dizzying industrial rush has created demand for 160,000 carloads a day on the railroads, but only 90,000 are available.[21] China plans to lay 62,000 miles of track by 2020, with one hundred rail projects already in the works, and to invest $240 billion in railroads by 2015. And while China's big cities already have new airports, the nation intends to spend more than $17 billion in order to build over forty additional airports by 2010.

China's most visible infrastructure project to date has been the building of new roads and highways. In 1989, China had just 168 miles of expressways; by 2004, it had built 21,500 miles. By 2010, it plans to have 40,000 miles and by 2020 nearly 55,000 miles,[22] equal to the total length of the entire American highway system. The developed world takes its roads for granted, but consider how the United States changed after building the interstate highway system: fresh vegetables from Iowa could be trucked to Chicago, giving farmers a bigger market for their corn. Factories could open in out-of-the-way towns, not just in neighborhoods near railroads and ports, bringing jobs to areas where farming or moving away had been the only options. Meanwhile, people began to drive from city to city, creating demand for cars, hotels, and even the roadside McDonald's hamburger.

The Chinese highways are already helping farmers and factory owners alike. Carl Walter, the chief executive officer of J. P. Morgan Chase Bank (China), enjoys long-distance drives across China. At a rural rest stop, he came across a truck with a thousand chickens in the back and stopped to talk to the driver. "I couldn't believe it," Mr. Walter said incredulously. The driver told him she was on a cross-country drive from the impoverished Jilin Province, northeast of Beijing, to the factory-filled Guangdong Province near Hong Kong—the equivalent of driving from Bangor, Maine, to Orlando, Florida. "She's arbitraging chickens between Manchuria and Guangdong," said Mr. Walter. "These guys way up there know they can get a better price for their chicken down there." Ten years ago, such a conversation would have been unimaginable; five years ago, it would have been shocking. Today it's surprising, but in just a few years it will no longer be taking place; there will simply be too many drivers converging from all across China.

Yet the highways—or rather, those traveling on them—mark severe geographical disparities in economic development. In China's rural areas, cars remain a rarity, and the new stretches of highway are eerily empty. It is different outside the big cities, where factories have overgrown farmland. Two kinds of motor-powered vehicles are prevalent there: luxury cars ferrying factory bosses between factories and city offices, and trucks piled high with goods bound for the nearest port. Both kinds zoom past a hodgepodge of bicycles hugging the shoulders of the new roads and race past wooden carts pulled by farm animals. Meanwhile, in China's big cities, where more and more Chinese can afford cars, rush-hour seas of bicycles have given way to epic traffic jams. The roads themselves seem to reflect the growing confidence of the Chinese people. In Shanghai, the expressways are brand-new, and the elevated portions often feature lights on the exterior walls, as if they were intended as a tourist attraction, the pride of a nation limited to pedal power until a decade ago. Near the international airport, the highway exteriors are lit in white neon; in the financial district, it is a show-off electric blue.

The pride does not seem out of place. After all, China's new infrastructure and its probusiness policies, combined with cheap labor, achieved what Chinese officials had hoped for. China has attracted thousands of factories and followed the successful economic model pioneered by Singapore, postwar Japan, and later Korea, creating jobs and prosperity through export-led development. Partnering with multinational corporations—the poster children of capitalism—was a gamble for China's Communist Party, but it paid off. Cities across China have metamorphosed like a real-life version of the computer game SimCity, as new housing developments and smoke-belching factories materialized alongside freshly laid roads paired with new electricity grids. Shenzhen, across the border from Hong Kong, was just a village when it was named one of China's first special economic zones. Within two decades, sleepy Shenzhen was transformed into a teeming city of over ten million people. It now has many skyscrapers, and because window washers there descend on a single rope from the roofs of buildings, they have earned a special name: spidermen.

○

CHINA NOW HAS HUNDREDS of central-government-regulated economic zones like Shenzhen and more than a thousand additional zones run by provincial governments.[23] Indeed, China's central, provincial, and local governments offered an array of benefits to persuade multinational companies to build factories in their respective zones, even competing with each other to attract the foreign investment that created so many jobs.

But it wasn't just jobs the Chinese were after; it was modernization itself. When foreign companies sought to open factories in China, the government insisted that foreign companies use, and teach Chinese workers how to use, their latest techniques, flooding a technologically antiquated country with know-how and spurring a speedy, latter-day industrial revolution. Aside from the requirements to transfer technology, the Chinese government made it more and more attractive for American and other foreign firms to build factories, hire Chinese workers, and bring in the modern world's expertise— whether the technology to run modern computer systems or the ability to build DVD players or modern cars—none of which China could do on its own.

Even with the lure of cheap wages and government incentives, however, it wasn't until the mid-1990s that foreign investment in China really began to take off. By 1995, China was on a tear; $38 billion worth of factories and other investments came its way that year, up from less than $5 billion in 1990, most of it in Beijing or Shanghai or elsewhere along China's coasts. By 2007, annual foreign investment was $67 billion, still well above the unprecedented level of $60 billion it had first reached in 2004. The stunning amounts invested,

along with what the Chinese government has spent building infrastructure, have allowed the nation to industrialize.

The transformation has been breathtaking in its scope and speed,
but there is still room for further changes: a quarter century after
reforms began, less than half the economy is truly part of the free
market, because the Chinese government still owns so many companies. By 2003, state-owned enterprises were down to 47.3 percent of
the economy, collectively owned enterprises stood at 6.8 percent, and
private companies made up the remaining 45.9 percent.[24]

Thus today China uses an unprecedented mix of economic models:
it remains a partly government-planned and government-owned
economy—a throwback to the nation's communist past—but a large
portion is now market oriented. The Chinese economy defies easy
description: it isn't fully communist, but it isn't fully capitalist
either. The University of Michigan China expert Kenneth Lieberthal
labels China's system "bureaucratic capitalism,"[25] and the China
scholar John Gittings calls it "state capitalism."[26] The Chinese political system is much easier to name: it is authoritarian. China remains
the domain of the Communist Party, which continues to censor the
press, quash political dissent, and shun democracy.

Despite the nation's economic gains, the human cost of China's
rise has been steep, particularly for the peasants, who, it turns out,
have seen a disproportionately small share of the benefits of recent
growth. While farmers were the big winners early in China's reform
efforts, in recent years their incomes have stalled in comparison
with those working in China's coastal cities, where incomes have
skyrocketed. Each of China's steps forward has exacted a price: building factories often meant lifelong farmers were thrown off land they
had tilled for decades and thus were deprived of their livelihood.
Breakneck development has caused terrible pollution. Water is
filthy, and worsening air pollution levels already trigger an estimated
750,000 premature deaths per year.[27] Horrific, preventable accidents
abound and often are blamed on local officials taking bribes to ignore
safety violations. Nearly 5,000 coal miners died in 2006 in China, for
instance, compared with 47 in the United States.[28] Some of the
abuses are free-market and some are government-planned. Despite

the low wages, many factory workers are forced to work overtime long into the night without pay, left unpaid for months at a time, or even locked in factory compounds like prisoners. And Chinese are being displaced by new economic policies under the current authoritarian regime just as they were under Mao. Outfitting big cities with newly planned roads and modern buildings often meant forcing the elderly to move from neighborhoods they had known all their lives.

Chinese government leaders have even coolly calculated that running roughshod over public opinion in the name of development will be harder in the future—and that they had better do it now while they can. When a Hong Kong tycoon[29] warned a Shanghai politician that he shouldn't encourage the construction of so many apartments, lest he trigger a housing bubble, the official insisted he had already considered the threat. The politician said that if the government wants to plan the city's real estate developments, they must be built now because when residents get richer, they'll make it harder for developers to clear their land. "In another ten years they won't budge," the politician said. "We're building like crazy because we have the opportunity."

Sometimes the Chinese government's coercion is a matter of life and death, not just real estate. Consider the one-child policy, which began in 1979. To enforce it, China formed a family-planning department with 300,000 workers nationwide. They are responsible for at least ten million coerced abortions and ten million sterilizations a year.[30] Although some families have evaded the rules, Chinese officials say that without the one-child policy, China would have 400 million more residents today[31]—a greater population surge than if every American picked up tomorrow and moved to China. As it did under Mao's communism, the Chinese government still places the perceived needs of the state well ahead of individual liberties. China tries to preserve stability by tamping down political dissent, censoring the Internet, newspapers, magazines, and television. Even eighteen years after the event, the government does not allow discussion of the Tiananmen Square massacre in mainland China. It has been remembered each year with a candlelight vigil in nearby Hong Kong, which Mainland Chinese newspapers are prohibited from mentioning. Students at China's most elite university, Beijing University, respond with blank looks when shown the famous photo of the Chinese man who faced down an approaching tank in Tiananmen Square; China's state-controlled media are still prohibited from publishing the tank man image, which is so famous in the rest of the world.[32]

Despite the continued political control, China's economic rise has moved the country forward and greatly benefited the majority of its people, and most Chinese would say they are far better off now than they or their families were a generation ago. Of course, nearly any-thing is an improvement over the starvation of Mao's famine. Peas-ants went from earning an average of $16 a year to earning $317 a year in twenty-five years, while the national average rose to $1,023. By 2008, the average income had reached about $1,165.[33] There are other ways to measure the gains. In 1978, the Chinese were involuntary vegetarians: just 5 percent of the average diet came from meat. By 2005, that proportion had jumped to 25 percent.[34]

Both urban and rural Chinese have prospered, but because there is such a gap between them, the Chinese government is now facing its biggest fear: instability. The number of demonstrations has risen sharply, particularly in rural areas. Farmers are frustrated because they see city dwellers earning much more money and because of the seemingly relentless corruption of local officials.

There are a lot of furious farmers. Tens of millions have become landless during China's breakneck race to build factories and infra-structure. Individual farmers now lease their land from the village collective rather than working for it directly, but many have had the land they tilled seized illegally by corrupt local officials, who pocket huge profits by selling it to developers. Farmers usually get little com-pensation. Others protest rampant pollution that has ruined farmland and rendered water undrinkable. They are behind many of the 87,000 local protests in 2005, which comes to 200 a day nationwide.

China has already been trying to even out economic development by connecting its thriving coastal cities with the struggling interior cities of western China via the new highways. "Within five years, they will have built what they need to connect central and western China to the coast," said Stephen Roach, chief economist of Morgan Stanley. The new roads will allow factories providing jobs and higher incomes to be built in areas that have been neglected in favor of the booming coastal regions near ports. "They have this basically infinite supply of labor and the further west they go, the cheaper wages are," Mr. Roach said. "The highways are key."[35] In 2000, during the eighth five-year plan, in order to head off protests and disaffection with growing income inequality as coastal areas boom, the government began its "Go West" campaign to develop western China. Between 2000 and 2005, construction began on sixty large-scale projects in western China costing $100 billion.[36] The central government has also been encouraging companies to build factories and real estate projects in China's hinterlands, where wages are lower. Seeking bargain labor in China's interior may not strike Westerners as worth the effort, since all Chinese labor seems bargain-priced compared with Western wages. But after years of development, workers in the coastal cities earn about four times more than those in the nation's interior cities. Western and Chinese companies alike are finding they can appease the Chinese government by fulfilling its development goals while lowering their own expenses by hiring cheaper workers in China's interior. China's efforts to bring parity to incomes in urban and rural areas are ongoing. During the eleventh five-year plan, which runs from 2006 to 2010, the Chinese government plans to build rural roads and irrigation systems and improve schooling and health care in the countryside.[37] The aim is to help pass along the gains of China's 577 million urban denizens to its 737 million rural residents[38]— before the government faces a full-blown rural revolt.

The government wants more of the country to look like China's flourishing coastal cities, where rice paddies have morphed into factories, millions of jobs have been created, and incomes have risen dramatically. Shanghai, for instance, has become a giant construction zone, its skyline dominated by skyscrapers and cranes. In 1978, Shanghai had just 15 skyscrapers. By 2006, there were 3,780 and counting, more than Chicago and Los Angeles combined.[39]

○

WHILE CHINA'S TOWERS reach toward the sky, Mao's image, but little of his philosophy, is still present in China. Tourists find his serene gaze staring out from posters, T-shirts, even novelty watches and other crassly commercial symbols of a changed China. While some Chinese can ignore his ubiquitous image in the way an American might ignore Mickey Mouse, few can claim to be free of his legacy. Tony Ma's life story mirrors much of the story of his country over the last half century.[40]

Today Mr. Ma is a well-trained executive working for an American company in China. But he remembers when that would have been impossible. And he remembers the cruelty of the Cultural Revolution. When Mr. Ma was a boy, Mao's Red Guards used to come in the middle of the night to visit the old lady who lived next door to his family. Her husband had criticized the Communists before he died, so the party blacklisted her. The noise piercing the quiet night is something he cannot forget. "The Red Guard made the lady kneel on hard wood and then beat her. The first night, they beat her for an hour," Mr. Ma said. "She cried so loud, she sounded like an animal." They came back and took everything she owned from the house, and then beat her five more times in the next two weeks. "It was scary."

A few years later, when Mr. Ma was fifteen, authorities dispatched his father, an Education Ministry official, to Fengyang County, the region where Xiaogang is located, to grow rice, feed cattle, and be "reeducated." The following year, Mr. Ma's schooling stopped, and he was sent to work at a steel mill near Beijing for two dollars a month. He cut metal all day long, studied in his dorm room at night, and for seven years—some 2,500 days of his life—he dreamed of getting out. "The scariest thing for me was that I might have to work in the steel mill the rest of my life," Mr. Ma said.

But "bourgeois" universities that were closed during Mao's Cultural Revolution suddenly reopened in 1977, and 400 of the steel mill's 2,000 workers were allowed to take the college entrance exam.

Mr. Ma was one of only three who were admitted to college. He studied chemistry in Beijing and met his wife there, and like many educated Chinese then, they dreamed of leaving the country. Mr. Ma won a coveted scholarship, and he and his wife moved to a different world—Stockton, California, and the University of the Pacific, where he earned his Ph.D. in biochemistry. Then it was on to Johns Hopkins for postdoctoral research.

When he finished, the former $2-a-month Chinese steelworker was hired as a scientist at Johnson & Johnson's consumer products lab in Skillman, New Jersey, where he earned $45,000 a year, as much as an entire Chinese town might have earned in the 1980s. He helped develop sweet-smelling shampoos and lotions. "I'm lucky," said Mr. Ma, now fifty-one, who has since joined B. F. Goodrich, where he spends half his time working in Hong Kong and half in Mainland China. His wife and two children are still in the United States. His son goes to Yale, and his daughter attends Duke.

Tony Ma's life in the last half century has followed the same track as his country's, all the way from poverty and brutality through to hope, hard work, and success. In fact, China has changed so much since he was marking time in the steelworks that today, young college graduates in Beijing know that a $15,000-a-year salary in China goes further there than a $45,000 salary in the United States, Mr. Ma said. They don't want to move to the United States or anyplace else, because they have lots of opportunities in the new China.

○

IT IS HARD TO BELIEVE that as recently as 1992, the same China that Westerners fear will soon dominate the world economy was still issuing ration coupons to its citizens. Middle-class families now own televisions, live in new apartments, and even pay to send their children to private schools. People have traded in their bicycles for motorcycles or even cars, some made by those same Western firms who dreamed of selling to China's masses. There is now a Starbucks Coffee shop on the Great Wall of China, and McDonald's has signed a deal with Sinopec, the huge Chinese gas station chain, to build drive-through restaurants along China's new roads. Over the past quarter century, China's gross domestic product has grown an average of 9.6 percent a year, a staggering figure.[41] By contrast, over the same twenty-five years, India's GDP has grown by 5.7 percent and the far larger and more mature U.S. economy by 3 percent.[42] The architect of Singapore's remarkably fast rise from poverty-stricken backwater to developed country said he is in awe of the breakneck development of China. "I go there every year, and I'm astonished each time at the speed," said Lee Kuan Yew.[43] In a few years, 100 million Chinese, a population greater than any European nation's, will have middle-class purchasing power. Modern China has arrived.

CHAPTER TWO

FROM THE SPINNING WHEEL
TO THE FIBER-OPTIC WIRE

Desperation brought economic change to India as swiftly as it had come to China, but more than one decade later and in an entirely different form. In 1991, India was flat broke. One hundred and ten million people had been thrown into poverty in just the preceding two years. Inflation of 17 percent ate into paltry incomes. By 1991, 330 million people, or two of every five Indians, lived below the poverty line. The government's finances had collapsed. India faced a crisis.

The nation's troubles weren't just economic, either. Rajiv Gandhi was running for prime minister. His family name has been as interwoven with twentieth-century Indian politics and just as star-crossed as the Kennedy name has been in America. With the nation's finances already in tatters, its politics hit bottom too: During a campaign stop on May 21, 1991, Rajiv Gandhi was assassinated. Out of the ashes of the ensuing nationwide emergency, India finally embarked on the economic reforms that would reconnect it so powerfully with the rest of the world. To understand today's India—and to forecast India's future—one must look back to those desperate times.

After Rajiv's assassination, his Congress Party won power partly on the sympathy vote. His widow, Sonia, was encouraged to become prime minister, but declined. Instead, the Congress Party chose P. V. Narasimha Rao as prime minister of a minority government, charting the course for a billion people struggling to get through the economic and political storm. In an echo of the grandfatherly Deng's ascension in China, Mr. Rao was an aging party warhorse, a seventy-year-old who had had heart-bypass surgery the year before. Mr. Rao was expected to be a caretaker leader, one placed in power in the twilight of his career until his teetering minority government fell.

Mr. Rao swore in his cabinet a month after Rajiv Gandhi's assassination. He named as finance minister the brilliant, upright, and utterly uncharismatic economist Manmohan Singh. Then he called ministers to a closed-door meeting and asked Mr. Singh to tell them the bad news: the nation was broke. Banks had cut off India's borrowings just as they might cancel a deadbeat's credit card. India's foreign exchange reserves had fallen to levels that would pay for only two weeks worth of oil imports. The International Monetary Fund (IMF) stood ready to help with a bailout, but only if India agreed to a number of reforms. Like a child whose parents threaten to cut off his allowance, India did not have much of a choice. Without external help, the lights would go out. Literally. Even more shocking to the politicians, for whom the early twentieth-century fight for independence from Britain still resonated, a planeload of India's gold reserves had been pledged to back new short-term loans from the West, and India's gold had been flown to London.[1]

The government reaction was swift and definitive. Mr. Rao announced to the nation that there was a financial crisis, and he immediately set about making changes on the recommendations of the technocratic Mr. Singh. From those blueprints came the basics of political and economic reform, many of the changes required by outsiders like the IMF. The economic crisis finally prompted India to race to unleash its economy.

As thermometers hit a scorching 105 degrees in New Delhi on Monday, July 1, 1991, India's historic reforms began. That day, Mr. Singh devalued India's currency by more than 9 percent in an effort to boost exports, paid for in much-needed foreign currency. On Tuesday, Commerce Minister P. Chidambaram announced he would lift long-standing restrictions on imports and make a number of structural reforms designed to further encourage exports. On Wednesday, the Reserve Bank of India raised interest rates to 11 percent to try to attract deposits. Meanwhile, Mr. Singh's currency move on Monday hadn't worked, so he devalued the rupee another 11 percent—a massive 20 percent drop against the U.S. dollar in the space of three days. On Thursday, Mr. Chidambaram abolished export subsidies as part of an effort to trim India's out-of-control budget deficit. Because those subsidies distorted trade, abolishing them had been on the IMF's wish list. The same day, the Central Bank governor announced that India would get a $2 billion loan from the IMF to avert the immediate crisis. On Friday, Mr. Singh declared that more "big structural reforms" would be coming, nothing short of a new industrial policy for the nation.

Messrs. Rao, Singh, and Chidambaram didn't stop after just one dramatic week. Over the next two years, the government introduced a reform nearly each week. The state-owned banking, airline, and oil industries were all opened to private investors. Led by Mr. Singh, India continued the reforms Rajiv Gandhi had started by eliminating the antimonopoly limits for big companies. Mr. Singh abolished much of the "license raj" that controlled both India's trade and industry by requiring licenses for many transactions—a move that cut red tape and corruption overnight. He lowered income taxes from 56 percent to 40 percent by 1993. And he allowed mutual funds and other institutional investors to buy shares in Indian companies on the Bombay stock market.[2]

For the nation as a whole, the effect was dramatic. The economy grew faster than it had in decades, and companies started hiring those out of work. Double-digit inflation dropped into the manageable single digits. Debt was paid down and the precious foreign exchange reserves built back up. Crisis had been averted. The lights were still on. India had had political freedom for almost five decades, but it wasn't until that hot July week in 1991 that the nation began an ultimately successful fight for economic freedom.

○

THOSE BROAD, ECONOMYWIDE ADJUSTMENTS produced dramatic consequences for ordinary families. When Narayan Rao (no relation to the former prime minister) was in college in the late

1980s, before India's historic economic reforms, jobs were so scarce that he wasn't sure what he would do for a living when he graduated. "Maybe I would've become a cop," said Mr. Rao. "My dad was a police inspector." Instead, he graduated with a computer science degree at just the right time, while India's economy was transforming. He and his brothers and sisters all have careers in India that were unimaginable before the changes of 1991. His little brother owns a company that makes jackets for Nike and Reebok. His little sister tests software for Novell. Mr. Rao works in Bangalore for Wipro Technologies, one of India's thriving tech firms. A recent assignment took him to Otis Elevators headquarters in Farmington, Connecticut, where he saw snow for the first time. His father was astounded when his eldest son outearned him only four years after finishing college.

To Westerners bred on the dream of advancement through higher education, Mr. Rao's story may seem routine. But in the India Mr. Rao was born into, his career trajectory was unthinkable until a few years ago. Today, millions of families like the Raos are prospering in ways that had never been possible in India.

○

BUT WHAT, EXACTLY, took so long? India had spent decades in self-imposed economic exile, and although it was a well-intentioned exclusion, it nonetheless kept its people mired in poverty. The roots of this isolation go back to India's fight for independence from Britain. The nation's emergence from colonial rule has colored every moment of postcolonial Indian history, from India's early moves to modernize its economy to political difficulties it has faced recently while reintroducing itself to the global business community.

Communism crippled China, but it was the reaction to colonialism that proved India's great handicap. India has been haunted by two lingering ghosts of the postcolonial period—Mahatma Gandhi's anti-industrialization tenets and Jawaharlal Nehru's socialism, which together caused India to withdraw from the world economy after winning its freedom from Britain in 1947.

Gandhi and Nehru were India's gurus, and, much as Mao's ghost hung (and hangs) over China, their philosophies and ideas were respected for decades after their deaths. By 1991, the nation was suffering because of the persistence of the views that Gandhi and Nehru had formed in their fight against colonialism. Their political views—socialism and economic nationalism—had been shaped by an India that was closer to the late nineteenth century than to the late twentieth.

Admired around the world for his advocacy of nonviolence and for his moral insistence on helping the poor, Gandhi supported policies that were meant to ensure India's economic independence from the industrialized West. He advocated traditional means of production, symbolized by his own daily use of a wooden spinning wheel, and asked Indians to stop wearing imported clothing and using imported goods, as a revolt against economic ties to a colonial power. Gandhi's insistence that only natural medicines be used led many, including his own wife, to forgo available vaccines and medicine. When his wife was dying of bronchitis in 1944, the British flew a supply of penicillin to her, but Gandhi refused to allow doctors to inject her with it, because he believed the use of needles violated his principles of nonviolence. He held her head as she died. Gandhi practiced celibacy for the last forty-two years of his life and believed that abstinence was the only acceptable form of birth control.[3] The result? India's population boomed and its scant resources were stretched because others were not as disciplined. His economic policies, too, grew to be just as impractical, for all their wealth of symbolic meaning.

Nehru, India's first prime minister, was a proponent of socialism. Central planning, as championed by China and the USSR, was popular during the post–World War II period. European nations, and even the United States, briefly used central planning, and India under Nehru was no exception.[4] During the fight for independence from Britain, Gandhi and Nehru dreamed of making India a self-sufficient nation. For most Indian politicians, support for economic nationalism went hand in hand with India's freedom movement. Fearing that foreign investors would become India's next British East India Company and effectively its new colonizers, Nehru made it difficult for foreign companies to invest in independent India, hard for Indian companies to export, and expensive for Indians to buy imported goods.

Gandhi was assassinated in 1948, but the Congress Party, nurtured by Gandhi and Nehru, continued its insistence on self-sufficiency and kept independent India from joining the booming postwar global economy. In the early years of independence, those autarkic policies helped homegrown Indian companies thrive, but over the decades, being shielded from outside pressure made many Indian companies lazy and uncompetitive.

○

INDIA'S BUSINESS ELITE was closely connected to the nation's freedom movement and, for the most part, shared its values. No business has paralleled India's nineteenth- and early twentieth-century history as consistently as the Tata Group. Jamsetji Tata, founder of the Tata Group in 1868, was a nationalist who dreamed of self-sufficiency for his country. In 1886, he started Swadeshi Mills to promote the purchase of Indian textiles instead of imported British clothing; decades later, Gandhi, with his spinning wheel, became the Swadeshi movement's most famous advocate. In 1902, Mr. Tata opened the Taj Mahal, the first Indian-owned luxury hotel, after being denied entry to a British hotel where he wanted to entertain clients. He thought India's independence as a nation depended on its economic strength, arguing that economic self-reliance was necessary for self-governance. He set out to make India self-sufficient in steel production, a dream he pursued until he died with a dogged search for deposits of the iron ore necessary for making steel. His son was able to realize the dream by founding India's first steel company, Tata Iron and Steel, in 1907.

His son's successor, J. R. D. Tata, supplied the steel needed for India's post-independence five-year plans. J. R. D. Tata was also a pilot, and founded India's first airline, which became Air India. At Nehru's request in 1952, he even created India's first cosmetics company, Lakme, so that women wouldn't complain when Nehru banned foreign cosmetics from India.

Having successfully campaigned for India's freedom, the Congress Party of Gandhi and Nehru stayed in power for decades as India became a democracy with one-party rule. Nehru's politics were heroic: his vision and idealism had led India to independence and left the vast nation, with all its social and economic divisions, an enduring democratic force in the world. But his economics, however well intentioned, kept India from realizing the commercial potential its size and natural resources should have allowed. Nehru's support for socialism, and the continuing support of his successors, kept many important companies state-owned or protected from world-class competition. They became sclerotic and hopelessly bureaucratic. In order to make their goods, many companies needed licenses granted by the government's "license raj," which became a semipermanent fixture.

By the 1970s and 1980s, laws that had been put in place with the best intentions in the early years of independence seemed hopelessly antiquated. Despite demand, a motorcycle maker like Bajaj couldn't make more scooters than it was licensed to produce, because it might violate India's antimonopoly rules, which had been designed to foster the creation of small companies nationwide as a way of encouraging self-sufficiency. Procter & Gamble's Indian arm once worried it would break the law if it made too much Vicks VapoRub during a flu epidemic.[5]

In the name of helping the poor, the Indian government passed laws granting lavish job guarantees to workers; back wages were owed even if their employers went bankrupt. Unfortunately, this made company leaders very reluctant to hire unless they could be sure a factory or office would be open for decades. (Today it still takes an average of ten years to close a money-losing factory because of India's job guarantees.) Government payrolls ballooned because layoffs were politically impossible. Since finding a job meant finding a job for life, political patronage became a way of life, and outlandish bureaucracy became a fact of life. Government salaries were low but conveyed power, and corruption festered at every level of government, as every license or permit processed provided an economic opportunity for the bureaucrat in charge.

The political dynasty of Gandhi and Nehru continued well beyond their lifetimes, and their successors shared not just their names but their economic theories as well. Jawaharlal Nehru's daughter, Indira, married a man named Feroze Gandhi, no relation to the Mahatma.[6]

Continuing her father's economic legacy, Indira Gandhi served as prime minister from 1966 to 1977 and again from 1980 until her own bodyguards assassinated her in 1984.

Only when Rajiv Gandhi became prime minister after his mother's death did it seem that a member of the dynasty finally recognized that India needed to change. In 1985, Rajiv Gandhi began to push through a set of reforms that repudiated his grandfather's and his mother's socialism. He changed laws to allow more imports and exports, cut taxes, and reduced the number of industries requiring licenses to produce goods. He raised the antimonopoly limits, allowing companies to grow to be worth as much as $80 million. That was still relatively small, but amounted to a fivefold increase. Indian bureaucrats following Gandhi's teachings claimed that telephones were luxuries, even in 1985, but Rajiv Gandhi allowed the number of telephones nationwide to double and trimmed waiting times. He lifted government price caps on goods like cement and aluminum. The consequences of all these actions were huge: the nation's economic growth doubled, and companies began hiring. Exports grew dramatically.[7]

But these boom times were short-lived. After two years, Rajiv Gandhi's reform effort withered in the face of opposition from government employees and farmers. He was defeated in elections in 1989 after high inflation squeezed voters. The overall economy was doing well, but the government, as well as individuals, faced a cash crunch as a result of some of his less farsighted policies: to fund India's increasing imports and greater spending, Rajiv Gandhi had begun using short-term borrowing from banks. It was like charging your weekly groceries to a credit card and making the minimum payment each month—it all goes smoothly until the bills and high interest rates compound over time.

This put India's finances in a precarious state, and then the perfect geopolitical storm hit India: oil prices spiked during the 1991 Gulf War just as the collapse of the Soviet Union put a damper on the barter system of trade between India and the USSR, in which neither used precious foreign reserves to buy goods from the other. At just this moment in history, while campaigning to return as prime minister, Rajiv Gandhi became the third famous Gandhi to fall victim to assassination. But Rajiv's economic ideas, like those of his grandfather Nehru and the Mahatma Gandhi, lived on after his death—and it was lucky for India, this time, that they did.

○

To Narayana Murthy,[8] the Bill Gates of India, the changes over that first, scorching-hot week in July 1991, as the nation reeled from Rajiv Gandhi's assassination, meant that his nation had stopped walling itself off from the world.

Mr. Murthy grew up in Mysore, a southern Indian city renowned for its silk. During his student days, he was a Marxist. He won a coveted spot in one of the nation's prestigious Indian Institutes of Technology in 1962, but he went to the local engineering college instead.[9] The tuition of $20 a month at IIT was out of the question, constituting nearly a third of the $66 salary on which his father, a local government employee, fed eight children. After graduating as a computer engineer, he worked for a software company in France, and later landed in Bombay and worked for Patni Computer Systems. In 1981, when Mr. Murthy was thirty-five, he persuaded a co-worker, Nandan Nilekani, and five others to borrow $250 from their wives[10] to start a company called Infosys Consultants. During their first decade in business, their little company, headquartered in Bangalore, just eighty-five miles from Mr. Murthy's hometown, did well by hiring Indian programmers to write software code for other Indian companies.

By 1991, Infosys had grown to 176 employees and even had an office in Boston, its first overseas. Of course, it wasn't easy for Mr. Murthy or any other Indian to get to Boston. Prior to 1991, trips abroad were nearly impossible. Consider that if Mr. Murthy wanted to visit his company's office in America, he first had to apply for permission from the Reserve Bank of India, the nation's central bank, to be allowed to convert his Indian rupees to U.S. dollars. For Americans, that would be like having to petition Alan Greenspan in order to go on a vacation to Mexico. But in July of 1991, Mr. Rao's government made the currency partially convertible,[11] and Indians suddenly needed no one's permission to go where they pleased.

Before 1991, when government-required paperwork was rampant and imports were discouraged, it wasn't easy to buy equipment from abroad. When Mr. Murthy or anyone else wanted to buy a computer and bring it to India, it took two years for him to win permission from New Delhi for an import license; by that time, whatever computer he had wanted to buy was hopelessly out of date. But when Mr. Singh in 1991 abolished most of the "license raj" that was responsible for those kinds of delays, companies like Infosys almost overnight were able to receive modern equipment, and India's factories rapidly modernized as well. Today Infosys still needs import licenses when it buys computers abroad, but the company can get them in half a day in Bangalore rather than in two years from New Delhi. The bureaucracy that had seemed onerous to Mr. Murthy and his fellow techies had been far worse for other industries. Because the technology industry was relatively new, it faced fewer rules from the "license raj." Companies in other fields rejoiced even more loudly as government restrictions were peeled away in 1991.

Starting in July of 1991, not only could Indian companies quickly get permission to import equipment duty free; they could suddenly buy imports at lower cost. As part of the old rules designed to foster self-sufficiency, India had at one time levied 150 percent duties on imported software, so a $100 Microsoft operating system would have cost a staggering $250—putting a computer far out of reach for most Indians, and making imported computers and software far too costly for most Indian companies. During the dramatic reforms that July, however, the Indian government abolished the duties on software, spearheading a computer revolution in India.

Other reforms were less welcome to Indian companies, and some even threatened to put Mr. Murthy's Infosys out of business. In 1991, the government allowed companies in certain industries, including technology, to be 100 percent owned by foreigners. In doing so, the Indian government was partially reversing a rule that in 1977 forced foreign companies doing business in many industries in India to give up control of their companies' Indian operations, typically by selling a majority of their Indian operations to the Indian public or to Indian firms.[12] The law was so controversial when it was adopted that IBM, Coca-Cola, and other big foreign investors threw up their hands and pulled out of the country. The rule had protected Indian companies from foreign competition, and striking it meant opening the doors to Microsoft, Oracle, and other powerhouse tech firms that could then compete with Infosys.

"A lot of my friends told me, 'Your future is destroyed,'" Mr. Murthy recalled. They said he should use his influence as president of the powerful Indian technology trade group NASSCOM to force the government to back off and leave the protectionist rule in place. He ignored them. "I always believed in free markets and I said no, we're not gonna do that."

Fortunately for him, there was more good with the bad. India has had a stock market since 1875—it was the earliest stock market in Asia—but for decades Indian companies had little incentive to use it. An office called the Controller of Capital Issues was in charge of deciding how much of a stake a company could sell on the stock market, and how much a company could charge for the shares in the initial public offering (IPO). The person in charge of deciding the price, typically a bureaucrat with no training in how stock markets worked, set prices arbitrarily, usually for low amounts that seldom reflected how much a company was worth. Mr. Murthy and his partners had a decision to make in the 1980s: should they take Infosys public, raising money on the stock market to expand faster? The Controller of Capital Issues would have set the price around 50 cents a share, about 25 rupees, even though the company was worth four times as much. So Mr. Murthy and his partners decided to hold off, refusing to sell the company they had built for a price they knew was absurd.

During the 1991 reform spree, the Indian government abolished the office that controlled stock market pricing and let companies and their investment banks decide on a fair offering price, just the way IPOs are handled at big stock markets around the world. The following year, Infosys went public. At 95 rupees a share, about $2, the IPO raised four times more money than it would have under the old rules.

Since then, his company—now called Infosys Technologies and a rival to Wipro, where Narayan Rao found work when he graduated from college—has grown from $2 million in revenue to more than $2 billion. Infosys, one of the nation's showcase tech companies, by 2008 employed more than 80,000 Indians at impressive salaries.[13] Mr. Murthy's Infosys has a Microsoft-like reputation in India: more than 300 of its employees became millionaires, thanks to stock options and the company's rising stock price. The same smart student whose family couldn't afford $20 a month for him to go to an elite school is now worth $1.7 billion, according to *Forbes* magazine. By creating jobs and hope for the future for so many young Indians, Mr. Murthy's much-admired Infosys represents a belated realization of Gandhi's and Nehru's dreams for a self-sufficient, independent India. Admirers have come from around the world. Microsoft's Bill Gates, China's Zhu Rongji, Singapore's Lee Kuan Yew, and even Britain's Tony Blair each commemorated his visit by planting a sapling on the spacious Infosys campus in Bangalore.[14]

○

THE CHANGES OF 1991 led to an economic boom not just for Infosys but for the nation. Yet the reform process that began with such a bang sputtered after only a few years. Once India put the 1991 crisis behind it, little sense of urgency remained. India's ideological left and entrenched interests hurt by the changes opposed the reform effort. In 1996, a massive corruption scandal caused voters to throw out the Congress Party and elect a left-leaning coalition of farmers and social justice parties. Economic reforms were all but halted. Since Mr. Rao's government fell in 1996, India's governments have been unstable; after decades of one-party rule, democratic India had five different administrations in the following decade. Economic reforms stalled, then restarted and generally lumbered forward, with some disappointing setbacks along the way.

Meanwhile, in the mid-1990s, India's intellectual, business, and political leaders started to talk about China's rise. India's intelligentsia believed that China's lightning-fast advancement was unsustainable. They predicted trouble after Britain handed free-wheeling

Hong Kong back to authoritarian China in 1997. They were wrong. After the handover, China remained stable and fast-growing, year after year, while India remained stuck at what professor Raj Krishna of the Delhi School of Economics called in the mid-1970s the "Hindu rate of growth," 3.5 percent a year, barely a third of China's growth rate. Soon India, like many other countries around the world, including the United States, became afraid of China's rise. The fear was that soon everything sold in India would be made in China. Indian government officials began to think, "China is really going to swamp us unless we do something," explained Ratan Tata,[15] scion of the Tata Group, now India's largest non-government-owned business group.[16]

China was just the latest threat. Many Indian businesses struggled to compete with more efficient foreign companies after the market-opening reforms, and many old-line Indian firms were unable to adapt. For instance, before 1991, 90 percent of India's refrigerators were Indian-made by stalwarts like Godrej & Boyce and Tata's Voltas unit. By 2006, foreign companies had overtaken the Indian brands: Korea's LG sold 30 percent of the refrigerators in India, Whirlpool sold 24 percent and Godrej was third with just 13 percent of the market.[17]

The challenges facing the century-old Tata Group once again paralleled those facing the nation. When Ratan Tata took the reins during the 1991 economic crisis, many of the conglomerate's complacent companies were unable to compete outside India or even against foreign companies selling in India. Voltas restructured, sold factories, jettisoned more than half its employees, and partnered with foreign brands to return to profitability. Venerable Tata Steel was one of the toughest cases. Despite its role as a pillar in company history and its proud association with India's independence movement, Tata Steel was so far behind the times by 1991 that Mr. Tata told management he would shut it down unless they turned it around. After managers recovered from the shock, they buckled down, and in a few years made it into one of the world's most efficient steel producers. The story was the same for company after company in the Tata stable.

Because he proved that even India's oldest companies could thrive on the world stage after India opened its economy, Mr. Tata became India's most respected business leader—GE's Jack Welch and renowned investor Warren Buffett rolled into one. When he arrives at work at Tata headquarters in Bombay, Mr. Tata walks past a white marble bust of his great-grandfather, the company founder, then a bronze bust of his predecessor, J.R.D. Tata. Most days, those monuments remain silent reminders of family and company history. But such is the affection for the Tata family that the birthdays of Ratan Tata's ancestors are marked by visits from company employees and other Bombayites, who come to adorn the statues with hundreds of fresh flower garlands as if they are Hindu deities in a temple.

Meanwhile, Ratan Tata, an American-educated architect, has continued his family's pioneering tradition. He built the nation's first India-developed passenger car, and created the Nano, a $2,500 automobile designed to make cars affordable to millions more Indians. Today his group of companies is at the head of a class of Indian businesses that are buying foreign companies, including Britain's Tetley Teas, The Pierre hotel in New York, and even AT&T's old undersea cable carrying telecommunications out of India.

But along with the rest of India's global business elite, Mr. Tata watched China race ahead, growing more and more frustrated that India had halted its own economic rise and thus forced much of its own population to remain poor, even as Chinese were climbing out of dire poverty. "Many of us were saying, 'Look at the growth rate in China, then look at ours!'" Mr. Tata said. "For a long while, there was denial, there were excuses. Suddenly, there was an awakening."

Indian politicians finally began to turn to China for inspiration, much as China once looked to Singapore's example. Back in 1994, the chief minister of the Indian state of Andhra Pradesh, N. Chandrababu Naidu, began dispatching waves of state government officials to Beijing, Shanghai, and the boomtown of Shenzhen. "He sent all his legislators to China with the mandate that they should come back and give him at least two ideas each about how India could improve," said Mr. Murthy of Infosys. "After our politicians went to China, they saw how China is creating a bigger and bigger difference in terms of infrastructure." This was the only way to persuade naysayers of the need for action, according to Mr. Naidu. He has since turned Andhra Pradesh, especially its capital city of Hyderabad, into a high-tech magnet. "I made it a point to talk about China," he said. "But ultimately, seeing it is believing."[18]

○

INDEED. BACK IN 2003, Prime Minister Vajpayee of India told his Chinese hosts in Beijing, "We are the two most populous countries of the world and we have the two fastest-growing economies in the world—yours faster than ours." Then Mr. Vajpayee got back on Air India One, flew back to Delhi, landed in his dilapidated airport, and was driven home along a bumpy road. At last, there was consensus among India's national leaders that rejoining the world economy as China had done was in India's best interest—a historic turn for a post-colonial nation that had for so long preferred self-reliance.

China is still far ahead, but India is finally on its tail. Both are rushing headlong into the modern world as Chinese and Indians are increasingly making what Westerners buy, answering their customer service phone calls, or themselves buying Western-branded goods. Globalization has clearly benefited both India and China greatly, lifting 200 million Indians and Chinese out of poverty during the 1990s[19] and catapulting tens of millions more far ahead into middle-class life.

Today India is frantically racing to catch up to China. Indians are still confident that reforms can be counted on to bring them up to speed. "Unfortunately, we started reforms late, but now reforms have taken off," said Mr. Naidu, and the average Indian is better off. "Even the rickshaw puller has a cell phone. Even a vegetable seller has a cell phone."

In the latest elections, the Congress Party president, Sonia Gandhi—widow of Nehru's grandson Rajiv—was reportedly again offered the chance to be prime minister, but she declined in favor of a trusted reformer, none other than Manmohan Singh, the liberal economist who was finance minister in 1991. He in turn has named Mr. Chidambaram, who helped him with the 1991 reforms, as his finance minister. There is a consensus within Mr. Singh's government that India needs to be more like China—to build roads and airports, and to draw in more foreign investment, leading to more jobs for Indians. "We got more done for the poor by pursuing the competition agenda for a few years than we got done by pursuing a poverty agenda for decades," the former Indian finance secretary Vijay Kelkar pointed out in a 2005 paper.[20]

The Indian government, looking to China's example, has finally promised not just to get out of the way but also to spur on the effort to reincarnate India's economy. "We recognize that infrastructure is our greatest problem," said the Indian commerce minister Kamal Nath.[21] Already, India has built 3,355 miles of highways, with another 1,600 under construction and an additional 3,700 miles planned. The government plans to spend an astonishing $150 billion on infrastructure between 2005 and 2010: $50 billion on the decrepit airports, ports, and roads; $75 billion on power plants to bring electricity to 125,000 villages and to keep the lights on elsewhere; and $25 billion for telecommunications.[22] The combined sum is more than India has ever spent. "Whether it is airports or ports or roads, India is taking off," Mr. Nath said. But Morgan Stanley noted that even spending $150 billion won't be enough to keep India growing at least 8 percent a year: China invested more than that—$200 billion—in 2005 alone, compared with India's paltry $28 billion.[23]

○

PROGRESS ON INDIA'S DEVELOPMENT PROJECTS is on again, off again, as if ambivalent India still can't decide whether it wants to be part of the modern world. The city of Bangalore's airport is a prime example. Originally built in 1942, the airport has changed little in the past sixty-plus years. Its white tile floors, poorly lit corridors, and shabby stained chairs—needed for the long wait at the luggage conveyor belt—make the airport look as if it belonged in the developing world. One might find a thin airport worker leaning against the wall, asleep, or another staffer eating his dinner at a table set up near passport control, not far from a neatly stacked pile of fifteen-foot-long tree branches.[24] A rumpled red carpet, held in place with duct tape, shows the way outside, where a crowd of perhaps 250 people—waiting relatives, taxi drivers, hotel touts—mill about at nearly any time of night or day.

But much of Bangalore, India's third-largest city, is no longer a part of the developing world. Bangalore is known as India's Silicon Valley and is home to the technological geniuses hired for some of America's most sophisticated computer programming. Infosys and Wipro both have enormous campuses in Bangalore, almost half of India's growing biotechnology industry is located there, and big Western companies including General Electric, Philips Electronics, Intel, and Nokia have office buildings in Bangalore filled with hundreds of white-collar employees connected to the global economy with high-speed Internet links. Luxury car dealerships, apartment buildings, and shopping malls have sprung up in recent years. But it was only when fast-hiring Infosys threatened the Bangalore government that it would move its jobs elsewhere unless a new airport was built that the city's infrastructure began to improve. High-tech Bangalore was first on the national list to get a new airport, but construction began three years late, and the project is already 30 percent over budget. By 2005, construction had begun—and stopped—on a series of highways in Bangalore. The new overpasses stop in midair, as if waiting for Infosys to invent technology that allows cars to fly.

Indians joke that India is like a drunk walking home: it takes one step forward, then two steps sideways, but eventually makes it home. Indian reforms, hampered especially by local politics, tend to lurch ahead, then jolt to a stop, only to hurl forward again.

"What we've tried to do is learn from China," explained Mr. Singh's dapper commerce minister, Kamal Nath.[25] India needs to study China's strengths, then "build it in our own pattern," he said. In addition to building roads, airports, and rail lines—India plans to spend $5 billion to build 6,000 miles of freight tracks, which should help exports reach seaports faster—India has been creating special economic zones similar to China's. India's zones also offer tax breaks and reduced red tape, but are small compared with China's and tend to be industry specific. For instance, one of India's planned zones is for pharmaceutical companies only. Modest size may limit the impact of the zones as well. In India, where it is difficult for developers to clear land from either legal residents or the many illegal squatters, economic zones average around four square kilometers, with many as small as one square kilometer. China's zones are giant, sometimes covering 400 square kilometers.

Mr. Nath, a veteran politician, says China was able to reform faster because it is authoritarian. "We are accountable to parliament and to our very, very free press," said Mr. Nath of the Commerce Ministry, which favors the zones. "China was able to take many shortcuts, not being a democracy—that's why they had this phenomenal growth." Indeed, China's Three Gorges Dam project alone inundated 365 towns with water, requiring about 1.2 million people to move, virtually all of it accomplished by government fiat. That couldn't be done in India.

There's an Indian joke that goes like this: "Deng Xiaoping is sitting in his car reading a newspaper, when his driver interrupts him and says, 'Comrade, there's a problem. The sign says turn Left for communism, turn Right for capitalism. Which way should I go?' Deng tells his driver, 'There's no problem. Just signal left and go right.' "

In India, the road to reform remains as bumpy as the streets. Indian politicians must be perceived to be helping the poor or risk being thrown out of office, as Mr. Vajpayee was in 2004, despite India's booming economy. "Our policy aim is not merely the survival of the fittest but the revival of the weakest," the smooth-talking Mr. Nath said. But he insists there is no turning back from the reforms. "The big change is the public has started viewing reforms as something we want and something we need."

In India, the government must gain consensus from various constituencies—multiple political parties, outspoken interest groups, local businesses, and residents. It can take years to coax wary voters to change. India tends to tackle issues one at a time: it slowly opens one dormant industry to competition, and then there is an explosion of activity and opportunities in that industry. Airlines are a good example. For decades, Indians flew Indian Airlines, the fusty state-owned carrier that began as Tata Air Lines before Nehru nationalized it in 1953. Forty years later, India reversed course, allowing private airlines once again. Along came Jet Airways—the dependable Southwest Airlines of India. Later came no-frills Air Deccan and Kingfisher

Airlines, along with several others. They are quickly overtaking Indian Airlines with better service, routes, and prices and much lower costs; Indian Airlines has 500 employees per plane, while Jet Airways has 150 and Kingfisher 70.[26] More and more Indians are traveling as prices for flights drop, to the point that some airfares are comparable to the price of a first-class train ticket. The telecom industry also exploded after India finally allowed in private companies. Until 1985, when India grudgingly began opening its telecommunications market, phone service featured high prices and calls that often failed to go through, all justified by arguments that government ownership was required to better serve the poor. Back then, it took a decade to get a phone installed, so people put their children on the waiting lists expecting they would have a phone by the time they were married. Since deregulation, cell phone use surged. Long-distance rates fell by two-thirds in five years, and the costs of sending mobile-phone messages has plunged by 80 percent. India had just 300,000 mobile phones nationwide in 1996, but by 2008, there were 230 million and Indians were buying nearly eight million cell phones a month,[27] many from foreign companies like Motorola. Connecting by cell phone service in India remains far more reliable than by land line.

○

SO WHILE CHANGE IS OVERDUE, India is making progress. "There is an overwhelming sense of confidence, which was not true 15 years ago," says Mr. Murthy's business partner, Nandan Nilekani, Infosys' chief executive officer. "The reforms are irreversible. Indian people will now feel disenchanted if growth rates fall below 6 percent." Economic progress "will not happen with the speed it now happens in China," Mr. Nilekani says. "It will improve in fits and starts."[28] The *Times of India* columnist Gurcharan Das agrees. "India will never be a tiger. It is an elephant that has begun to lumber and move ahead," Mr. Das said in his excellent account of India's post-independence economic history, *India Unbound*. "It will never have speed, but it will always have stamina."[29] The commerce minister puts it in more competitive terms. "We are the fastest-growing free-market democracy in the world," said Mr. Nath. "China is winning the sprint, and we are going to win the marathon."

India and China have both won a marathon of sorts, one measured in metal. Steel was so important to Mao that he starved his people while trying to produce more of it than Britain. Now that China has repudiated Mao's policies, it manufactures more than four times more steel than any other country in the world.[30] Indians like Jamsetji Tata viewed being self-sufficient in steel as critical to the nation's ability to win independence. In 2007, the once anemic Tata Steel bought the former British Steel.[31] Today India makes three times as much steel as its former colonial master, the United Kingdom.

CHAPTER THREE

MADE BY AMERICA IN CHINA

There are many ways to measure China's economic growth: by counting its skyscrapers, the fruits of its factories, or the miles of highways, or even by monitoring changes in the diet of its people.

But a Dutchman in Shanghai takes a more voyeuristic approach.

"I look at apartments at night," said Pieter de Haan, the Dutch general manager of Royal Philips Electronics' Lighting Division in China. He measures the nation's economic and social progress by its lightbulbs, one out of every ten of which is sold by Philips. In rural Chinese homes, the average number of lights has gone from zero to three since China opened its economy, and in Shanghai the numbers are even greater. Poor urban families have four lights, and middle-class families have about ten. The growing class of affluent Chinese families will have twenty lights in a three-room apartment, Mr. de Haan has noticed.[1] Using Mr. de Haan's measuring stick, we need only simple arithmetic to calculate how much China has grown, or how much Philips, a $35 billion company, has profited as a result of that growth.

For multinational companies like Philips, and for the Chinese, China's development has been a virtuous circle—as companies have built more factories, the nation has gotten richer, enabling people to buy more of its light bulbs and other products. Philips figures that China has 200 million middle-class people, 80 million of whom are very well off. They bought $4.1 billion worth of Philips goods in 2005. Even a small increase in the average income of the Chinese people is cause for celebration for company stockholders and for employees at Philips headquarters in Amsterdam. That's because Shanghai alone has the same population as Philips' entire home country of Holland, around 17 million people. Like other multinational companies in the globalization era, Philips is in some ways a modern incarnation of the Dutch East India Company, the famous maritime trader along the Spice Route that linked India and Europe in the seventeenth and eighteenth centuries.[2] Like the Dutch East India Company, Philips ships goods from Asia to eager buyers in the West—not cinnamon and pepper on galleons that took up to a year to get to Europe, but consumer gadgets on modern container ships that in the twenty-first century can go all the way from China to Los Angeles in just eleven days.

A close look at the business decisions of a single company, Philips, shows the dynamics at work in China that are typical for foreign investors there—whether large companies like Philips or much smaller ones. Those company decisions affect tens of thousands of people around the world. Some are workers—in Europe, the United States, China, or India—and some are consumers. In either case, the way foreign companies like Philips approach China has broad ramifications. And when tens of thousands of other companies are walking along the same path, the effects go far beyond the business world.

For instance, seizing the opportunities presented by new infrastructure, tax breaks, and special economic zones designed specifically to entice foreign companies, Philips shifted large parts of its production to China and became one of the nation's largest foreign investors. Opening Chinese factories and closing factories in the West allowed Philips to cut its costs dramatically on goods that appear on American and European shelves, and today Philips has thirty-two Chinese factories with 18,000 employees, plus another 30,000 Chinese workers employed by subcontractors. As India starts to supply the refined brains for the new global economy, China continues to provide the raw brawn. Chinese factory workers, whether making light bulbs, talking toys, or tennis shoes, earn each day about what Americans pay for a latte at Starbucks. But cheap labor isn't the only force behind China's rise. Wages across Africa, much of Southeast Asia, South America, and even India are lower, and if miniature paychecks were all that mattered, the jobs of the world would long since have left China.

Just like the consumer electronics industry, much of the world's commerce has connected with China because the Chinese government has spared no incentive in wooing foreign companies to build factories there. China's modernization drive has combined its developing-world, low-cost labor with nearly state-of-the-art technology and an export-friendly infrastructure. Meanwhile, China's huge population has provided companies with a giant pool of low-wage workers in the same place where they have found a potentially large set of new customers, enabling mass-market factories to produce both for the export market and for the growing Chinese market. In addition, the abundance of new factories and office buildings in China means that many Western companies can make money selling goods to each other, further stimulating the economy. This dramatic confluence of factors, a "perfect storm" of commerce, has allowed China to sprint way out ahead of India and other developing countries that simply cannot offer the full combination of attractions for foreign investment.

Put it all together, and China amounts to a double dream for Western companies—corporate one-stop-shopping for both cost cuts and revenue growth. The first dream is that companies can use China's cheap labor to make light bulbs, state-of-the-art laptops, clothes, or just about any of the other goods that fill shelves, catalogs, and online shopping carts back in the United States and Europe. Cheap Chinese manufacturing has saved companies billions of dollars; some of these savings have been passed on to consumers in the form of lower prices and some have been absorbed as company profit. Andy Xie, Morgan Stanley's managing director specializing in China, estimates that U.S. companies saved up to $70 billion in 2005 alone by moving production to China, adding that amount to their profits. They have passed on a further $100 billion in savings to American consumers.[3]

The second dream is that when a billion Chinese see their incomes rise as a result of the new, better-paying jobs, they can finally afford to buy Western goods sold in China. This dream is taking longer to achieve, yet slowly but surely the Chinese are buying their first wallets—and filling (and then emptying) them. 110 million Chinese were able to afford nonessential goods by 2007, a number expected to balloon to 200 million by 2010,[4] creating a market nearly the size of America or Europe, albeit with lower income levels. Consider cell phones: in 1997, China had just 10 million subscribers, but by 2008, it had nearly 550 million cell phone users[5]—more than every man, woman, and child in the United States.

Surprisingly, some of the vestiges of communism are often actually helping foreign businesses profit in China. China's government planning system still shapes almost every aspect of business, which can both benefit and stymie Western companies. To the system's credit, there isn't much guesswork about what the Chinese government or Chinese businesses will buy once the government lays out its economic development plans. The consistency of Beijing's policy, and its generally strong track record of economic policy-making, is one of the unexpected strengths of a nation that does not have much experience with the market economy system. The government will name a new priority in a five-year plan and spend billions modernizing. Western companies then dive in to sell to their new Chinese customers— whether selling asphalt needed for paving new highways, airplanes for the opening of new airports, or light bulbs for new homes. For instance, when the Chinese government decided to build a modern highway system more extensive than America's, foreign and local companies rushed to cash in on the asphalt boom. Philips doesn't sell asphalt, but it benefitted anyway because roads must be lit up for night driving. Philips sold $195 million worth of streetlights alone in 2005, one out of every three streetlights in China.

Because the Chinese government places a high priority on enticing foreign companies to build factories in China, many of Philips' most profitable customers are other multinational companies there. For example, Philips makes light bulbs for car taillights in China and sells them to Volkswagen for the cars it manufactures in China—the cars driving on all the new highways. Most of the tens of thousands of new factories and office buildings in China are illuminated with fluorescent lights, a Philips specialty. In response to the new demand, Philips opened a fluorescent light bulb factory outside Shanghai. Because so many of the goods that Philips and other companies make in China can be sold in China as well as overseas, multinational companies have built huge, hyperefficient factories. The existence of these economies of scale is rare in developing countries, but common in China because of the growing domestic market for many goods combined with the giant export market.

Chinese government plans have even caused Philips to reverse its business strategy for some products. The Chinese government decided to modernize the nation's decaying hospitals and has built nearly 2,500 in the past five years,[6] most of them in big cities. The modernization plan has not only meant the difference between life and death for tens of millions of well-off Chinese who finally have access to modern medical care but has also created in its wake a huge market for companies selling medical equipment, including Philips.[7] There wasn't much local competition: because Chinese hospitals made do for decades without buying new machines, few Chinese companies made X-ray machines, blood-pressure monitors, or ultrasound machines. At the snap of government fingers, China went from a land of fifty-year-old X-ray machines to the second-largest medical equipment market in the world after the United States. The Chinese government can also snap its fingers and cause dramatic consequences for companies doing business in China. In the case of hospital modernization, the consequences were hugely positive for foreign companies. In 2004, Chinese hospitals bought $1.25 billion worth of imaging equipment alone—heart monitors, magnetic resonance imaging (MRI) machines, X-ray machines, and the like. Philips alone sold $185 million worth of equipment.

So why would Philips change business strategies? Although China's best urban hospitals look much like those found in the United States, they serve just 20 percent of the Chinese population. That still leaves 80 percent, more than one billion people, with poor access to health care. As the hospital modernization effort continues, smaller Chinese hospitals are starting to replace their ancient equipment too, albeit on lower budgets. Philips feared it would be left out of that potentially huge market because its longtime strategy has been to sell only the most expensive and sophisticated medical machines worldwide. Because the Chinese market is so big and is growing so rapidly, the company changed its entire hospital equipment strategy. It hired six hundred Chinese workers and opened a factory in Shenyang, in northeastern China, to make cheaper, simpler MRI, ultrasound, and X-ray machines. Philips plans to sell them all in China at first, then export the machines to other developing countries when there is demand. This is just one example of the way Chinese government priorities are triggering big changes for Philips and other multinational companies doing business in China.

On some matters, Philips has been fighting the Chinese government, however, and it has been an uphill battle. Like almost every foreign company doing business in China, Philips has had huge headaches with the protection of intellectual property. For instance, China now makes 90 percent of the world's DVD players, but for a decade Chinese DVD player makers refused to pay Philips royalties for the DVD technology Philips invented. "T.I.C.," shrugged David Chang, Philips' chief executive in China, who has learned to be patient. "This is China." Finally, after China joined the World Trade Organization, the pirates agreed to pay up. Currently, Philips gets $200 million a year in royalties from DVD makers. That's not bad for a company that got its start in 1891 by "borrowing" Thomas Edison's design for the light bulb and manufacturing lights for Europe. "That was way back when we were the Chinese of Europe," jokes Philips' chief executive Gerard Kleisterlee. Light bulbs are not a laughing matter for the company, however: Philips has nine lighting factories in China.

One of these factories is in Malu, an hour's drive from the corporate offices in Shanghai, past the downtown skyscrapers and along one of China's new highways. Outside the city, homes give way to mile after mile of factories. On the busy road, dusty trucks carrying building materials bully past the chauffeured cars carrying factory bosses, both flying past a smattering of bicycles and a handful of riders on motor scooters. When Philips began building this light bulb factory in 1995, Malu was a small town surrounded by farmland.

Today Malu is a modern city with hotels, apartment buildings, home furnishing stores, a barber shop—and factories that stretch as far as the eye can see.

Inside the Philips factory in Malu, 1,600 Chinese workers in blue uniforms—blue is the company color—operate the largely automated assembly lines. One stands watch as a machine drops an empty glass shell over a spindly metal filament, then yellow flames whoosh up from spigots to seal the light bulbs. At the end of the assembly line, a pair of Chinese workers packs each of the finished, tested light bulbs in a thin, rectangular box, ready for display on the shelves of a store in China, Europe, or the United States. More than half the light bulbs Philips makes in China leave the country, replacing bulbs that were until recently made in now-closed factories in Canada or Spain.

○

CHINA'S ECONOMY seems to have taken off like a rocket, but the rise hasn't always been smooth. In the early years of China's reopening, the dream of selling to a billion Chinese became a nightmare for many companies. During the early 1990s, foreign companies tiptoed into the China market,[8] and by the mid-1990s a sprint had begun. Foreign investment in China really took off in the mid-1990s, as American and European executives dreamed greedily about winning over a billion new customers. But many got burned in the process.[9]

Part of the blame for that rests on a Chinese government policy requiring foreign companies in some industries to partner with Chinese companies—the less rosy side of the Chinese government's strong hold on business. That policy led to situations in which a Chinese company in control of the resulting joint partnership turned out to be run by a local Communist Party branch, or by crooked or incompetent managers. The Chinese and the foreigners were, as the Chinese saying goes, "sleeping in the same bed, dreaming different dreams." In other cases, foreigners looked at the percentage growth in Chinese incomes and believed that the market in China for their products would soon become huge. Some were right: mobile-phone makers like Motorola, Nokia, and Ericsson made billions,[10] and fast-food sellers like KFC did quite nicely. But during the 1990s, most of the foreign companies found they were wrong about the profit predictions, even though they were right that Chinese incomes would more than double in a decade. After all, a nation that reached an average GDP per capita of $2,000 only in 2007[11] still cannot afford many toys, computers, or even toothbrushes. A 1998 survey by A. T. Kearney showed that just 38 percent of all foreign-invested manufacturers were covering their operating costs in China.[12]

Chinese companies struggled too. As China entered the international market, hardly any of its citizens had the faintest idea of how to manage a free-market business. And it has shown. Most Chinese companies have struggled. When China opened to outside commerce, managers new to both the ways of the free market and to modern business theories were unable to compete with private companies and efficient factories run by foreign multinationals. They typically had at least twice as many workers on the payroll as needed and came equipped with old-fashioned command-and-control management techniques and antiquated technology. Workers were used to the Iron Rice Bowl of the communist era and didn't work very hard.

The contrast was strongest at joint ventures set up between Chinese and foreigners. For instance, back in 2000, a joint venture between Jeep and the Beijing branch of the Communist Party had so many extra workers that some would recline the seats of Jeeps moving down the assembly line and sleep there. Managers from Detroit not only weren't allowed to downsize the workforce but could barely get the Chinese government to pay for the Jeeps it bought. When the government paid, it was with suitcases full of cash. The American CEO trying to run the enterprise had his phones tapped and his office ransacked—by his own joint-venture partners. Even today, many foreign partners simply accept that they won't be allowed to lay off unneeded Chinese workers. To keep from losing money, they merely expand their factories, making twice as much cement or twice as many trucks as they did before with the same numbers of workers.

After a few years of practice, many foreign companies learned better how to protect themselves. The Chinese government also began allowing foreign companies in many industries to have full ownership or management of their enterprises in China. In 1990, American companies with operations or joint ventures in China broke even doing business in China. By 2004, they had earned a combined $3 billion; by 2005, they were pulling in $3.3 billion, according to the U.S. Commerce Department's Bureau of Economic Analysis, and about 80 percent of the American companies in China were profitable. The gains from cost savings came on top of that. Indeed, when profit forecasts fell short for Chinese sales, many U.S. companies began to shift their strategies away from converting China's billions to customers and toward using their Chinese factories purely for export, sometimes hiring Chinese, Hong Kong, or Taiwanese companies to make goods in China on their behalf instead of trying to own the factories themselves.

○

By THE FOURTEENTH CENTURY, China had become a pillar of international trade by moving goods along the Silk Road—overland trading routes across China, through the Arab world, and on to Europe. Back then, China was a technological leader, and it prospered as a result. China's inventions included paper, gunpowder, the magnetic compass, and even wallpaper, and one of its biggest exports was porcelain, which Europeans couldn't duplicate for more than a century. What a sharp contrast to the manner in which China successfully trades today: Instead of doing the inventing as the West watches on with envy, China excels at building Western inventions cheaper than Westerners can build them at home. China has shifted from a hub of invention to one of rote production.

The movement in recent years toward using China as a production hub was an unparalleled success for Western business, and the companies involved are not even close to maximizing its potential. Foreign companies have already turned China into a huge subcontractor, using the cheap labor in China to make goods for their American, European, Korean, and Japanese customers. In a 2005 survey by McKinsey & Company of U.S. companies active in China, the companies reported that they bought just 30 percent of the goods they could buy in China, but planned to increase that to half by 2008.[13] Chinese workers have seen incomes go up, but the lion's share of the winnings has gone straight to the foreign companies and foreign consumers, who are paying lower prices than they otherwise would. On the average, if China exports a shoe that sells for $100 in the United States, just $15 of the price stays in China in the form of workers' wages, transportation costs, or other value.[14] American companies keep the remaining $85. The same holds true for computers: the average laptop exported from China is worth $700, but the Chinese company that makes the computers earns only $15 each.[15]

The real boom in China is the global economy itself. Much of it has simply moved to China, and it is owned and run by the same multinationals that controlled it before. While tens of millions of Chinese workers have benefited because of the new jobs created there, a larger share of the gains from the business migration to China has gone not to Chinese companies but to American, European, and Japanese companies and to consumers in those countries.

Yet as the outside world watches China's numbers rise and rise—economic growth is sizzling, exports are skyrocketing, skyscrapers are rising—a panic has ensued. Seemingly overnight, China has become an economic powerhouse. Just look at the trade deficit: the United States alone imported a record $237 billion more from China than it exported to China in the first eleven months of 2007 alone, the largest trade deficit the United States has ever run with any country. The European Union's trade deficit with China reached 132 billion euros for the first ten months of 2007,[16] and China's economy is growing so fast that it is poised to overtake Germany as the world's third-largest economy as soon as 2008, having passed the United Kingdom to become the fourth-largest economy in 2005.[17]

However, a reality check shows that despite trade deficits that alarm the West, a high percentage of China's much ballyhooed economic muscle belongs to foreigners. A large portion of the frighteningly lopsided trade deficit can be traced to goods made by Western companies in China, then shipped home for sale. China's world-beating exports are indeed thriving, but only four of China's top twenty-five exporters are Chinese companies. Foreign companies and their Chinese joint-venture partners produced 88 percent of China's high-tech exports in 2005.[17] In practice, "Made in China" often really means "Made by America in China" or "Made by Europe in China."

China's most profitable business activities are out of the hands of mainland Chinese. China, it seems, has not been invited to its own coming-out party.

Whereas the global part of the Chinese economy—the part dominated by American and other foreign companies—is flourishing, the Chinese-controlled portion has an uncertain future. China must transform itself further if it is to reap the full rewards of its own economic rise. More than half of China's incredible 10 percent GDP growth comes from government and foreign direct investment. If you strip that away, China's growth rate is closer to the American growth rate. China's phantom GDP is fine as long as the heavy investment continues, but it will cause a painful recession if the investment stops. China spent a whopping $201 billion on infrastructure in 2005 alone,[19] with much of the infrastructure supporting exports as well as creating jobs for Chinese construction workers. Foreign investment, which hit $67 billion in 2007, pays mostly for new factories being built in China by multinational corporations or by Hong Kong, Taiwanese, or other Asian companies that sell to them. The numbers give China an illusion of strength, but the nation's economy is not as strong as it appears.

○

INDEED, LURING WESTERN BUSINESSES to China has cost China hundreds of billions of dollars. Chinese government investments pay for many of the new highways, power plants, office buildings, railroads, and other infrastructure being built furiously in China. The money for this comes primarily from loans from Chinese banks, plus some government-issued bonds, most of which are sold to Chinese banks. The bank loans have created a problem: China's banks are broke, and the government is having a hard time cleaning them up. Ernst & Young "conservatively" estimated that the Chinese banking system had $911 billion in bad loans in 2006,[20] six times the magnitude of the American S&L crisis.[21]

Almost all of China's banks remain state-owned, although the biggest are selling stakes to big foreign banks and selling shares on stock exchanges outside mainland China. Under communism, China didn't have commercial banks—after all, its people didn't have any money to put in them. The People's Bank of China was both bank and treasury for the Chinese government. In the early 1980s, China began creating a separate banking system by spinning off four giant state-owned banks. They didn't function like profit-minded Western banks, though: they existed as the government's piggy banks, told to lend money needed by the state-owned companies or for whatever special projects politicians planned in a city or town. Not until a government reorganization in 1994 were Chinese banks told to operate on a profit-and-loss basis like Western banks.[22] Today many of the glorious high-rises, shopping malls, apartment buildings, highways, and other infrastructure projects are financial white elephants, paid for by bank loans that aren't being paid back. Some of this is due to corruption, particularly among local officials who take kickbacks from real estate developers and then order Chinese banks to lend to their projects.

In addition to trying to stamp out corruption, Beijing has been trying to transform the banking system by writing off past bad loans and changing banking practices. The government has allowed foreign banks like Citibank and HSBC to buy minority stakes in China's biggest banks in hopes that foreigners will not only pressure them to modernize but also teach them how to do so. The largest Chinese banks are selling shares on global stock markets, with the government counting on investors to pressure the banks to continue their much-needed reforms. International bankers concur that Chinese banks are vastly improved, but like the habit of planning the economy, local government officials' penchant for telling banks where to lend die hard. Even China's Central Bank chief conceded that one of the largest, the Agricultural Bank of China, was so hopeless despite years of reform efforts that it should just be broken up, its headquarters closed, and its branches parceled out to other banks.[23]

The central government is trying to rein in China's worst corruption, which is prevalent nationwide and not restricted to the banking industry. The government has executed hundreds of local officials to send a message that corruption isn't tolerated, but this is another practice proving hard to stop, particularly after so many decades of poverty. The central government is especially worried about the widespread corruption because it has contributed to social unrest. Whereas American law prohibits payment of bribery, and American companies typically refuse to make direct payments, many Chinese consider bribery to be business as usual. Foreign companies paying bribes hire consultants to help facilitate projects and don't ask too many questions about where the exorbitant "consultant fees" are going. Foreigners report that in China, at least the corruption is efficient: it can amount to 20–40 percent of a particular project's cost, but a onetime payment can fast-track local government approvals that pave the way for profits for years to come.

○

AS WESTERN COMPANIES found in the mid-1990s, the miracle growth of Chinese incomes is partly a real force for the future and partly exaggerated. A tiny slice of the Chinese population had already gotten extremely rich. In a single generation, Mao's nation of former peasants has spawned 320,000 millionaires.[24] This group, and others with high incomes, has become a bonanza for luxury-goods companies. Chinese malls have Prada, Armani, and Louis Vuitton stores, and BMWs, Mercedes, and Audis glide along China's streets. Glitzy malls in Shanghai are filled with deserted luxury stores, but once every few days a man will visit from a distant Chinese city like Wuhan and spend $25,000 on purses, shoes, and clothes for his wife or girlfriend, keeping those deserted stores operating at a profit.[25] Sophisticated Chinese shoppers, like their Japanese counterparts, strive to buy expensive luxury brands. In the past decade, China has become the third-largest luxury-goods market in the world after Japan and the United States, with the Chinese spending $2 billion a year. By 2015, Ernst & Young expects, China will pass the United States to buy as much in luxury goods as Japan, nearly one-third of the global market. Today China's luxury market is dwarfed by that of the United States. But within this generation, China is expected to have a new market as big as America's. Because the Chinese population is so large, even a small percentage rising to the middle class creates a market as big as many European countries boast. By the mid-2020s, Shanghai combined with the five fastest-growing provinces in

China—a group with a population 27 percent larger than the United States—is expected to have the same standard of living as the United States in terms of per capita GDP.[26]

While China's big spenders balloon the market for luxury goods, overall incomes remain low. Chinese officials predict that China's annual per capita GDP level will rise to $3,000—but not until 2010.[27] Even as most of China's 1.3 billion people have watched their incomes rise dramatically, the majority of China's people remain poor; they are just less poor than they were before. Per capita disposable income in the countryside, where most Chinese live, was just $400 in 2005, compared with an average $1,300 in cities.[28] Less than 8 percent of Chinese babies wear disposable diapers.[29] Toddlers wear trousers called *kai dang ku*, which have a large slit at the bottom. That's messier but far cheaper.

O

THE FORTUNES OF CHINESE COMPANIES mirror those of China's citizens—a small proportion is unthinkably rich and sophisticated, but the vast majority is poor. Some Chinese companies are making lots of money in China, even some still owned by the Communist government. A few of the biggest state-owned enterprises, like PetroChina, China Mobile, and China Telecom, are very profitable.[30] But most Chinese companies are shaky, despite the nation's overall progress. After all, they don't have much experience with free-market capitalism.

Under Mao's communism, when the government owned all companies, they didn't operate under normal business rules: they produced as many units as government planners told them to, regardless of customer demand. They sent almost all proceeds to the central or local government, which reallocated the money as needed among different companies or regions. The companies provided workers—comrades—with food, housing, medical care, school, and care during retirement.

In 1997, the Chinese government began the process of selling off and closing down unprofitable state-owned companies and collectives, from hotels to cooking-oil producers and bicycle makers.[31]

Back then, most of the state-owned enterprises were bankrupt and had been shutting down and laying off millions of workers each year. Between 1996 and 2004, 67 million workers at these enterprises and collectives were let go.[32] When Chinese workers lose their jobs, they lose their iron rice bowls—their once ironclad right to care and benefits provided by their government-owned employers under communism. State-owned hospitals, desperate to earn a profit, today refuse to treat patients who cannot pay. Schools now charge tuition to avoid shutting down. There is such uncertainty among Chinese workers that the average Chinese saves 30 percent of his or her income.[33] The state has shifted social spending to ordinary Chinese, who are living in fear of catastrophic medical bills for themselves or their parents, or facing tuition bills for once free schools for their children. The answer for many Chinese is to land one of the millions of new jobs created by foreign or privately owned Chinese companies opening factories and offices in China, or perhaps to depend on relatives who have done so.

New jobs created by the booming economy have provided livelihoods for an astonishing number of Chinese: about 145 million people found jobs in the new factories built or offices opened between 1996 and 2004, and their family incomes have risen as a result. There is a nearly bottomless supply of unskilled factory workers in China, given that an additional 150 million rural residents are earning so little from farming that they are effectively unemployed. Millions migrate to cities each year in search of work in the factories.

But white-collar job candidates are also plentiful. Managers have realized that after the educational desolation of the Cultural Revolution, China is again producing university graduates. Since reopening universities in 1977, China has quickly been increasing the numbers of college places each year. For a nation of a billion people, China's total pool of college graduates remained small in 2005: about 8.5 million, 2.3 million of whom completed science and engineering degrees.[34] Nonetheless, the supply of well-educated Chinese engineers and other highly skilled workers is growing fast, creating a huge pool of potential white-collar workers—one being tapped by American, European, and Japanese companies. In 2007, about 5 million Chinese graduated from college, at least 800,000 of them in the science and technology fields favored by American companies hiring in China.[35] Even though a much larger percentage of Americans go to college, just 1.3 million students finish college each year in the United States, fewer than in China, which has a vastly larger population. The American workforce comprises 40 million college graduates, about 10 million of whom have science and engineering degrees,[36] but in about a decade, China should have a larger pool of science and engineering graduates than the United States.

Of the Chinese graduates, only 10 percent are suitable for work in multinational companies, largely because of their poor English-language skills and China's emphasis on rote learning rather than creativity, problem solving, and teamwork. But Chinese students are upgrading their skills, fast. A decade ago, only a handful of China's top universities offered computer science degrees, with students trained on outdated systems. Now, even China's education system is boosted by foreigners: none other than Microsoft executives lecture at Chinese universities to be sure the company will have a qualified pool of tech graduates to choose from when it hires. In Shanghai, more than 300 Chinese Microsoft employees offer tech support and customer service to customers in Asia, Europe, and the United States. Meetings are held in English, and Harry Potter posters decorate cubicles near the ping-pong table. "It is much easier to get a software engineer here than in the U.S.," said Dennis Lam, director of Microsoft's Global Technical Engineering Center in Shanghai. "The talent pool is pretty impressive." Perhaps the most sought-after Chinese white-collar workers are the *hai gui pai*, like Tony Ma of B. F. Goodrich. These "sea turtles" were born in China, went to university abroad, often in the United States, and have since returned to China. There were 120,000 Chinese students studying abroad in 2003, half of them in the United States.[37] Some of China's most successful managers and its best-paid bankers, engineers, and other white-collar workers are returnees.

Even though Chinese workers have been the big winners overall because their incomes have risen, they have few rights and little recourse to fair courts, so it is easy for unscrupulous, newly capitalist bosses to take advantage of them. China's army of migrant workers, the tens of millions who pour from the countryside into the cities hoping to find work, are particularly powerless and often wind up as construction workers or factory hands. Just 6 percent of construction workers, the very heart of the Chinese development miracle, are paid on time each month, according to Qiao Jian, head of the labor union department at the China Institute of Industrial Relations.

The other big losers from the shift of the global economy to China are American workers whose jobs have been moved to China, and they are hard to count because the rise of China is creating some jobs in America at the same time it eliminates others. Just as the effect of China's strong economic growth on America is more complex than it appears at first glance, so is the effect on American jobs. The bulk of China's job gains have come from factory work, and most Americans no longer work in factories but in the service industries. Yet they, too, have reason to worry: increasingly, American companies and other multinationals are hiring Chinese workers to do white-collar work.

Just as an American parent might work overtime on the assembly line to pay for a child's college tuition and thus training for white-collar work, China is trying to encourage its next generation to work with their minds rather than their hands. As factories move to China, products that are built in China are increasingly designed and engineered there as well. This is partly at the insistence of the Chinese government, which has asked foreign companies to create research and development facilities, not just factories. Foreign companies have rushed to do so, at first to curry favor with government officials and later to take advantage of low Chinese white-collar wages. Over 700 foreign-funded investors have set up R&D centers in China in recent years.[38] Some Chinese researchers are developing advanced technology for companies like Microsoft and Intel, while many others are researching or designing more mundane products built in Chinese factories. In 2005, just 14 percent of companies surveyed designed their Chinese-built products in China; by 2008, half expect to do so, creating more and more well-paid design and engineering jobs in China.[39] Philips was one of the foreign companies that answered the Chinese government's call to build a research center, and since 2000 it has hired 400 Chinese white-collar workers. Other Western companies have hired hundreds of thousands more Chinese engineers and office workers, creating China's first modern middle-class workforce. In this next stage of development, the Chinese government is once again setting the nation up to prosper in world markets by using low wages to entice foreign companies to employ—and thus train—its skilled workforce, not just its factory workers.

CHAPTER FOUR

THE INTERNET'S
SPICE ROUTE

Despite the steps its leaders took to maintain independence and self-sufficiency, India is still shaped by its colonial past. Stately Victorian buildings punctuate city blocks, standing frozen in time amid the perpetual hustle of the streets. British-style parliamentary democracy flourishes. Perhaps most strikingly, though, the English language lingers, and its continuing presence in India is now supercharging the former colony's economic growth. India's more than 100 million English-speakers—about twice as many as live in the United Kingdom itself—are attracting millions of new jobs, propelling its once crumbling economy into the twenty-first century. In the process, middle-class Americans and Britons are growing increasingly worried that their jobs will be moved from Boston to Bangalore, or from Manchester to Mumbai.

The fears of these Western workers are justified. More than a million white-collar, service-industry jobs have already moved to India, and more are on the way. As many as 300,000 American jobs each year will move overseas for the next thirty years—9 million jobs in all, estimates the McKinsey Global Institute, McKinsey & Company's economics think tank.[1] On behalf of foreign companies, Indians answer phone calls, write computer code, and increasingly take on far more sophisticated tasks—from accounting to investment banking—that previously were performed strictly in corporate offices across America and Europe. As China has famously become the factory to the world, India is becoming the world's back office. The birth of the remote back office has turbocharged the Indian economy, reorganizing the way business is done in India and around the world and spreading India fever among foreign companies. Fueled by gold rush dreams of massive profits through cost-cutting, international companies are rushing headfirst into India, and they will leave in their wake millions of white-collar workers in the West, all of whom will need to find new jobs and some of whom will have to find new careers.

Stunningly significant changes are coming. "I don't think most people appreciate the magnitude of the change in the world's workforce; this is a tsunami coming our way," said Intel's chairman, Craig Barrett. "Over the next ten years you are going to see major, major dislocation."[2] He should know. Intel has already hired 3,000 Indian workers. Of the world's 500 largest companies, 400 send middle-class work to India, up from 150 in 2000.[3]

○

THE NEW PRACTICE of moving white-collar work overseas is called offshoring, and it put long-ignored India on the map as a market for foreign companies. Private jets are landing in dusty Indian airports, carrying powerful CEOs and corporate board members from some of the world's biggest companies, eager to evaluate the hype for themselves. Most have come to check out the offices their companies have already opened to tackle offshored work. Now that India has become a part of their businesses, they consider the next steps. Can Indians do other work for them cheaply, and can they sell their products in India? Most conclude yes in both cases, and place even bigger bets on the Indian market. In 2005, Microsoft, Intel, and Cisco each announced they would invest more than $1 billion in India.[4] Six months later, IBM said it would invest $4 billion. "IBM is not going to miss this opportunity," said Samuel J. Palmisano, chief executive of IBM. His company already has 73,000 employees in fourteen Indian cities—more Indian knowledge workers than Philips has factory workers in China. "In the next three years we will triple our investment in India, from $2 billion over the last three years to nearly $6 billion in the next three years," Mr. Palmisano announced in Bangalore in June 2006. IBM already runs IT systems for 225 of its client companies entirely from India. Offshoring has infected the business world with India fever. In November 2006, the U.S. Commerce Department led a business development mission to India, and executives from 186 U.S. companies attended. It was the U.S. government's largest-ever overseas visit.[5]

Offshoring is simply the movement of white-collar jobs overseas, whether within the same company or farmed out to an outside contractor like IBM, which in turn moves the jobs overseas. So Microsoft might open a call center in India and hire hundreds of Indians to field questions about its computer programs from Americans dialing 800 numbers. Or Microsoft might hire another company—an American outsourcing company like EDS, or an Indian firm like Wipro—to run the Indian call center on its behalf. Offshoring is different from hiring staff overseas to work on business in those overseas markets, as when Microsoft hires Indian sales staff to sell its computer programs in India or opens a call center in Delhi to answer queries from Indian customers. In the case of offshoring, the customers or end users are usually in the United States, Europe, or another developed country, while the workers are elsewhere. A variation is "outsourcing," in which a company farms out some of its work to another firm, whether that firm is in the same country or abroad. Microsoft would be outsourcing work if it hired EDS to run a call center for it, whether EDS's call center was in the state of Texas or in the Indian state of Tamil Nadu.

The new jobs typically move overseas in one of three ways. Big multinationals doing business around the globe have been realizing, as they chase new customers in low-wage countries like India and China, that they can cut costs by opening offices overseas and moving much of their own white-collar work to those nations. Or they hire large Indian firms like Infosys, Wipro, or Tata Consultancy Services to provide workers in the same way companies outsource factory work to China. In addition, Western companies are outsourcing their back offices to big U.S. firms like EDS or HP or IBM. Many of those outsourced jobs wind up offshore, too, like the 43,000 that IBM now has in India. Offshored work is cheap and, as ossified back-office processes are taken over by hyperefficient back-office specialists, also more effective. Sometimes big companies don't even know where their phones are answered or their computers are programmed. As long as the work is high in quality and low in cost, why should companies care?

Workers, on the other hand, have every reason to care. White-collar workers have never before had to worry about their jobs' migrating overseas. The very concept of exporting services is revolutionary. Since the birth of the Silk Road, exports have always been goods, whether they traveled by camel or later by ship, by truck, or by airplane. Now, with the Internet and inexpensive telephone service connecting the world, developing countries with educated workforces can export their intellectual work, too, not just the products of their factories. More workers can rely on the strength of their brains instead of their backs to make a living. The wages—typically one-half to one-tenth of Western rates—are a bargain for companies in the United States and other developed countries, and make it worth the trouble of hiring faraway workers. The ability to export services easily and inexpensively, thanks to new technology developed in the last two decades, has made offshoring possible and represents a remarkable advance for the global economy.

But technology is not the only reason that offshoring has taken off. Massive populations with low wage expectations are an equally essential part of the equation, and linking workers up with modern technology has been the key to bringing in white-collar jobs. India's English-speaking population also facilitates a direct connection between India and the largest economy in the world. U.S. companies are by far the most active offshorers: American businesses had moved 1 million white-collar jobs offshore by 2003 and have picked up the pace since then, with most jobs going to India. By 2003, British companies had moved 250,000 service-industry jobs overseas. By 2008, the United States will have moved 2.3 million service-industry jobs overseas, and the United Kingdom will have offshored 650,000.[6] Germany, with many English-speakers, is the next-largest offshorer.

○

ALTHOUGH THE CREATION of offshoring seems like a logical business move, it came about by accident. The invention of the Internet and other technological advances in the United States laid the groundwork. The late 1990s technology boom led to the creation of hundreds of new high-tech companies, extravagant parties in Silicon Valley, and stratospheric salaries for computer programmers, who were suddenly in short supply. American tech companies began using temporary immigrant visas[7] to bring programmers from India to Silicon Valley to help during the crunch. Shortly before the new millennium, the Y2K computer panic sent companies scrambling to rewrite their software in order to keep their systems from crashing at midnight on December 31, 1999, when the century rolled over on computer calendars. Even with the temporary hires, American companies faced a drastic shortage of techies who could write the tedious computer code required to prevent Y2K glitches. In desperation, they began the first large-scale experiment with offshoring: they frantically moved overflowing computer coding work to India and crossed their fingers that the Indian programmers would be up to the job.

The Indian rookies proved more than capable, and suddenly corporate America had a nearly inexhaustible source of cheap programmers halfway around the world. Companies that had hired Indian programmers during the Y2K scare began turning to India even after that when they needed programming work done. In the meantime, the world was being wired together by undersea fiber-optic cables that made possible fast and reliable phone and computer communications across oceans. Later, Silicon Valley's new technology enabled companies to cheaply route phone calls over the Internet. In the wake of the success of the Indian programmers, some companies experimented with moving call centers to India. That worked, too. Gradually, companies began asking what other kinds of white-collar work could be sent to India, and Indian companies began aggressively marketing their ability to do work for big American companies at huge cost savings. American companies led the charge, but European companies and those from other nations started to move work to India, too.

In 2001, the tech bubble went bust, triggering layoffs in America and costing many Indian programmers on temporary employment visas their jobs. The grim joke then was that the definition of "B2B," an Internet industry term meaning "business to business," changed to "back to Bangalore." The industry's crash triggered bankruptcies for many American technology companies and forced others to lay off some American employees and move work to low-wage India to avoid going out of business. As a result, Indians who had been sent back from California found that the tech boom followed them home to India. Now India has its own Silicon Valley-esque techie haven—Bangalore, in southern India. It not only has sunny weather like LA but also is the hometown of giant Indian offshoring firms like Wipro and Mr. Murthy's Infosys. In cities across the nation, entire new suburbs have sprung up to house call centers and other offshoring offices. In India, micromarkets are sprouting up around this megatrend. Small businesses have emerged to train would-be workers to speak in either an American or a British accent at call centers specializing in serving customers from the United States or the United Kingdom. In Silicon Valley and London alike, Western consulting companies like neoIT have prospered by advising companies on how to move jobs out of their home markets to places like India where white-collar wages are lower.

In the Western suburbs of Mumbai, there is a new-from-the-ground-up, privately guarded minicity called Mindspace. The development could have sprung up in Chicago or Dallas. Right around the corner from a Toyota showroom, Mindspace's freshly built office towers are clustered around luxury apartment buildings and a grocery store. The new office buildings are home to familiar names like GE, Siemens, HSBC, IBM, Accenture, and EDS, as well as Indian companies working on behalf of other American and British companies. Employees sit in cubicles wearing saris or turbans—or new shirts and slacks—and answer phone calls from overseas.

Lots of new office buildings and housing complexes like Mumbai's Mindspace boomtown are cropping up around the country as those who have landed new jobs in the offshoring industry are settling into spacious apartments with pristine swimming pools and playgrounds for their children. But outside their security fences and guarded gates live the Indians who aren't part of the global economy. Millions of people in Mumbai alone live in slums or along roadsides, crammed in dirt-floored rooms, with walls made from discarded wood or aluminum siding or plastic sheets. When there is work for them, it is usually road repair or construction. The pay is around twenty-five cents a day. India's ubiquitous poor remain the stereotypical image of India for many Westerners, even as the nation's educated elite has made India a magnet for Western jobs. To escape India's specter of poverty, generations have sacrificed whatever they have to educate their children in some of the world's most competitive schools. Now, finally, young English-speaking graduates are finding good white-collar jobs that pay at least $2,500 a year—a ticket to the middle class in India, where the cost of living is drastically lower than in the United States.

The competition for jobs is so fierce that a newspaper classified ad yields 250 applicants for every call-center job. American companies are rushing to move jobs offshore, where they can pay workers less. When EDS began hiring for its call center in the Mindspace complex, 6,000 people applied for just 110 jobs with a starting salary of $250 a month, or $3,000 a year, for college graduates. Even if companies could attract college graduates in the United States to work in call centers, they would have to pay them more than $250 a week. In India, they can hire better-educated workers to do the same jobs for less.

IBM, General Electric, and Microsoft have each invested billions of dollars and hired tens of thousands of Indians to work for them from India, and scores of other leading American companies have hired thousands more Indian workers. The big Indian offshoring companies TCS, Wipro, and Infosys have a combined 220,000 workers, most of them doing work on behalf of American customers. Mr. Murthy's Infosys alone is growing so fast that it added more than 28,000 employees in twelve months; its employee ranks have grown an average of more than 40 percent a year each year of the past decade, and the firm reached 70,000 employees in 2007.

As America worries about layoffs, Infosys and other Indian companies worry about how to train all their new recruits fast enough. The entire nation's IT and call-center market has mushroomed, accounting for 5.4 percent of the country's GDP and employing 1.6 million Indians. Thousands of companies have latched on to the trend, moving service sector jobs not just to India but also to Eastern Europe, China, Malaysia, the Philippines, and other developing countries that offer first-world skills at third-world wages. French companies like France Telecom have moved work to Vietnam, and Japanese companies have hired Japanese-speaking Chinese workers. U.S. companies alone have 900,000 service workers overseas, with the lion's share located in India.[8]

○

IT ISN'T JUST America's $18,000-a-year call-answering jobs or $65,000-a-year computer programming jobs that are moving, although many companies portray offshoring as such. In fact, companies are scouring their payrolls to find all the jobs that could be done at lower cost in developing countries—ranging from some of the simplest entry-level work to some of the most sophisticated research-and-development jobs. Alan Blinder, the former Federal Reserve Board member who is now director of Princeton University's Center for Economic Policy Studies, argues that what will decide whether jobs are moved overseas is not how high the salary is in the United States, but the nature of the work. Work involving "personal services" like plastic surgery or lawn mowing will stay in the United States, while "impersonal services," like jobs for movie animators and call-center operators, may move. Some jobs in each category are well paid. Already, India is home to increasing numbers of the world's travel agents, legal researchers, business consultants, tax preparers, and bankers. Jobs that require Ph.D.'s and pay $150,000 a year in the United States are also on the move, as insurance companies instead pay India-based workers $50,000 a year to create sophisticated mathematical analysis that allows them to decide what rates to charge for life insurance back in the United States.[9]

The six-figure salaries at blue-chip firms mark the newest wave of a labor exodus that began almost unnoticed but has quickly gathered steam. Millions of college-educated workers in developed countries have just watched their wages become uncompetitive now that India has joined the world's labor market. India has about 2.7 million college graduates each year[10]—more than twice the 1.3 million graduating every year in the United States. Between 250,000 and 625,000 of the Indian graduates are qualified to staff the back offices of American and British companies, according to McKinsey, which is itself rushing to move jobs to India. Every year, more engineers graduate from college in a single Indian state, Andhra Pradesh, than in the entire United States.[11]

What is the big draw? Do the math: at IBM, for instance, moving about 5,000 tech jobs to low-cost countries like China and India will save the company $168 million annually within a few years. IBM can use the savings to cut prices to sell more, to pay better returns to shareholders, or to spiral prices downward for the entire industry, forcing competitors to move their own jobs overseas if they hope to stay in the game. The United States will lose 3.3 million jobs to offshoring by 2015, about 2 percent of the entire U.S. workforce. Those jobs would have paid a combined $136 billion a year in wages.[12] Companies in most industries have done the math, too, and are rushing to hire in India at far lower wages than they normally pay. Morgan Stanley, America Online, J. P. Morgan, British Telecom, Goldman, Sachs, Maersk Sealand, Union Pacific Railroad, Norwich Union, Deutsche Bank, Yahoo, and UBS are not far behind IBM. HSBC is hiring thousands in India, China, and Malaysia to take over work once done in New Jersey, Tokyo, London, Hong Kong, and Singapore. Even Britain's National Health Service is sending jobs to India. General Electric alone is in the process of moving nearly 100,000 jobs to India and thousands more to China. "The talent pool is just enormous and it is highly, highly skilled," said Chandramowli Srinivasan, president of EDS India. He has already helped his company hire 20,000 workers in India. "It is very addictive, once companies learn what is possible." Some companies are opening their own offices in India, and others have outsourced their work to companies like EDS. Either way, few customers notice the change, much less object to it.

While the trend toward offshoring is alarming, the sheer number of jobs involved is not, at least not for now. The loss of up to 300,000 white-collar jobs a year, or 6,000 jobs a week, isn't as worrisome when you consider that, at the typical high pace of job turnover in the United States, one million Americans lose jobs every two weeks, and a greater number find new ones.[13] But for Western workers, there are three big problems caused by offshoring. First, certain industries, like computer programming, are being hit very hard by job losses. Second, for those industries where there is less job movement, wages can still be held down by the fact that the jobs could be moved overseas, even if they are not. Third, with the labor market globalized, workers should expect that their jobs and careers will be less stable over decades as businesses continually evaluate where they can most effi-ciently have work done. Not all the news is bad for American work-ers—some of the job movement will even create jobs in the United States at higher wages. It will certainly result in a churning labor mar-ket. Americans in many fields will have to get used to changing jobs, or even careers, more often. "There will be more jobs, but a higher level of job turnover," according to Diana Farrell, director of the McKinsey Global Institute, a pioneer in research on offshoring.[14] She argues that while the United States is losing jobs to offshoring, it is gaining new ones fast enough to replace them. More soberingly, she points out that many American white-collar workers who lose their jobs don't find new ones quickly and, on the average, accept salaries 11 percent below their previous ones.[15] The more specialized the job lost, the harder it is to find a comparable replacement or quickly to retrain, especially for hard-hit industries like computer programming.

Economists are locked in arguments about how vast the changes will be. Princeton's Blinder calls offshoring "the third industrial rev-olution" and believes that it will require massive economic and social adjustments for Americans, even though he doesn't believe that it will produce massive unemployment.[16] When factory jobs began moving to low-wage countries like Mexico, Poland, and China, many hourly workers responded by making sure their children went to col-lege and moved into supposedly safe service-sector jobs. Today many of those very workers may need to find something else to do as they watch their own jobs move offshore, just as their parents' jobs migrated a generation before. Indeed, the reason offshoring is so unusual, and so unsettling, is that no one knows what will come next.

○

DURING THE 2004 U.S. presidential election, there was a noisy debate about offshoring that drew ordinary Americans' focus to the issue. Senator John Kerry railed against "Benedict Arnold CEOs" who moved jobs overseas. This got the attention of many companies that hadn't before thought of moving jobs to India, even prompting some to move work overseas. Marcus Courtney, president of the Washington Alliance of Technology Workers, has been issuing warnings on the effect that offshoring will have on America's workforce. "We are talking about our highest-paying and best-skilled jobs that corporate America is getting ready to export," said Mr. Courtney. "It will only lead to increased unemployment, lower wages, and fewer benefits for America's middle class."[17]

American workers get uncomfortable when they come face-to-face with their new foreign co-workers. Nalani Thite, an employee of Mr. Murthy's Infosys, was assigned to live in Seattle for a few months to work at Nordstrom's offices there. She remembered that her co-workers weren't always quick to cooperate with her or the other temporary employees brought from India to work in Nordstrom's home office. They seemed on edge about whether their jobs were safe. "The person you're dealing with is scared that their job might go if Infosys does well, or if this Indian lady can do it better than me."

Those whose jobs are on the line are keenly aware of the threat to their careers, but most Americans and Europeans don't realize that hundreds of thousands of low-wage white-collar workers are being hired overseas. The public is unaware because companies conceal their new hiring practices. Companies sending jobs overseas often insist that workers there be trained to camouflage their accents to sound more like their Western customers. Many telephone calls are answered by eager young Indian college graduates who try to blend in by adopting American or British accents, using fake Western names and talking about football or soccer scores from the caller's region. Indians learn that when they are talking to Americans, biscuits become cookies, lifts become elevators, and barristers become attorneys. At General Motors' landmark building in downtown Detroit, employees who dial 0 usually assume the operator is downstairs in the lobby. They are off by eight thousand miles. "Welcome to General Motors, my name is Andy, how may I help you?" says Amit, picking up the phone in Bombay.

The extent of the change has also gone unnoticed because many of the jobs on the move are those that customers wouldn't normally see. Ford Motor Company has two hundred accountants in Chennai who prepare corporate tax returns worldwide, jobs that were not visible to Ford customers before they were in India. Techies running companies' IT systems were out of sight to customers even when they were in the United States. Companies give lots of excuses for not publicizing the job moves: they see the strategy as a competitive advantage and don't want to tip off rivals; or they say that hiring workers in Asia lets work continue around the world's time zones, speeding goods to market; or they claim they aren't firing anyone, just placing new jobs or overtime work abroad; or they regret that there aren't enough qualified workers in the United States. Behind the rhetoric stands the simple logic of half-price wages, the most common and compelling reason jobs land on Indian shores.

Indian businessmen say Americans should not worry about the jobs' migrating to India, because Americans can always find something else to do for a living. "I'm always amazed at how most Americans underestimate the resilience of the U.S. economy," said Sunil Mehta, vice president of India's National Association of Software and Service Companies. "It is inevitable as part of a globalized economy that you have to have free trade." The stakes are high for India. Across the street from Mehta's office in Delhi is a construction site that is also home to the builders and their families. For them, home is a blue plastic sheet draped over a bamboo pole. Children play and laundry dries in the 100-degree heat as women and men steadily carry baskets of red mud on their heads. One carries a stack of ten bricks on his head.[18]

As India races into the modern world, the mix of poverty and aspiration can be incongruous. In Bombay, bedraggled children prowl through traffic, begging or selling sticks of gum, plastic toys, or flowers to be offered to the gods. Child beggars are nothing new for India, but the scrawny kids peddling bootleg copies of *Harvard Business Review* for $3.25 a copy[19] suggest that the economic revolution has left its mark, if not its bounties, on Indians far outside the realm of universities and call centers.

○

A BIOTECH COMPANY called Lupin, located in an unlikely spot a three hours' drive east of Mumbai, provides more evidence of the economic revolution. Getting to its labs takes a sturdy vehicle: you leave the highway and zigzag up a dirt road into hills where locals shoo goats out of the way of oncoming traffic. Around a bend, a starkly white minimalist building emerges from the ancient, dusty landscape like an optical illusion. Behind a tall gate and security checkpoint, hundreds of white-coated scientists are racing to invent new drugs.[20] They are part of India's thriving biotechnology industry, which began as a vehicle for widespread production of generic drugs and copycatting of other drug companies' inventions but has grown into an innovative industry. India already has seventy-five pharmaceutical plants approved by the U.S. Food and Drug Administration—more than any nation except the United States itself.[21] Meanwhile, big Western drug companies are tapping India's well-trained doctors to conduct clinical trials for drugs under development.

The scientists and call-center workers alike have being spending their newfound paychecks, further boosting the economy. However worrying for Westerners, the success of the offshoring movement has been a catalyst for economic growth in India. Hearing that economic powerhouses like America are worrying about competing with India has instilled pride in business and government leaders as well as in workers. The creation of just a million jobs for college graduates in a land with a billion people has had a disproportionate effect. It has bred optimism about the future in young Indians entering the job market. It has stimulated other parts of the economy by creating spinoff jobs—restaurants have opened because prosperous Indians now go out to eat more often, and construction companies are hiring because companies are building new offices. Motorcycle and car factories are running overtime, as computer programmers spend their paychecks on new sets of wheels; motorcycle sales have nearly quadrupled since reforms began, reaching 7.4 million a year in 2007. Car sales have skyrocketed from fewer than 200,000 a year in 1991 to 1.5 million in 2007[22] and are on pace to double to 2 million by 2010.[23] The explosion of new jobs and new spending has helped India's economy grow quickly, almost as rapidly as China's and more than double the standard "Hindu rate of growth," reaching a blistering rate of 8.9 percent a year in 2006.

So far, dramatic advances have come despite the nation's fickle relationship with reform and the slow-paced Indian bureaucracy. Because offshoring has thrived and created millions of new jobs, the Indian government has drawn criticism for not helping other Indian industries compete in the global economy. India's red tape, historic antibusiness bias, and truly abysmal infrastructure has held back the rest of the nation's economy, allowing only a small sliver to flourish. Indeed, one reason high-tech industries have thrived in India is that they were less tangled in India's notorious red tape: because the technologies were new, the "license raj" didn't have a chance to invent nearly as much mind-numbing regulation for them. Nor did companies like Infosys and Wipro require decent infrastructure to prosper. Rather than shipping exports over bumpy roads to slow-moving seaports, they were able to send exports over computer wires, telephone lines, and satellite links.

It is easy to see why India has not yet attracted many new factories. India's developing-world infrastructure prevents companies from exporting their goods cheaply and quickly. James P. Holden, then running Chrysler, toured India in 2000, considering whether to produce and sell cars there. He returned to Detroit and summarized his visit with a smirk: "Call me when you've built some roads." The lack of an expressway in Mumbai, for instance, makes for a three-hour crosstown drive over potholed, backed-up local roads, which loitering cows occasionally block. India doesn't have enough power plants, and electricity supplies are so unreliable that lights—and computer screens—regularly flicker in downtown business districts. Small, high-tech companies keep stacks of car batteries on hand as backup electricity supplies. Indian airports are so shabby they have become a national embarrassment. Broadly speaking, India is competitive in manufacturing only after goods make it to the airport or the seaport where they are exported, and that is much more time-consuming in India than in China. There are a number of inefficiencies beyond infrastructure, both in exporting and even in selling to the Indian market. Companies must navigate antiquated customs processing, variations in taxes and byzantine rules for transporting goods between Indian states in addition to the crumbling highways, decrepit airports, and what-me-hurry ports.

○

As a result, while India increasingly supplies the brains foreign companies need, it doesn't yet provide much of the brawn. Yet the Indian government needs factories exporting goods around the world to make good on its promise to spread the benefits of new jobs among more citizens. While India's well-educated, English-speaking elite can find work in the new office buildings, the majority of Indians aren't trained for white-collar work. Fully 39 percent of Indians are illiterate.[24] Many could work in factories, but because there aren't enough manufacturing jobs, millions are unemployed or continue to eke out a living in farming. Tens of millions of Indians would have different lives, and better opportunities to offer their children, if the nation had the modern infrastructure necessary to persuade foreign companies to build factories in India to export goods to buyers in the United States, Europe, and the rest of the world.

But India has always been an anomaly and, unlike other developing countries, has gained more attention for foreign investment that creates white-collar jobs rather than blue-collar work. Still, as the rush to move service-industry jobs offshore gives foreign investors confidence in India, the nation's manufacturing industry is also benefiting. Foreign companies are anticipating that India will become a giant market as more and more Indians can afford to spend. Other foreign companies are beginning to look to India as a manufacturer because they have already moved so many factories to China and are worried about becoming overdependent on the output of a single nation, especially one like China with a potentially volatile political future. If a company overextends itself in a single country, political turmoil, disease, or even natural disaster halfway around the world can halt the company's entire production in a matter of days.

Foreign companies are discovering that, partly because of the legacy of Gandhi and Nehru, who encouraged the development of small companies and handmade items, Indian factories are among the most competitive in the world at producing, say, 5,000 copies of a hand-beaded shirt, or 500 copies of a specialized part. By contrast, China excels at churning out 50,000 or 100,000 copies of the same item. Most Indian factories haven't been allowed to grow large enough over the decades to adapt to modern methods for mass production. As a result, foreign companies that need relatively small runs of goods made are increasingly turning to India for those products. In mass production, India is learning how to thrive in one industry at a time. For instance, Toyota was an early foreign investor in Indian manufacturing: the Japanese company invested $200 million in six joint ventures with Indian companies that make auto parts. Because Toyota sets the benchmark in auto manufacturing and its engineers have trained the company's Indian suppliers in sophisticated Japanese production techniques, manufacturing quality has been brought to world-class levels in the auto supply industry, helping Indian companies grow by selling parts to Indian car companies, to Toyota, and to other foreign car makers. After a few years, the Indian auto parts companies are just beginning to gain the kinds of economies of scale that make exports viable. Many of the world's big auto makers now buy labor-intensive parts from Indian companies. As a result, India's auto parts exports have been growing by 25 percent a year and are expected to rival China's by 2015.[25] Every auto parts factory opened could mean hundreds or even thousands of new jobs for India's ranks of unskilled workers.

○

FOREIGN COMPANIES eager to do business in India do best when they follow strategies that differ radically from their approach to doing business in China. A close look at one multinational company's approach to both markets illustrates the differences between the two Asian countries. Philips has been in India since 1930, but follows different strategies in India and China.

In the northwestern Indian town of Mohali, 1,400 miles away from the tech oasis of Bangalore, Philips has a factory making light bulbs. At one end of the factory, sand combined with soda ash is heated to 2,732 degrees. The mixture becomes a three-foot-deep, colorless river of molten glass flowing through the factory. The clear liquid streams into molds that shape the light bulbs. Along simple assembly lines, workers insert the filament and support wires to shells of light bulbs moving steadily down the line, and watch as they are lit up in quality tests. The Indian light bulb factory looks much like the Chinese factory, except for one difference: nonconformist Indians wear what they want, not the Philips-blue uniforms worn by their Chinese counterparts. The fruit of this factory is the source of the majority of Philips' profits in India—a whopping 40 percent of light bulbs sold in the nation are Philips bulbs.

The Indian factory with its 1,000 workers is the most efficient the company has anywhere in Asia—Chinese factories don't come close. Yet the Indian factory can't compete in global exports because of India's poor infrastructure. Sailings from India's ports aren't frequent enough for the global economy. Even for shipment within India, light bulbs have to be packaged in corrugated cardboard tubes instead of the thin boxes used elsewhere in the world; otherwise they break when bumping around in the back of a truck along India's rutted roads. For competitive exports—even to keep its exports in one piece—Philips, like many other companies, must turn to China.

Until the 1991 reforms, many foreign companies, including Philips, weren't allowed to own majority stakes in their Indian operations, and thus couldn't control their own business. After the 1991 reforms, Philips executives stationed in India argued that headquarters should move more white-collar jobs to India, but for years they were met with skepticism. Finally, in 1996, Philips opened a small software development center in Bangalore. In 2003, the entire Philips board met in India and toured other companies' back-office operations. They were immediately sold on the offshoring concept, and then the movement of jobs to India accelerated. Philips created a back-office service center in Chennai and financial executives from all the company's divisions were told to transfer as much white-collar work as possible east. Today about three hundred accountants and financial analysts work in Chennai on behalf of Philips offices in North America. The next two hundred workers hired there will do back-office work for offices in Europe and elsewhere.[26]

O

WHILE THE OFFSHORING industry has served as a catalyst for economic growth in India and infected the Indian middle-class workforce with optimism, a parallel change is happening for some companies doing business there. As they strive to sell to Indian customers, they are questioning business models that work well in well-developed Western economies. In those established markets, many multinationals concentrate on selling their goods to the top-earning 20 percent of customers—those at the top of a pyramid of incomes. The rule of thumb is that 80 percent of a company's goods are sold to that group. The challenges of the Indian market have turned that idea upside down: the vast majority of the money in the Indian market is at the bottom of the income pyramid. C. K. Prahalad, an eminent University of Michigan Business School professor, argues that selling products to "the bottom of the pyramid" is the future of global business because of the sheer numbers of potential customers now available in India and China. If he is right, that would prove to be a dramatic change of focus for big business. Worldwide, there are 4 billion people at the bottom of the pyramid, and they spend $5 trillion a year, according to the World Bank.[27]

Many of the experiments to find out whether his theories are profitable are happening in India. For Philips, too, India serves as a test bed for consumer products aimed at the poor, in part because it finds Indian employees more creative than Chinese at dreaming up new products and strategies, and in part because, thanks to the tradition of Gandhi rather than of Mao, it finds both employees and company managers rather more concerned about the plight of the poor. For $5, Philips sells a hand-crank radio for the rural Indian market, where electricity is scarce, and has sold 90,000 of them, worth $450,000. The company also invented a low-pollution wood-burning stove, important because 1.6 million deaths worldwide—more than 400,000 of them in India alone—are caused by indoor air pollution, chiefly from cooking fires. It began selling the low-priced stove in pilot projects in 2006. Perhaps most notably, Philips is experimenting with providing pay-per-use services, not just selling goods, to rural Indians. In partnership with the nation's space research organization (which provides satellite access), with a nongovernment organization, and with a large hospital chain called Apollo, Philips has outfitted a van that travels to rural areas where doctors are rare. The van carries doctors as well as diagnostic equipment like X-ray and MRI machines for those who need care. Because images from the machines are transmitted by satellite to specialists in big-city hospitals, sick rural residents who might not otherwise make it to a doctor can get diagnosis and care without leaving their villages. "How do you move away from the temptation of providing a portfolio only for the affluent?" asks Philips' India CEO, Ram Ramachandran.[28] "You have to be part of the economy where you're working." Besides, he argues, the real buying power in India comes from the poor. "Imagine a billion people spending a little, little bit of money, which adds up to a helluva lot." Philips doesn't bother with rural customers in China now, but if the India projects work, products developed for the Indian market could be offered in China and across the developing world. The strategy change parallels Philips' decision to market low-end medical equipment for the corporate market in China, but in India it is aimed at consumers, not companies.

Meanwhile, the Philips "Innovation Campus" in Bangalore has already grown to 1,700 employees and is expected to reach 3,000 employees by 2008. Employees there write computer programs that run all kinds of gadgets made by Philips, from televisions and DVD players to cell phones and coffeemakers, and they are paid a quarter of what Americans working in Silicon Valley would be paid. The company's employees in India write 20 percent of Philips software worldwide, much of which winds up in products made across the border in China with the brawn of 50,000 factory workers churning out Philips goods.[29] Indian business leaders see many potential synergies between India and China.

"If we orient ourselves to working together, we could be a formidable force of two nations," says Ratan Tata, whose offshoring firm, Tata Consultancy Services, already has more than 500 employees in Hangzhou, China, serving Chinese customers as well as multinational companies doing business in Korea, Japan, Singapore, Taiwan, and elsewhere—most with factories in China. "China is really the factory of the world. India can be the knowledge center of this region," Mr. Tata says. "If we could put those two together, it could be very synergetic."[30]

○

AND SO IT IS that China's government-planned development has turned it into the factory to the world and is in the process of transforming it, like India, into a powerful magnet for foreign companies' white-collar work. India, meanwhile, is finally following China's example, first attracting back-office jobs and more recently interesting foreign companies in opening factories. The two nations have taken opposite approaches, but they share one important trait: they are the fastest-growing big economies in the world.

Because each is growing about three times as fast as the United States and Japan and far faster than Europe, India and China represent the unavoidable future for companies around the world. Established companies have already saturated the large American and European markets, and must fight ferociously there just for the opportunity to continue to grow slowly. The two emerging-market giants are the only places where most big companies can grow rapidly, their only hope for adding vast numbers of new customers, and thus for pleasing stockholders and corporate boards. Capitalism is forcing old-line companies to figure out how to go after the world's newest and poorest consumer markets.

The meeting points of China and corporate America can be incongruous: visitors to Shanghai can sit in a hotel lobby listening to a Chinese band playing John Denver songs while midwestern M.B.A. types marvel that Chinese eat chicken feet instead of buffalo wings. Some of the world's biggest IPOs are those of Chinese companies controlled by the Communist Party, capitalism's new best friend. The corporate bellwether General Electric says that in the next decade 60 percent of its revenue growth will come from developing countries, primarily India and China. By contrast, just 20 percent of GE's revenue came from developing countries in the past decade. Intel's chairman, Craig Barrett, saw the possibilities in hiring cheap white-collar workers in India and China early on, but also recognized the potential for selling more semiconductors in both countries. Because Intel's annual sales growth is flat in the United States but has reached 30 percent in India, Intel has gone to the trouble of persuading Indian banks to create affordable loans for computer buyers there. Now Indians can buy a PC with installment payments of $11.45 a month, suddenly putting computers within reach for millions and creating demand for more Intel chips. By bringing the global economy to India and China—both by hiring Indians and Chinese and by selling products to them—Western companies are changing the face of the world economy and thus the way we live, those of us in the East as well as those of us in the West.

And as we'll see in the next chapter, the ability to connect cheap workers in India and China with the modern technology and infrastructure of the global economy is not just changing the lives of workers worldwide. It is not merely changing companies' fortunes. It is also changing the very way business is done—a revolution that has not been equaled since Henry Ford unleashed the assembly line.

CHAPTER FIVE

THE DISASSEMBLY LINE

In a ritual reprised late each afternoon, a well-worn legion of trucks lumbers out of the gates of southern Chinese factories, piled precariously high with the goods produced that day. The trucks are bound for Hong Kong, the vital intersection between mainland China and the West. As the sun sets over Hong Kong's harbor, the trucks reach a nearby neighborhood filled with shipping warehouses. Up and down the streets, the story is the same: a truck from China pulls up, and wiry men wearing shorts and T-shirts clamber over its back and sides, scrambling to reach the cardboard boxes it carries, the fruits of a day of Chinese factory labor. Mesmerizingly efficient, the men carry the boxes from the trucks to a nearby scale inside the warehouse before striding back to the truck for the next load. Meanwhile, others weigh and measure the boxes individually and slap each one with a sticker showing bar-coded information about the contents—not so different from a neighborhood UPS or FedEx package. Yet another set of workers stacks the labeled boxes into enormous metal shipping containers that can be loaded straight into the hold of an airplane or a container ship like giant steel suitcases. When the truck from the factory has been stripped bare, it is driven back across the Chinese border to collect more boxes ready for export. Moments after the empty truck leaves the warehouse, another pulls into its place and stays just long enough for the men to load the filled metal shipping container onto it for the short journey either to the airport cargo facility or to Hong Kong's giant container port.

But the most surprising part of this shipping cycle is that so many of the boxes are not filled with finished products headed from a Chinese factory to Western shelves. Instead, the boxes contain partly finished goods being shipped from one factory to another. A single component may undergo several voyages inside shipping containers before its final exodus to a Wisconsin Wal-Mart or a London stereo shop, often arriving at a factory, being integrated into a product moving along an assembly line, and being shipped out in a single day. At a warehouse owned by the Hong Kong shipping company Trans Global Logistics, boxloads of made-in-China car windows are loaded at sunset into a shipping container headed for a Korean auto assembly plant. Next there's a stack of boxes filled with half-finished Treo cell phone handsets being shipped from mainland China to a Taiwanese factory that adds high-tech components. In the same warehouse sits fabric woven in China but bound for London. Some boxes go the other way: stacks of microchips made in Japan are destined for a mainland Chinese factory, where they will become the brains of computers assembled there. Other shipments are finished goods, many of which have been pieced together from components from several factories: a twenty-foot-high stack of boxes containing about two thousand pairs of New Balance tennis shoes assembled in China is on its way to Footlocker stores in Los Angeles. Nearby, a few hundred pairs of Chinese-made Wrangler zip-fly blue jeans are waiting to be shipped to Pakistan. Next to the jeans are boxes filled with designer sweaters that began as flax from France, which was spun into yarn in central China, and then knitted into sweaters in southern China. The completed sweaters, having journeyed through several Chinese factories, are being air-shipped to Eileen Fisher's New York warehouse, via Seoul, Korea, on Asiana Airlines. Although few Chinese can afford the luxury of travel, except a one-way bus ride to a waiting job, many of China's exported goods experience a zigzagging itinerary that would weary even the most experienced globetrotter.

The way the world does business has changed because what Americans and Europeans buy on store shelves is flowing down a new kind of assembly line, one that stretches back and forth between disparate countries around the world. Ten years ago, this indirect, pinball-like path from factory to customer was not an option. But during the 1990s, companies began searching for the lowest-cost place to make each component of their products. At the same time, sophisticated technology made reality of what had once been a logistical pipe dream: creating a seamless connection between multiple factories, sometimes in multiple countries. Cost-cutting efforts combined with powerful new technology allowed companies to change the way they build most consumer products.

The last time a manufacturing revolution of this magnitude occurred was in the early twentieth century, when Henry Ford revolutionized the business world by popularizing the assembly line. He brought all the materials and components needed to make a car into one place, lined up workers, and had each of them manufacture and install one piece until they had cooperated to make a car. Iron ore brought to Detroit by boat from northern Michigan went in one end of Ford's factory, and a finished car rolled out the other end. In between, the iron ore was turned into steel, which was pressed into hoods and doors, which were attached to an engine and hundreds of other parts, until finally a complete car was driven out of the factory. During the 1920s, forty thousand workers, a whole town's worth, toiled in a single Ford factory complex in Detroit making Model Ts. Wave after wave of immigrants moved to Detroit to work in the auto factories, and customers could buy a car in any color they wanted— as long as it was black.[1]

In the twenty-first century, everything has changed. Henry Ford's assembly line has shattered into a thousand pieces and scattered around the world. The new system—call it a disassembly line—is the result of companies rushing to break up their products into specialized subassemblies to drive down costs, ratchet up quality, and reduce the time it takes to get the product to market. The manufacturing process is so different from that of the last century that the term "assembly line" has been replaced by the phrase "supply chain." Each step in the production process is now like one link in a flexible chain, which is hooked to the next piece, then to the next, and so on. The traditional assembly line for shoes, laptop computers, sweaters, toys, and most other consumer goods has fragmented. For expensive products like cars, the supply chain is extremely sophisticated—each car has an average of five thousand pieces, coming together from around the world. Even a cheap toy might be assembled from pieces made in a dozen different factories strewn across a Chinese province. Making sure that goods move along the supply chain efficiently has become so complex and critical that managers now study this process in business school and use specialized computer programs to track all the various components coming together from around the world. Toyota and other big manufacturers require suppliers to slap radio-frequency identification tags on individual parts to help Toyota's computers send them from trucks at loading docks, down conveyor belts to the final assembly line at just the right time. Putting the pieces together is a dizzying dance that involves a combination of quickly evolving technology, truly global companies, and hundreds of thousands of factories around the world.

○

HERE'S HOW TODAY'S DISASSEMBLY LINE WORKS: a clothing company like J. C. Penney might order 100,000 copies of a shirt. First, it might buy yarn from a Korean producer, then ship the yarn to Taiwan to be dyed and woven into cloth. The clothing company might order buttons from a specialized Japanese company with a factory in China, but ship the buttons plus the freshly woven cloth to Thailand to be cut and sewn into a shirt. Because fashions are changing quickly and the store would want the shirt on its shelves as soon as possible, the cloth and buttons might be sent to five different Thai factories so that each could rush to finish and ship 20,000 shirts, completing the 100,000-piece order faster than if one factory produced the entire lot. Five weeks after they are ordered, identical shirts can be found on store shelves halfway around the world. It may sound needlessly complicated, but this shipping frenzy pays for itself by leading to fewer remaindered goods, which occur if the shirts hit store shelves after fickle customers have moved on to newer fashions.

Because so many different factories are now involved in making each product and sophisticated technology tracks which parts should be added as it is assembled, it is easier for companies to customize orders for customers. That's another major departure from Henry Ford's assembly line method, which produced a single make in a single color.[2] One reason that Nike can let customers design their own tennis shoes over the Internet is that the subcontractor responsible for the upper parts is specialized enough to sew together different-colored variations requested by the customers. Dell Computer can configure each computer as ordered because it doesn't have to make each piece itself; instead, Dell installs various components made by different outside suppliers. For today's customers, choosing a color is just the beginning: many products are customizable down to the last detail. So much for the homogeneity of the black Model T Ford.

The disassembly line is the backbone of globalization. The ability to fragment the assembly line and stretch it across the world has dramatically changed the roles of companies and their workers. People don't move to Detroit to work in enormous Ford factories anymore. Instead, auto companies break up their long assembly lines and move work to wherever they find cheap labor alongside decent shipping pipelines to the rest of the world. Today, jobs are emigrating instead of people. Fifteen percent of North American companies and 29 percent of European ones no longer manufacture any of their products in their home markets, according to Deloitte Touche Tohmatsu.[3]

The disassembly line has let companies become extremely efficient, by building each piece of a finished good in the country where it is cheapest, then moving the part on to the next factory in line. This approach also allows each company to focus on what it does most productively, driving down prices for consumers around the world and spreading jobs across the globe. Thomas Hout, senior adviser to the Boston Consulting Group, calculates that globalized supply chains reduce the prices of factory goods sold in the United States by 5 percent.[4] The average price American importers paid for a T-shirt fell 30 percent over a decade, from $2.14 in 1996 to $1.51 by the end of 2005, according to the Progressive Policy Institute.[5]

Seasoned Western companies and scrappy Asian businesses alike are specializing in unprecedented ways. One company in the southern Chinese city of Shenzhen makes thousands of varieties of plastic eyes for toys and dolls. Just eyes.[6] And so the Shenzhen factory has become a link in many dolls' very global supply chain.

The result of all this specialization is that lots of companies either no longer make what they sell or no longer sell what they make. Leading companies now concentrate only on what they can do better than others, hiring specialist subcontractors to make pieces of their goods or even to put the various pieces from other contractors together and box up the finished product, ready for shipment to customers. Thus, the world's most established companies are counting on developing-country businesses to build the products they sell, whether they make dolls or shoes or computers. The industrialized world is busy deindustrializing, while the developing world is industrializing.

Many leading-edge American companies have concluded that their real role is in inventing new products or marketing finished products, not in trudging through the dirty work of crafting each component or putting the pieces together. Few Western companies are the cheapest and best at assembling what they sell, so they have hired other companies to do it for them. Apple created the iPod and markets it, but the chip that powers it—the brains of the iPod—was invented by PortalPlayer, a small Indian company in Hyderabad, and the devices are made in China and shipped around the world. Wal-Mart builds giant stores and orders what Americans want to buy from those selling for low prices. Even though it sells more goods than any other American company, it doesn't own any factories. Wal-mart alone imports from China nearly as much as the entire country of Canada imports from China.

Why do companies go to the trouble of radically changing the way they do business? The aim is to lower costs, and few schemes would be considered too elaborate in the pursuit of that goal. Consider Ford's assembly line. In 2006, the Ford Motor Company paid its American workers $27 an hour—$52 if you include the cost of health insurance and other benefits. These highly skilled members of the United Automobile Workers union are perfectly capable of building dashboards, for instance, along Ford's assembly lines. But if Ford instead hires a unionized Michigan auto parts supplier to deliver the dashboard, then pays the Ford employees only to attach it to the rest of the car, it will be much cheaper because the supplier pays its workers about $15 an hour, or $25 an hour including benefits. And if Ford hires a non-union supplier, say, in North Carolina, to build the dashboard, wages are closer to $10 an hour, $16 with benefits. That gives Ford a cheaper way to get its dashboard. If Ford's supplier subcontracts to other companies around the globe to build pieces of the dashboard, it can deliver the dashboard to Ford for even less. So the supplier might buy speedometers from a factory in China that pays $2 a day, have the behind-the-dashboard wiring sent from a $4-a-day factory in Mexico, and buy the heating vents from yet another Chinese factory, where workers earn a dollar a day. Because the plastic for the dashboard is formed with expensive, high-tech molding machines, it would likely be made in the supplier's American factory, which would then pay its workers to combine all the pieces into a finished dashboard and deliver it to Ford. Building a globalized dashboard—even after including the cost of shipping the parts overseas between factories—costs significantly less than using Henry Ford's assembly line model of having workers at one huge factory make speedometers, wiring harnesses, heating vents, engines, and other components and bolt them all together to form a car.

The shift from assembly lines to disassembly lines didn't happen overnight. First the supply chain for American auto companies moved outside of Detroit to auto parts factories in other states with lower wages. Then the simplest, most labor-intensive components were imported from low-wage Mexican factories. Now more and more parts of increasing sophistication are bought from factories in China, India, and other Asian countries and shipped across the ocean before being installed in America's cars. Leading companies still make their most valuable, difficult-to-manufacture goods—and the ones that rely on proprietary knowledge—in high-wage factories at home. But overseas factories are increasingly skilled at turning out specialized components for all kinds of consumer goods, and many of those factories are in China. Most disassembly lines touch China at least once because the nation, with its low wages and modern infrastructure, makes a very compelling manufacturing spot. But today's disassembly lines are remarkably global because other countries remain cheaper or more efficient than China for making certain kinds of goods and components.

While China's seemingly bottomless pool of low-wage workers is essential, it isn't enough by itself. Other countries have lower wages than China's, including most of Africa and nearby Bangladesh, Cambodia, Vietnam, and parts of India. Jobs move around the world in search of lower wages, but low pay rates aren't the only reason for the migration. China is very cost competitive when it comes to the final assembly of large volumes of labor-intensive goods like clothing, shoes, or DVD players, even if some high-precision components are made elsewhere. The United States, Europe, Japan, and Korea remain more efficient than China when it comes to manufacturing goods or components that require few workers but call for heavy investments in expensive machinery like robots. Fragmented assembly lines allow each task to be done at the place in the world best suited for efficiently producing one piece of a product.

○

GLOBAL TRANSPORTATION has gotten cheaper, too, with trucks, trains, ships, and planes functioning as a seamless system of globe-spanning arteries. An unassuming UPS warehouse just a five-minute drive from the Shanghai airport is an important nerve center for an incredible variety of the world's widgets. Cardboard boxes and wooden crates are stacked neatly in numbered rows in what looks like an oversized garage. Every month, the 140 UPS workers there handle 8,000 tons of goods flowing out of China and 3,000 tons of imports. One spring day, a wooden box filled with electronics equipment flown from New York's John F. Kennedy Airport to Shanghai was parked in a row near a tall stack of what looked like rolled-up carpets. The rolls turned out to be expensive Japanese fabric bound for a Chinese clothing factory. Next to the fabric was a four-foot-tall cardboard box holding the weekly shipment of car radio antennas made in a General Motors factory in Australia and bound for GM's Shanghai factory. Nearby were two pallets of miniature ball bearings. The ball bearings were on their way to a factory in Wuxi, about a two-hour drive from Shanghai, run by Seagate Technology, an American company that makes storage drives for computers, videogames, digital cameras, MP3 players, and other gadgets. A tall wooden crate held a mobile X-ray machine made by Philips in the Netherlands and ordered by a hospital in Ningbo, China. In one corner was a secure warehouse within the UPS warehouse where expensive microprocessors were kept before being shipped out to computer assembly plants in nearby Suzhou. The sophisticated microprocessors came from California's Advanced Micro Devices, and a single cardboard box in the padlocked AMD room could be worth $100,000.[7]

Dwarfing the rows of imported goods are the constant export shipments. Every night, starting at midnight, the first of ten trucks carrying hard drives—fruits of a day's work at a Chinese factory—pulls up to the warehouse. UPS workers weigh, count, and record the shipments, fill out Chinese customs paperwork, and stack the cardboard boxes in the warehouse for a few hours until trucks arrive to carry the boxes to the airport. The hard drives are made at the Seagate factory in China and shipped from Shanghai to Chicago, Los Angeles, Dallas, Malaysia, and Hong Kong—an average of 250,000 hard drives a day, one of which may be powering your computer. Meanwhile, a beaten-up blue truck pulls up from a factory in Ningbo, China, a three-hour drive away. An orange UPS forklift scoots to the back of the truck to unload wooden crates full of auto parts bound for the Dana Corporation in Youngstown, Ohio. Next, UPS workers load a white truck with cardboard boxes containing computer screens made by Quanta Computer, a Taiwanese company with a factory in Shanghai. The driver starts the engine, then heads for the Shanghai airport, where the screens will be loaded onto a flight bound for Penang, Malaysia. That's where Dell assembles computers before shipping them to the United States, meeting the made-to-order requests of Dell's customers.

○

BUT THE MODERN disassembly line isn't just for factory goods: even services are starting to follow the example of factory assembly lines and are fragmenting globally. Henry Ford's pioneering assembly idea was used first for cars, then adopted by nearly every other manufacturing industry, and eventually used for services in addition to goods. The founder of Motown Records, Berry Gordy Jr., pioneered applying the assembly line concept to services. Mr. Gordy churned out hit songs for his record label in the 1960s by using the production process he observed while working on an assembly line building Fords. His Motown artists followed a standardized process: first there was song writing, then recording, then the quality-control department, and finally promotion. Today Motown's assembly line approach to services is also being disassembled into a global supply chain—not to produce songs but to write computer programs, design consumer goods, create movie animation, process bank loans, or produce PowerPoint presentations for consulting firms. In recent decades, more and more companies have outsourced their white-collar service work just as Ford and other auto makers gradually outsourced manufacturing tasks. First they outsourced the work to other American firms, then moved the jobs overseas, often to India, when reliable communications connected cheap labor to supply chains in the same way that China's highway infrastructure hooked up its factories to global trade.

While China is adding white-collar exports to its repertoire and India is increasing factory exports, infrastructure is determining which low-wage country proves more competitive in each field. India's infrastructure is well-educated English speakers, who are wired to the West through modern telecom and computer technology, and that has given India the edge in luring white-collar jobs. The Chinese government's drive to build superior physical infrastructure—tens of thousands of miles of highways and modern airports—allowed China to dominate manufacturing exports. Without high-capacity, dependable modern infrastructure, the world's sophisticated supply chains simply don't work. The existence of new factories in China and call centers in India has hastened the fragmentation of traditional assembly lines, supercharging China's manufacturing power and India's service industry.

○

Now that India and China have reconnected themselves to the rest of the world, disassembly lines have redrawn the map of world commerce entirely. For developing countries, the changes have been a big boost, lifting hundreds of millions of the world's poorest people out of poverty through jobs at new factories. The combined growth of India and China during the past two decades has cut the portion of the world living in extreme poverty from 40 percent to 20 percent, according to the World Bank. The stakes are high: India's government figures that if it can keep the economy growing at 8 percent a year for the next decade, it will lift 350 million people out of poverty.[8]

As millions of jobs move across the globe, nearly every nation has grown concerned about the future of its labor force. But China and India are not sucking up all the world's work. While China was becoming the world's factory, its Asian neighbors were terrified there would be no room left for them in world trade. Contrary to their fears, trade has increased, though their roles have changed dramatically. Because of the popularity of the disassembly line model, developing countries have found they have unexpected new roles to play in the global economy. Bangladesh or Vietnam might not have the manufacturing sophistication to turn out an entire laptop computer or a whole car suitable for export—including silicon wafers and state-of-the-art engines—but they certainly have factories capable of making simple components that can become pieces of those complex products. Developing countries without high-technology capabilities have made themselves the origins of supply chains—doing the first, simplest few steps, such as weaving cloth for blouses or making a car's wiring harness—before the goods move on to the next step in the production process, and often on to assembly in China. Twenty years ago, developing countries provided just 14 percent of rich countries' manufacturing imports, but by 2006 that figure had increased to 40 percent, and by 2030 it should rise to more than 65 percent, according to the World Bank, which predicts that global trade will have increased dramatically by then.[9] Thanks to the speedy operations at shipping warehouses in Hong Kong and Shanghai, even small companies in underdeveloped, otherwise stagnant countries can now form a link in the supply chain for globalized goods, rather than losing out to other countries entirely.

The same goes for India. Because companies are becoming ever more virtual, India and China are frequently parts of the same global production lines. Companies that are comfortable fragmenting their assembly lines into supply chains and scattering them around the world are hiring Indians to do white-collar work in order to support the blue-collar work sent to China. That is to say, Indian engineers are designing car parts to be manufactured in China, just as the Philips engineers in Bangalore write computer code for the digital TVs, cell phones, and DVD players its Chinese factory workers snap together. India and China form complementary links, rather than competing links, in many companies' disassembly lines. Using the two developing nations together is a powerful, almost irresistible, tool for Western companies trying to ratchet down their costs and speed up production cycles.

In addition to its significant benefits, globalization presents extensive risks for companies that choose to wade in its waters. A problem at a single link in these ever-lengthening supply chains—anything from a tsunami or blizzard to a fire at a local warehouse or a strike by dockworkers at a port—can temporarily shut down all sales of a product, disappointing buyers and devastating company profits. So far, companies have found that the enormous cost savings offset the dangers. Still, lingering concerns about China's political stability or America's vulnerability to terrorism or even dangers posed by diseases like bird flu could shift the valuation of the risks of globalizing.

Moving jobs overseas also allows companies in America to rely on higher-paid American workforces for more sophisticated work while factories in China do the dirty work of building their goods, and cubicle farms in India do their boring back-office work. But the jobs of some of those who used to work in American factories—or call centers or mortgage-processing offices or law firms—have been eliminated as entire offices have moved overseas. Some of the American workers whose jobs were slashed will find new, more interesting work. But many won't have the skills and may be left behind.

○

THE MASTERS OF SUPPLY CHAIN MANAGEMENT—and the people responsible for bringing many foreign-made goods to the United

States and Europe—are a couple of brothers from Hong Kong. Think of them as Chinese Henry Fords, business pioneers for this century. They run a Hong Kong company called Li & Fung. Few Westerners have heard of it, but it touches millions of Western consumers. With little fanfare, Li & Fung accounted for 3.7 percent of the United States' clothing imports in 2005, some $2.7 billion worth. Li & Fung finds factories that can make just about anything you would find in a department store, from garden tools and screwdriver sets to towels, tennis shoes, toys, and clothing. But even though it ships about 1.7 billion pieces of all kinds of goods from fifty countries, Li & Fung doesn't own a single factory. Put simply, the firm takes orders from companies in the West that no longer make what they sell, and it finds factories to make the goods, whatever they are. "We're the ultimate outsourcer," says William Fung, managing director.[10] He and his brother Victor run the company, which greases the wheels of global trade by putting buyers and sellers together.

The company's evolution mirrors that of China, but it also shows a way forward for companies and countries caught in fresh competition from lower-wage countries. A century ago, when China was shipping porcelain to the West, a Chinese man who spoke English decided he would rather go into the shipping business for himself than work as a translator for the American or British merchants buying goods in China and selling them at home. That was Victor and William Fung's grandfather, Fung Pak-liu, who with his partner Li To-ming formed Li & Fung in 1906 in Canton, a southern Chinese city today known as Guangzhou.

When the Communists won power in 1949, the Fung family, like many merchants, lost all its property in mainland China. As China closed its doors to the world, the Fung family escaped to Hong Kong. There was heartbreaking chaos for many of those who made it out of China: desperate, impoverished Chinese refugees streamed into Hong Kong—some overland, some even swimming from Macao through shark-infested waters. On arrival, thousands of wretched Chinese immigrants lived packed in boardinghouses whose rooms for rent were literally metal cages. The lucky ones found relatives, friends, or jobs quickly. By comparison, the prosperous Fung family was very fortunate: despite having lost everything in China, many family members had already settled in Hong Kong. But the family company suddenly had no way to make the goods its customers wanted to buy. The Chinese factories that it relied upon were, in an instant, cut off when China closed itself to the world.

Like the city of Hong Kong itself, Li & Fung adapted quickly. All across Hong Kong, factories sprang up to make the goods that Chinese factories had produced. The Chinese immigrants washing ashore in the then-British colony provided cheap factory labor, just as they had back in mainland China. The new factories triggered a boom in Hong Kong, and enough jobs were generated to absorb the flood of immigrants. Li & Fung soon had Hong Kong factories making plastic flowers, toys, firecrackers—all kinds of goods—and the company resumed its exports to the West. Over the decades, the family company grew alongside Hong Kong, whose people moved from poverty to prosperity, from low wages to high wages, and propelled the city into one of the fast-growing Asian tiger economies in the 1980s and 1990s.[11]

As the family company prospered, Victor and William were sent to college in America, to MIT and Princeton, respectively. William then went to Harvard Business School, and later his older brother, Victor, taught there. They came back to Hong Kong in the early 1970s and shook up the family company, insisting it use the business methods they learned in the West—no more absentee aunts and uncles and cousins on the payroll. But they had a problem: wages got so high that most of Hong Kong's factories had to move to Taiwan, Korea, or elsewhere. In other words, the city of Hong Kong successfully transformed itself from a place of desperate refugees into a manufacturing powerhouse and eventually into a city of white-collar service workers. After Hong Kong had lifted itself out of poverty, salaries grew so high that its factory workers were no longer competitive with those of its neighbor countries in manufacturing—much like the United States, Europe, Japan, and Korea today. The Fungs had to transform the company again as manufacturing began to move away from Hong Kong, adjusting their company to the tides of the global economy just like Western companies are adjusting to the rise of China and India today.

When mainland China reopened in 1978, Victor and William bet that China would become the factory to the world. Their family company could return to its roots, but not quite by using their grandfather's approach, or by expecting companies to use Henry Ford's assembly line. Instead, the brothers promoted today's disassembly line method. Rather than hiring Chinese factories to produce finished products for Western markets—the porcelain cups and saucers of their grandfather's time—William and Victor figured that China could most efficiently export components found along the supply chains of multinational companies. During the past decade, the brothers have added factories in India and around the world to their stable of companies connected by supply chains. They have built relationships with manufacturers all over the world, so if a customer needs to know where to make 85,000 pairs of slacks or 20,000 stuffed animals, Li & Fung can get the goods delivered at a good price. They have helped supply chains grow longer and more complex. William refers to the 7,500 factories his company contracts with as "the manufacturing diaspora" for the 350 Western companies that are his customers. "We're in the age of radical outsourcing," says William Fung. "Nothing is sacred." His brother Victor says what we are watching as global commerce transforms is the "atomization of the supply chain."

○

FOLLOWING THE CIRCUITOUS JOURNEY of one of the products Li & Fung shepherd through the global economy shows that, by any name, the model for manufacturing increasingly used today is not their grandfather's—nor is it Henry Ford's assembly line. For instance, the Hong Kong company finds all the factories used to make an Eileen Fisher linen sweater, which then takes a long march to store shelves. The sweaters begin as a raw material (flax) grown in France. China grows flax, too, and Chinese flax is cheaper but does not feel as soft, so Eileen Fisher uses higher-quality French flax for its sweater. The expensive flax for the sweaters comes by boat from France to Tianjin, on China's eastern seaboard. It is then trucked 255 miles west to a yarn factory in a city called Shuozhou in a region that is better known for its coal mines than for its clothing factories. The flax is dropped off in a warehouse that looks and smells much like a hay barn. At one end are twenty-foot-high stacks of flax bales, which resemble unkempt hay. At another end are a dozen women sitting amid piles of flax, wearing winter jackets against the cold. The older women tie scarves over their heads, and several younger ones wear identical bright yellow baseball hats bearing the Nike logo. Their job is to pick straw and other impurities out of the flax for not quite a dollar a day.

It is in this unlikely spot in the middle of China that the sweater starts its journey along a disassembly line that will take it from raw flax to a luxury linen sweater that will later be worn all over the United States. This is everyday globalization. The yarn factory, Shanxi Shuofang Flax Textile Company, is a Chinese state-owned enterprise, a relic of China's communist past struggling to find a place in the nation's future. Down the street is a huge, coal-burning electricity plant where two smokestacks belch white into the gray sky— the same white that settles over the city, leaving an almost sheer film on windshields, motorcycle seats, anything that sits still long enough. Shuozhou's four-lane streets look as if they were built in the last few years. With streetlights, traffic lights, and even security cameras at intersections, this city of 1.3 million could be modern-day Kansas City, but for the remnants of the old Chinese way of life. At stoplights, there are scores of bicycle riders. Enormous trucks carrying high piles of coal roar past them, and the bicyclists also share the road with overcrowded buses and donkeys pulling wooden carts piled high with leeks. Inside the yarn factory gates, a wizened man with a homemade broom sweeps the driveway.

A couple of men load the cleaned flax onto a little truck and drive it from the warehouse to the factory next door, where an enormous green machine the length of a basketball court sits ready. The factory's baby-faced general manager, Jiang Hou Wen, points to the machine and stands a little taller as he says that this is the most sophisticated flax-combing machine in all of China. It was made in France and shipped here after a French company closed its yarn factory at home, partnered with this state-owned Chinese company, and began making yarn here in Shuozhou. At one end of the giant machine, two workers flatten strands of rough, raw flax and feed them into the maw of hundreds of metal combs: the machine straightens and irons the flax until it comes out the other end looking and feeling like ponytail-wide strands of soft blond hair. The strands are coiled into three-foot-high barrels, an industrial take on Rapunzel's hair. The flax ponytails are taken to other machines that further comb the flax and combine the fibers into one long strand. The flax continues its transformation: another set of machines turns the straw-colored strands to yarn and whirls the soft thread onto foot-high plastic spools. The spools of yarn are taken to the next room, and 144 of them at a time are dipped into vats of bleach for six hours. "These machines were made in Russia," Mr. Jiang says, pointing to some of the bleaching room equipment. "And those are from Hong Kong." Next, a set of machines made in Germany transforms the thick strands of now white flax into fine threads and rolls it into six-inch-tall spools—two thousand spools a day. The raw flax takes three days to go from the rough bales to neat spools of thread. Flax dust quickly coats clothing and machines, but few of the factory workers wear masks.

The factory equipment may be up to global standards, but both the pay and the lodging for workers are decidedly local. Inside the factory complex is a brick-walled dormitory. A smell of noodles mixed with urine hangs in the hallways. The rooms, each with six beds with blankets and thin mattresses, are fairly spacious and heated, but the shared bathrooms are revolting, their traditional Chinese hole-in-the-floor toilets clogged. Dorm rooms are nonetheless decorated with dreams: there's a poster of a racy black sports car above one door, and across the hall an advertisement torn from the newspaper hangs on the wall, showing a shiny Philips mobile phone. There are 750 workers at this yarn factory, and they take turns working three eight-hour shifts a day. Night-shift workers earn $100 a month, but day-shift workers earn as little as $37 a month, barely a dollar a day.

Mr. Jiang explains that the factory, with its United Nations array of machines, came to be in Shuozhou because in the early 1990s a French company was allowed to partner with the Chinese government to build the factory and take a 30 percent stake. The idea was that the French would sell flax to the Chinese joint venture and then export the yarn to its high-end customers in Italy and Brazil. The French ran the factory for a decade, adding more and more machines until their stake had increased to 48 percent. The remainder is split among Chinese government branches: the provincial government owns 27 percent, the regional government 11 percent, and the city of Shuozhou 14 percent. In fact, a competing yarn company sprang up suddenly next to this one, run by the same Chinese manager who then ran the joint-venture factory. Mr. Jiang explained that after the French company brought over the machinery and taught the Chinese how to run it, it "made investment mistakes" and went bankrupt. The French company no longer has any workers in Shuozhou, and it doesn't collect its half of the profits. Apparently, this out-of-the-way company, with its Byzantine mix of Chinese government ownership, was one of those French "investment mistakes." Times are still tough for the yarn factory. Because there are now more yarn factories in China, including the competitor directly next to this one, yarn prices have fallen, and profits are hard to come by. Mr. Jiang said his factory made profits of just $12,500 in 2004.[12]

Mr. Jiang's low-profit yarn factory is just the first way station on a long international road leading to an Eileen Fisher sweater or other articles of clothing. For some customers, the white thread is shipped to Thailand, Japan, or India for dyeing, and who knows where next for weaving into cloth. Spools destined for the Eileen Fisher sweaters are instead put on a truck for a two-day, 1,116-mile drive to a factory in Guangzhou, in southern China, where the thread is dyed purple, coral, pink, or lime green. Then the colorful spools of yarn are loaded onto yet another truck, this one bound for a clothing factory in nearby Dongguan, China, called the Everbright Knitting Factory.

At Everbright, workers stand in front of four hundred knitting machines in a room lit by bright fluorescent lights and cooled by fans. One machine turns a spool of yarn into linen panels for a sweater in cheerful pink; another churns out panels in lime green. In an air-conditioned room nearby, skilled workers sit on plastic stools and operate special, rounded sewing machines that link one linen sweater panel to the next to form a sweater's shape. They are paid $245 a month, or $8.15 a day, and those running the simpler looms earn about half that. Both are well above the minimum wage for this region of $70 a month. Since they live in factory dormitories and have few expenses, most can afford cell phones: there is a shared rack where dozens of cell phones are left charging during the workday. The workers are in their early twenties, and they are hundreds of miles from home. Most come from villages in Sichuan and Hunan provinces, where they went to school until they were around twelve years old, then worked in the village taking care of children or farming, until moving away to work at Everbright or another engine of China's export boom. These $8-a-day factory workers are the big breadwinners for the entire family: often they earn more in a few months than their parents earn in a year. When they go home during the weeklong Chinese New Year holiday each spring, they often come back from the countryside with friends or cousins eager to land jobs in the clothing factory.[13]

The colorful sweaters are washed and dried, then laid on special tables, ironed, and checked for flaws. Those that pass inspection land at a table where, every fifteen seconds, a worker reaches into a small box filled with Eileen Fisher labels and hand-stitches the designer label to a sweater. The linen sweaters take up just one of the assembly lines in the Everbright factory. The Limited, Target, and others also hire this factory to make some of the clothes they sell. Next to the Eileen Fisher sweaters is a table with stacks of white sweaters by Guess Jeans, and next to that is a table covered by enormous black sweaters with white stripes on the sleeves. They are men's sweaters, and each is large enough to fit two of the sewing factory workers inside, perhaps three. The sweaters are both too big and too expensive for those who create them. Workers use a special gun to attach price tags ready for U.S. stores: the white Guess Jeans sweaters sell for $69, the monthly minimum wage in this part of China. The Eileen Fisher sweaters cost $148, more than a month's salary for most of those working in this factory. Workers fold each Eileen Fisher sweater and put it in a plastic bag, then pack the sweaters in a cardboard box for the two-hour truck ride to the Trans Global Logistics warehouse in Hong Kong. Trans Global fills a metal container with the sweaters and drives them to the cargo section of the Hong Kong airport. Seven minutes after reaching the airport, the sweater shipment glides down a giant conveyor belt to be X-rayed and loaded onto the belly of the airplane, soon to be worn all over America. Those swank sweaters will have journeyed from France to China to the United States via one boat, five trucks, three factories, and an airplane on an odyssey now common for products found in American shopping malls. These days, most clothing is far better traveled than its wearer.

CHAPTER SIX

INDIA'S CULTURAL REVOLUTION

In the fall of 1991, when Stawan Kadepurkar entered college in Pune, not far from Bombay, only 60 percent of those who graduated earlier that year had found jobs. By the time he graduated in 1995, India's economy had lurched into high gear, and Mr. Kadepurkar and his graduating class found a far rosier future. Almost no one worried about graduating into unemployment. Mr. Kadepurkar landed a job as an electronics engineer at Siemens in Bombay and was paid $1,500 a year, a terrific salary at the time. For Mr. Kadepurkar, as for most Indian tech workers who graduated after 1991, the good times were just beginning. Two years out of college, he joined Infosys in Bangalore, the company created by Narayana Murthy and Nandan Nilekani. His salary rose to $5,000 a year, more than the combined earnings of his parents, both teachers. While helping Infosys' client Cisco write code that allowed phone calls to be transmitted over the Internet, Mr. Kadepurkar, like most of his classmates, lived with his parents and saved enough to buy a motorcycle. When he was all of twenty-five, he bought a house. At twenty-nine, he bought his first car, a Hyundai Accent.

"In my parents' generation, they ended up buying a house in their forties and a car even later," Mr. Kadepurkar said. "When we were in college, I don't think anyone dreamed we would be doing it so early in life." His salary rose to a princely $20,000 a year, then $40,000, and he marveled as those who joined Infosys just a few years after him exuberantly cashed in their first paychecks to buy the latest cell phones. "They are unhesitatingly buying things like cars and motorbikes, and taking out loans to do it," he said. "They've really not seen a lean period." Like many of his Infosys colleagues, Mr. Kadepurkar was sent to work in the United States for months at a time. Most recently, he has been transferred to California, where he earns a whopping $120,000 a year. He plans to work in California for a few years before returning to India. Meanwhile, back in Bangalore, he said, the new Infosys hires are no longer content with buying cell phones. They have been opening Internet stock-trading accounts so that they can invest in all the Indian companies going public. "Colleagues are getting more and more ambitious in terms of what they want to do in life," he said.[1]

While the glut of shiny new cell phones and motorcycles may be symbolic of India's economic success, it also signals a radical shift in culture. Millions of young, well-educated Indians live in a world different from that of their parents, who struggled to make ends meet on far lower salaries. They even differ from their older sisters and brothers, whose ambitions and dreams were much more modest. For the young and educated, India has been reincarnated as a land of prosperity and boundless opportunity. Many denizens of the New India work on behalf of American companies and can count on finding intellectually rewarding work while earning enough money to eat in restaurants, to buy homes and cars, to chat on cell phones with their friends, and to travel. They finally have the things most American college graduates take for granted. "Outsourcing has shown we can compete in the world and win," said Mr. Nilekani, the Infosys CEO.[2] As India connects itself to the global economy, young Indians' clothing, food, and even marriage rituals are starting to mirror what they see on their new color televisions—whether Bollywood films, American television shows, or advertisements for foreign brands.

Mr. Kadepurkar's story is the norm, not the exception, for successful Indians of his post-1991 generation. The people who are "taking away America's jobs" may be paid just a tenth of America's wages, but they have a fantastic standard of living in India. Salaries go much further in Bangalore or Mumbai than in Silicon Valley or Manhattan.

Mr. Kadepurkar earns $120,000 a year when working in California because that pays for the same lifestyle as a $40,000 salary does in Bangalore. A luxury three-bedroom apartment for a Bangalore family, in a complex with a swimming pool and children's play area, rents for $500 a month. Middle-class Indian families routinely hire full-time housekeepers and cooks, who earn just $55 a month, the same amount they would be paid for a single day's work in the United States. Cell phone service starts at $5 a month. Most of those who can afford cars can afford full-time drivers, who earn $125 a month. India's boom has minted hundreds of thousands of young IT maharajahs—by night kings and queens of their castles in gated communities, by day cubicle dwellers programming computers, answering phones, or performing research on behalf of foreigners.

○

TO VISIT INFOSYS' BANGALORE HEADQUARTERS is to see not just the newly emerging India but also the entire global economy on the move. Outside the gates of the complex, barefoot children walk to school on the noisy, traffic-choked streets. But inside the guarded gates is an idealized re-creation of an American college campus: Infosys' office buildings sit quietly among grassy expanses bisected by sidewalks and peppered with basketball and volleyball courts. There's a Domino's pizza restaurant and a giant parking deck. Back when the Infosys campus was built, in 1994, most workers rode buses or motorcycles. A decade later, new cars are replacing two-wheeled transport.

In cubicles across the Infosys campus, "Infoscions" tap away at the everyday jobs that keep the global economy running smoothly. Vishwas Jain, twenty-eight, an electrical engineer with an M.B.A. who earns $14,000 a year, helped Sony build a business-to-business website. But Mr. Jain's job isn't as simple as plugging in numbers and code. "We can't sit here and just build it," he said. "We need to understand their business processes."[3]

Infosys employees take their jobs seriously; 1.4 million people applied for jobs there in 2006. For Mr. Jain, Mr. Kadepurkar, and their colleagues, landing a job at Infosys is as coveted as landing a job at Microsoft is for Americans. By working for Infosys, they end up working for a Who's Who of corporate America and multinationals around the world. In Infosys' welcome area, a slick video shows earnest workers, and the lobby shows off a partial list of Infosys' clients: PepsiCo, Gap, Amazon.com, Nordstrom, DHL International, Apple Computer, Cisco Systems, Reebok, International Business Machines, J. Sainsbury, Mercedes, Airbus, Aetna, Toshiba, Johnson Controls, Boeing, Monsanto, and Porsche. "Infosys welcomes Kraft Foods, Bank of America, UBS and Allianz Cornhill Insurance," reads a sign in the lobby one December morning.[4] Another day, the sign welcomes a delegation from Kazakhstan and one from Nortel.[5] For visitors, the sight of the Infosys campus and others like it "has helped to brand India as a knowledge nation, not as snake charmers," said Mr. Nilekani.[6]

While Indian firms like Infosys are known for code-writing, they are quickly expanding into new areas, everything from low-end call centers to sophisticated research and development work. A short walk across the corporate campus from company headquarters, past the employees' gym, golf putting green, and swimming pool—luxuries most Indians have never seen—is a separate building for the Infosys subsidiary that serves as the back office of various multinational companies. Alpana Sinha, twenty-five, sits in one cubicle there and helps close home loans for Americans who borrow from GreenPoint Mortgage. If a loan applicant claims to earn $30,000 a year, she checks the figures against income statements to be sure. Ms. Sinha earns less than $3,600 a year,[7] and couldn't afford a home in America, but she isn't complaining. She and her colleagues, 55 percent of whom are women, marvel at the world that has become open to them. "The world we are living in—the way we are living now—it has changed completely," said Ms. Sinha. Her boss observed that the young employees are part of something much bigger—the rise of India itself.[8]

"This is part of a big wave," said Akshaya Bhargava, CEO of the back-office subsidiary. "It is not something you get to see more than once in your lifetime." He himself left India for London in 1989 and never thought he would have a reason to return. He had grown tired of India's barely functioning basic services, tired of the Indian bureaucracy's habit of denying every request. "In your mind, in your heart, you give up," Mr. Bhargava remembered. Today, he said, working with overseas customers is producing a change in the mind-sets of young Indians. Demanding American customers don't accept excuses for why they cannot qualify for a loan or receive an express package on time, and that has rubbed off on the Indians listening to their complaints at call centers and others working for the increasing number of Western companies in India. "You're creating a body of people who will say it is not okay" when companies or governments fail to meet their requests, he said. Just like their troublesome clients, Indian yuppies simply expect things to work. They are demanding more from their government, Infosys CEO Nandan Nilekani said. "After buying that car and scooter, you find there is no place to drive it," because of India's poor roads. Indians—not just foreign investors—are demanding better infrastructure, he said.[9] Young Indians expect to be able to get a telephone as soon as they can afford one. They expect to be able to land a job. They expect a bright future in India.

In the past, many of India's elite went to college overseas and found they needed to stay outside India if they wanted to earn high salaries. Many of the most successful, best-educated Indians left the country. Doctors, professors, and professionals of all stripes emigrated to the United States, the United Kingdom, and elsewhere. That brain drain is now reversing as India's economy booms and everything from shopping to getting a phone installed becomes less of a struggle. First the best minds of the tech industry began to return. Now many Indians who didn't want to live in the India of the past are happily moving back, sometimes to help care for aging parents, and often embracing Indian traditions for their children rather than assimilating in foreign countries. In Bangalore alone, between 30,000 and 40,000 Indians have returned from overseas in the past decade.[10] Among Indian returnees as well as call center and IT workers, the very attitude toward employment is changing. There is no longer an expectation from those hired that they have found a job for life. Poor performers are fired, and, at the same time, employees job-hop when they have chances for higher pay. In India, this is a radical change.[11] While those working in the offshoring industry are India's vanguard, change is coming slowly in other slices of the nation.

There are so many professional opportunities in India that Indian managers gossip about skyrocketing pay packages for experienced executives willing to return to India. The percentage of high-income Indians is tiny but growing. India had 83,000 millionaires in 2005.[12] The consultants McKinsey & Company found that in 2005 some 1.2 million well-off Indian households had incomes of $10,000 a year—the equivalent of more than $45,000 in the United States—and estimated that the number is increasing by 20 percent a year. About 40 million Indian households—about 200 million people—have incomes between $4,000 and $10,000 a year—the equivalent of Americans with household incomes between $20,000 and $45,000 a year. That group has been growing by about 10 percent a year, should reach 65 million households by 2010, and has become the prime target for American companies trying to sell goods in India, according to McKinsey.[13] As India's economic reforms bring even greater prosperity, some of the profits from the newly flush Indian customers go to Indian businesses and some go to Western companies. The prosperity of Indian technology companies and their workers has indirectly created 3 million Indian jobs outside the industry, some in construction and some through employees' increased spending at restaurants, nightclubs, and shops.[14] Indian airlines and hotels are packed as business travel booms and as more Indians can afford to fly instead of ride trains.

As each month passes, the Indian market becomes more attractive to Western companies looking for new customers. Even as Americans watch jobs moving to India, American companies are benefiting from the boom there. U.S. companies are selling more products in India for two reasons: first, Indians simply have more money to spend; and, second, as India opens more to the outside world, its middle class is adopting some elements of Western culture. Because of its colonial history, India shares many tastes with Britain—not only in British-influenced accents, but in habits like drinking tea rather than coffee in northern India, for instance.[15] Now the cultural center of gravity for India's yuppies leans toward the United States, partly because the majority of call center and technology job clients are American. Call center workers are trained to imitate the American accent and to learn American pop culture, and tens of thousands of offshoring employees like Mr. Kadepurkar have become familiar with America because they have worked with clients there. During working lunches in offshoring firms, employees are as likely to order in from Domino's or Pizza Hut as from restaurants serving Indian food.

American brands are both newly available and coveted in India. Indians have been able to buy Western goods easily only since the laws that favored Indian producers were relaxed during the 1990s, but now malls are cropping up, selling Western fashions and American brands. Made-in-Chennai Fords clog India's potholed roads. Even India's poor are target customers for some products: cups of Pepsi sell for six rupees, about a penny, in rural India. As India gets richer and rejoins the world economy, it is costing some American jobs but allowing the United States to export its way of life. The American dream has been reborn halfway around world, and for Indians, purchasing American products is part of that dream. American brands are synonymous with prosperity and success, even McDonald's and Pizza Hut.

Indian women are experiencing the most significant changes. Traditionally, Indian women depended financially on their families until they married, at which point they depended on their husbands. In the face of rising wages and spreading Western values, these conventions are fading. For example, during the early years of the offshoring boom, call center offices had to invite parents to visit along with job applicants because the older generation could not understand what kind of respectable company would ask young women to work late into the night making phone calls to strangers. Now the jobs are viewed with prestige. As more women work, they are trading in traditional flowing saris for Western clothes or the less formal *salwar kameez*, slacks worn with a loose tunic. In heavily Muslim Hyderabad in the offices of the offshoring firm 24/7 Customer, new female recruits who wear burkas to work often shed them for less restraining clothing in a few weeks.[16]

Even marriage traditions are changing. Young people with careers are marrying later. After the wedding, women are resisting traditional duties like home cooking the family's meals, packing lunch for their husbands, and home pasteurizing the family's milk. Just a decade ago, most young, middle-class Indians accepted the practice of an arranged marriage, but now many of India's financially independent young women are shunning arranged marriages of the sort that even their older sisters were compelled to accept a few years earlier. In the past, parents would meet with other parents or even marriage brokers to find suitable matches for their children, then introduce the potential bride and groom briefly before the wedding. Now, even when arranged marriages prevail, it is common for would-be brides and grooms to be introduced to a number of potential mates until they find someone acceptable to them, not just to their parents. In addition, jobs in off-shoring firms serve as a new sort of matchmaking service for young workers. R. N. Koushik joined Infosys in 1991, when the company had just 135 employees and paid him a mere $55 a month. He met his wife there. "We were the sixth Infosys couple," he said proudly, list-ing the names of co-workers who had married after meeting at Infosys.[17] Young Indians colorfully debate the benefits of "love mar-riages" on Internet chat rooms. And many young Indians, like West-erners, are relying on Internet dating services to find true love. Ads proclaim Shaadi.com "the world's largest matrimonial service," and India's Rediff Matchmaker has more than 30 million online users.

To Indians, the most shocking example of how much has changed for women is the story of Nisha Sharma, a software engineer. On the night of her wedding, she dialed police on her cell phone to ask them to arrest her fiancé. The reason: minutes before the wedding, his fam-ily had suddenly demanded a dowry of $27,000 and a new car from her father.[18] Officially, dowries were banned in India in 1961, but the practice of a bride's family's giving expensive gifts to the groom's fam-ily remains so widespread that brides' families are frequently pestered for years after the wedding for further gifts. Ms. Sharma's fiancé was jailed, and, at the age of twenty-one, she became a celebrity nation-wide, with government officials hailing her as a role model and chil-dren studying her courageous story in textbooks.

○

WHILE INDIAN UNIVERSITY GRADUATES line up for jobs that can propel them into the newly vibrant middle class, for India's rural and urban poor, change has been interminably delayed. Expectations, like incomes, are rising across India, and not just for those working in call centers. Even as the New India cohort thrives, much of the rest of India is making much slower gains or even being left behind, creating social and political tensions that cloud India's impressive strides forward. The lowest-paid workers in the offshoring industry—those working in call centers—earn median wages of $275 a month.[19] But most Indians still earn less than $60 a month, or just $2 a day.

Change has come in small increments to India's villages, where 70 percent of the population lives. Many villages now have a communal television, and those who can afford a computer often have dial-up Internet access, which is helping raise awareness of the world beyond. But time has stood still on many more pressing, day-to-day problems. Many villages still lack running water, electricity, and reliable access to medical care. In 2006, in an effort to cut down on diseases like diarrhea, the government embarked on a high-profile campaign to persuade Indian villagers to install outhouses and stop using nearby fields as toilets. This is the very same hygiene mantra Gandhi championed seventy years earlier.

A village in eastern India called Idulbera shows that even villages that have made big gains have not managed to lift residents into the middle class. Negi Singh Sadar, seventy, is the leader of Idulbera, where children tend cows and goats while adults work the fields or travel over bumpy dirt roads to the nearby city of Jamshedpur to look for work. Entire families live in one-room, dirt-floored homes, and the sight of a car or motorcycle is a rarity, despite the eight-mile distance to the nearest city. With a $6,500 donation from charities and a $4,000 contribution from villagers, his village changed its planting practices and tripled village incomes in five years.[20] "We had one crop a year—rice," said Mr. Sadar, a four-foot-tall man with gray hair, a quick smile, and pride in the gains his village of a few hundred people has experienced since 1997, when it managed to buy a communal water pump. Villagers can rent the pump for thirty cents an hour plus the cost of the diesel it uses, enabling them to water their fields and squeeze additional plantings into the growing season. Now, in addition to rice, the village grows green beans, okra, and eggplants to sell at Jamshedpur's market. Even more profitably, villagers grow bright orange marigolds, make them into garlands, and sell them—two for a quarter—to worshipers in Hindu temples in nearby Jamshedpur. In a land where only 70 percent of children nationwide are vaccinated,[21] all the children in Idulbera have received immunizations, Mr. Sadar said. He is already planning for their future: he used some of the village profits to plant a stand of teak trees, which won't be ready to harvest until the village's children are grown up. Yet, even with all these improvements, Idulbera's villagers remain poor and isolated, living in what seems an era different from that of their own countrymen in Bangalore.

"The frustrating thing about India," the Indian Nobel Prize–winning economist Amartya Sen has noted, "is that whatever you can rightly say about India, the opposite is also true." The nation simply does not give in easily to generalizations, providing ironies, complexities, and contradictions to nearly any statement of fact about it.

What is clear is that the separation of New India and Old India is not merely the walking distance between village and city. Some rural residents give up farming and move to cities to look for work. With cities already critically short of housing, they often wind up living in some of the world's most horrific slums. India's rural poor, like China's, are out of sight for many visitors, but its urban poor are extremely visible. The poor in India's cities also seem to live in a country different from that of their yuppie neighbors, with fewer chances to escape the grind of poverty, much as America's inner-city residents seem to be stuck in a world different from that of America's middle-class denizens.

Just when first-time visitors to Bombay recover from the surprise of landing at such an outmoded airport after hearing about India's fast economic growth, a drive downtown takes them past a shocking sight: Asia's largest slum. Shacks defy gravity to stand on top of other rickety shacks until slum neighborhoods reach several stories tall. Like every number in a city of 16 million people, in a nation of 1.1 billion people, the numbers of those living in this slum are staggering to people from anywhere else: this single Bombay slum, Dharavi, has about 600,000 residents, over half of them children.[22] The slum, with its muddy alleyways, dusty workshops, open drains, and vastly outnumbered toilets and showers,[23] is home to as many people as live in

Kansas City, Seattle, Washington, D.C., or Frankfurt, Germany. The amassed poor are especially shocking to Westerners, who are used to seeing the poor in small groups—the homeless sleeping over warm grates on a New York winter's night, for instance. First-time visitors find the poverty in Dharavi as appalling as foreigners found the sight of America's underclass, broadcast worldwide when Hurricane Katrina flooded New Orleans.

Even more shocking, Dharavi is a "rich" slum. There is little unemployment. Residents are drivers and housecleaners, aircraft mechanics and college students, office clerks and factory workers, tannery workers or casual laborers. Many residents work building roads at 25 cents a day, work that has been easier to find since the 1991 reforms. Housewives there take on freelance embroidery jobs. Dharavi's narrow alleys are interrupted with the whirr of saws from tiny furniture-making shops. Rows of homes are encroached upon by the pungent presence of a leather-tanning shop, where on one summer day, whitish sheepskins were piled five feet high, near a separate pile of goatskins. Two workers dozed on wooden cots in the workshop, unfazed by the smell of curing leather or the determined flies. Children played in trash-strewn open areas, chasing the occasional chicken or stray dog. In Dharavi, the average 100-square-foot home rents for $22 a month, while a family-sized apartment of perhaps 220 square feet rents for $55 a month. Whole families live in a single room, but they have electricity and televisions. Most of Dharavi's residents have lived there for years, even decades, and while they are not rich, they are a powerful group. To politicians, they are a bank of hundreds of thousands of potential votes to be wooed with the placement of additional shared showers or the promise not to tear down the neighborhood, despite its valuable location near downtown.

However horrific Dharavi looks to outsiders, most residents believe the alternatives are worse. They may be right. Bombay's slum dwellers are not to be confused with its pavement dwellers, the 25,000 families living alongside Bombay's streets in illegal, but seemingly permanent, tumbledown shanties. Along one stretch, concrete pipes awaiting installation along the street served as impromptu children's playgrounds. The shacks along the road house the poorest of the city's poor. They cannot afford to live in Dharavi. The slum is too expensive.

○

WIDESPREAD POVERTY like that found in urban shantytowns and in villages like Idulbera lingers because incomes are rising from such a low base. India's 1991 reforms stimulated overall economic growth, and India's average incomes have nearly doubled in the past decade. Since then, hundreds of millions of Indians moved up from extreme poverty to the ranks of the merely poor. In Bangalore's biggest slum, Ejipura, huts with plastic sheets for roofs have been upgraded to tiny concrete houses in recent years.[24] Nonetheless, in 2005, about 36 percent of the Indian population still lived on less than one dollar a day and 81 percent on less than two dollars a day, according to the Asian Development Bank.

Still, all the call center jobs in the world wouldn't solve India's poverty problem. First, few of the very poor would qualify to work in call centers: despite the Indian elite's reputation for educational success, 35 percent of all Indians are illiterate.[25] While India's colleges are renowned for turning out terrific engineers, the nation's primary schools remain in shambles. Compulsory—and free—primary education became the law only in 2001. Just 15 percent of India's students reach high school, and only 7 percent graduate. Nearly three-quarters of Indian boys are literate, but just half of Indian girls can read and write; many wouldn't qualify to work in modern factory jobs if India did manage to attract foreign investors on China's scale. Classes are overcrowded, and teacher absenteeism is rampant. Parents are so desperate to enroll their children in quality schools that private schools are proliferating, and even poor families scrimp to pay for tuition starting at around $25 a year.

The advances of the glittering New India mask stubborn problems, such as high child-mortality rates, violence against women, caste-based discrimination, and religious strife. As well-educated women like Nisha Sharma and her call center colleagues take an ever-increasing role in the global economy, poor women remain especially disadvantaged. In much of India, the birth of sons is celebrated, while the birth

FORGING FREEDOM: The Tata Steelworks in Jamshedpur is part of the legacy of Nationalist Jamsetji Tata, who viewed self-sufficiency in steel as critical to India's drive for independence. *Rajat Ghosh/www.rajatghosh.com*

THE "RICH" SLUM: In addition to tiny rooms housing entire families, Bombay's biggest slum, Dharavi, teems with small businesses like this leather-working shop. *Robyn Meredith*

WORKING THE LAND: A boy watches what could be his future: his father plows with the help of the family cow in Geetilata village in the state of Jharkhand.
Rajat Ghosh/www.rajatghosh.com

A STRONG BACK: Handcarts, motorcycles, and cars share the streets in Calcutta, now known as Kolkata. *Rajat Ghosh/www.rajatghosh.com*

LEFT BEHIND: While hundreds of millions of Indians have been lifted out of abject poverty by the nation's recent growth spurt, poverty remains hard to shake for hundreds of millions more, like these women working in Calcutta. They earn less than $2 a day selling leaves used for worshipping deities.

Rajat Ghosh/www.rajatghosh.com

A STRONG MIND: A boy living in Bombay's slums studies alongside nonstop traffic. *Rajat Ghosh/www.rajatghosh.com*

RELIGIOUS FESTIVAL: In an annual Hindu festival, an image of Ganesh is immersed in the sea off Bombay's most famous beach, Chowpatty. *Rajat Ghosh/www.rajatghosh.com*

OLD INDIA ALONGSIDE NEW: One of India's few new highways stretches from Bangalore to Pune, and, along it, buses share the road with more ancient forms of transportation. *Rajat Ghosh/www.rajatghosh.com*

CLEAN POWER: Like China, India must confront its pollution problem. Most of its electricity is fueled by coal, but India is increasingly relying on windmills like these found in Maharashtra state. *Rajat Ghosh/www.rajatghosh.com*

THE ROAD AHEAD: India's crumbling infrastructure has delayed its economic development, but the nation is finally beginning to build new overpasses and expressways to speed up growth. *Rajat Ghosh/www.rajatghosh.com*

THE WORLD'S BACK OFFICE: The futuristic Bangalore campus of Infosys Technologies, founded by Narayana Murthy and Nandan Nilekani, is where tens of thousands of white-collar jobs once found in the United States and Europe have migrated. *Infosys Technologies*

THE KEY TO JOB CREATION: South Korea's Hyundai Motor Company built a modern car factory in Chennai, formerly called Madras. More and more foreign manufacturing companies are building factories in India.

Rajat Ghosh/www.rajatghosh.com

5,000 YEARS OF HISTORY: A woman carries drinking water past the village lake near Yangshuo, China. *Grischa Rueschendorf/www.rupho.com*

MAO'S DREAM SURPASSED: China is now the world's largest steel producer, but it pays a heavy price in pollution. These are the smoke-stacks of China's oldest steelworks in Anshan, Liaoning Province, China. *Grischa Rueschendorf/www.rupho.com*

TWO CHINAS: Construction workers and other Chinese laborers eat a modest lunch in the shadow of Shanghai's glitziest skyscrapers.
Grischa Rueschendorf/www.rupho.com

INCREASING PROTESTS: Demonstrators block a street with their bicycles in Shenyang, Liaoning Province, protesting layoffs.

Grischa Rueschendorf/www.rupho.com

STILL STANDING: Chairman Mao, who championed Chinese communism, in the glare of today's capitalism in Chengdu, Sichuan Province.

Grischa Rueschendorf/www.rupho.com

PEDAL POWER: A roadside bicycle-repair business in Benxi, a Liaoning Province city so polluted that it reportedly disappeared from satellite photos in the 1980s before a cleanup effort was begun. *Grischa Rueschendorf/www.rupho.com*

OLD MEETS NEW: China's tallest skyscraper, the Jin Mao Tower in Shanghai, towers over the ancient buildings of Yuyuan Garden. *Grischa Rueschendorf/www.rupho.com*

WELCOME TO CHINA: The skyscrapers of Shanghai's Pudong district light up the night. *Grischa Rueschendorf/www.rupho.com*

MADE BY AMERICA IN CHINA: AT&T telephones being made in Dongguan, in Guangdong Province, by VTech, a company better known in the United States for making electronic toys.

Grischa Rueschendorf/www.rupho.com

TAKING OFF: The airport in Guangzhou, Guangdong Province, under construction in 2002. The airport, now one of China's largest, already plans an expansion that will allow it to serve 38 million passengers in 2010.

Grischa Rueschendorf/www.rupho.com

BEYOND SWEATSHOPS: Workers make components of hard disk drives at one of SAE Magnetics' factories in Dongguan, China.

Grischa Rueschendorf/www.rupho.com

THE MODERN SILK ROAD: Chinese-made goods start the journey west in warehouses like this one owned by China Merchants Logistics Group in Shekou, on the Pearl River near Hong Kong.

Grischa Rueschendorf/www.rupho.com

of daughters is viewed as a future financial strain because of the wide-spread practice of brides' families paying dowries. The result is sex-selective abortion and female infanticide. Just 90 girls were born for every 100 boys on the average, and in some regions just 75 girls are born for every 100 boys.[26] India cannot seem to shake traditions the rest of the world assumes are long abandoned. India still has child brides. More than half of rural girls are married off before they turn eighteen, only to become field workers or servants in their husband's family. Even when they are of age, some brides face abuse, particularly in the impoverished North: As recently as 2005, there were at least 6,700 dowry murders, in which a husband's family killed a woman whose family could not meet additional demands for dowry.[27] A common murder method involves dousing the bride in kerosene and setting her on fire, then claiming she died in a cooking accident. In many parts of India, widows are still treated as pariahs, cast out into poverty by their families. Since half of Indian women are illiterate, it is hard for them to escape poverty by finding well-paid work.

Even the caste system persists. While caste is generally no longer a consideration in social interactions or in the workplace in India's larger cities, and the intercaste marriages that were considered radical a decade ago are now more common, caste is not yet as extinct as slavery, and like the ensuing racism in America, caste-related discrimination persists in India. Lower-caste Indians as well as tribal populations face persistent discrimination, particularly outside India's cities. There are four hundred different tribal groups in India, numbering 60 million people. Members of these tribal groups, called *adivasis*, along with members of India's "untouchable" castes, known as *dalits*, remain socially and economically marginalized in India. Twenty percent of rural residents are *dalits*, but 38 percent of the very poor are *dalits*, and similarly 11 percent of the rural population is *adivasis*, but 48 percent of the very poor belong to the tribal groups.[28]

Finally, the partition of India during independence in 1947 failed to curb religious strife. Today 142 million Muslims remain in India, more than the 140 million who live in Pakistan. Even as once taboo marriages between Hindus and Muslims are becoming more common, religious rivalry remains. From time to time, terrorists ignite the simmering Hindu-Muslim rivalry by bombing trains, temples, or mosques. A stubborn urban gang war between Hindus and Muslims persists in Mumbai.[29] And on the international front, diplomatic strains linger between India and Pakistan, two nuclear-armed neighbors that still dispute control of the northern region of Kashmir. It is easy to forget those long-simmering tensions as attention turns to India's economy and efforts to bring prosperity to all Indians.

Bringing India's poor along on the ride to a New India would require vast job creation. That is likely to come only with the addition of thousands of factories, myriad construction projects, or the nurturing of a big increase in agricultural exports—or all three.

A lot depends on how soon India modernizes its infrastructure. Until more roads are built to connect factories and farms with ports and railways, neither factories nor farmers are likely to see a China-style export boom that would create hundreds of millions of jobs. However haltingly, India has finally begun building roads and highways, and that has not only created jobs laying asphalt but also helped connect remote towns and villages to cities. That has enabled some farmers to get produce to markets more efficiently and allowed other villagers to commute to better-paying city jobs. A road-building boom would beget the construction of new factories, but no one can say when this boom will come. Until then, workers will be stuck gaining ground slowly.

Despite the lack of modern infrastructure, India has already seen noticeable gains in factory work, and as manufacturing industries finally look to India, the numbers are beginning to add up. For instance, because Indian gem cutters earn 20 percent of what Europeans earn for the same work, much of the diamond-cutting and -polishing industry has migrated from Belgium to India, creating at least 500,000 jobs for Indians.[30] With India's 140-million-strong mobile-phone market growing fast, Motorola and Nokia are building handset factories in India. The German auto parts maker Robert Bosch doubled its initially planned investment to $390 million. General Motors announced it would build a second car factory in India, betting that more and more Indians will soon be able to afford cars as more jobs are created. Some of the gains come when developed nations level the playing field: when the United States and Europe removed thirty-year-old textile quotas in 2005, Indian textile factories prospered. Exports to the United States alone jumped 36 percent, with Indians delivering textiles for The Gap, Crate & Barrel, and the like.

While Chinese development favors factory exports, perhaps the biggest potential source of growth in India comes from the countryside, where most Indians live. Sixty percent of India's workers and a third of its economic output are dependent on agriculture.[31] Politicians dream of creating jobs in rural areas as a quick way to bring gains to India's poorest, and as a way to discourage mass migration into already teeming cities. The developed world is partly to blame for the fact that India does not export more from its farms. Western nations have balked at cutting subsidies for their farmers, which often price Indian exports out of the market. The European Union famously pays its farmers two dollars per cow in daily subsidies,[32] more than most Indian *people* subsist on each day.

But India's lack of infrastructure is a big hurdle even to farmers. Not only do many villages do without the electricity and water pumps that could help irrigate fields, but they are also hamstrung by India's poor highway network after they manage to harvest crops. With little refrigeration available, 40 percent of India's fruits and vegetables spoil before reaching markets because getting them from farms to stores over India's dirt roads and potholed highways takes so long. One of India's leading businessmen, Mukesh Ambani, chairman of Reliance Industries, India's biggest company, plans to change all that. He is spending a remarkable $5 billion to change the way India's agricultural industry works—from the financing of seeds to where produce is sold.

First Mr. Ambani plans to build 1,600 farm-supply stores nationwide, which will sell seeds, fertilizer, and fuel and provide farmers with credit to buy them. When fields are harvested, farmers could sell their crops to the same stores. Mr. Ambani's plan is patterned after one pioneered in northern India by Tata Chemicals, the chemical and fertilizer arm of the Tata Group. Its Kisan Sansar ("farm center") network of one-stop farming stores caters to more than twenty thousand villages and four million farmers in three provinces, but outdated Indian regulations prevent Tata from expanding the network nationwide.[33] These farming centers are revolutionary in India. Up until now, farmers had to pay usurious rates to borrow from local moneylenders who sometimes charge more than 10 percent per day. A bad monsoon season typically cripples the harvest and bankrupts farmers who cannot repay the costly loans, their debt rising to perhaps $1,000. In 2005, hundreds of farmers escaped their debt by killing themselves, often by drinking fertilizer.[34] The existence of loans for farmers at fair prices would make the consequences of a failed harvest much less tragic. Mr. Ambani also plans to build eighty-five modern logistics hubs to move the produce from the farm-supply stores to customers, some in India and some overseas.

Perhaps the most ambitious part of his plan is to change the way the food is sold, bypassing India's remarkable number of mom-and-pop shops, which now sell 96 percent of India's goods. Mr. Ambani wants to build the Wal-Mart of India, creating a chain of stores across India to sell the produce and other goods. At the same time, a modern distribution system would get produce to ports and airports, creating $20 billion in agricultural exports, by Mr. Ambani's estimation.[35]

○

IN 2030, DEMOGRAPHERS PREDICT, India will become the most populous nation on Earth, overtaking China around the point when both reach 1.45 billion people.[36] Also in 2030, economists predict, India will surpass Japan to become the world's third-largest economy after the United States and China.[37] And in 2030, India will have by far the largest workforce in the world because 68 percent of its population will be of working age—a particularly high percentage of workers compared with retirees and children dependent on workers' incomes. India will have 986 million working-age people in 2030, an increase of 270 million from 2006.[38] Demographers call this a "demographic dividend" phase, a kind of demographic sweet spot that normally helps a nation's economy grow faster because its large economically active cohort tends to have a higher savings rate and higher investment level at the same time that it has more income to spend on consumer goods. Demographers say that, all things being equal, economies boom when countries have larger labor forces, just as the American economy boomed after baby boomers entered the workforce.

For India, however, the demographic dividend could prove a grave threat. Today India has a young population; half of its 1.1 billion people are under twenty-five,[39] and 31 percent are less than sixteen years old, not yet working age.[40] More important, India's working-age population—those aged fifteen to sixty—is growing faster than its population as a whole. When India's young demographic bubble begins to reach working age, India will need far more jobs than currently exist to keep living standards from declining. Creating vast numbers of jobs for India's poor is crucial, literally a matter of life and death. India today doesn't have enough good jobs for its existing workers, much less for millions of new ones. If it cannot better educate its children and create jobs for them once they reach working age, India faces a population time bomb: the nation will grow poorer and not richer, with hundreds of millions of people stuck in poverty. The challenge is vast: by 2050, India is expected to have a population of 1.6 billion people, more than China's 1.4 billion. Demographers project that India will have 230 million[41] more workers than China and about 500 million more than the United States.

India is at a critical juncture. If the nation fails to create jobs for its fast-growing population of workers, it risks being mired in poverty and hopelessness. The Indian government is portraying the nation's population growth as a huge global advantage. For that to prove true, the government must not squander an opportunity to promote the economic growth that will provide jobs for all those new workers in coming decades. Because the offshoring phenomenon has attracted the attention of foreign companies, India is finally having its moment on the world economic stage. The Indian government must seize this historic chance. It must further reform its economy and modernize the nation's infrastructure, encouraging

Indian companies to grow at the same time it attracts the foreign-built factories that will create jobs at home, much as China has done so successfully during the past decade.

"A unique constellation of factors now objectively indicate that India is now on the threshold of a golden age of growth," said the former finance secretary Vijay Kelkar. "If we seize this moment, India can transit out of poverty, and coming generations can enjoy an era of unprecedented prosperity and a decisive voice in shaping the global economic order and world politics." But he offered a warning too: "It is necessary that we choose wisely because wrong choices now can mean all future generations would remain poor forever."[42]

So far, India's record is frustratingly mixed, and the challenge is primarily political. Foreign political commentators were stunned when the government of Prime Minister Atal Bihari Vajpayee was resoundingly defeated in 2004. They were surprised because India's economy was prospering, its offshoring industry creating so many new jobs that Vajpayee's campaign slogan was "India Shining." The poor—the majority—revolted and voted him out of office. India was not shining for them. In fact, the poor were watching compatriots get ahead while their lives had changed little. Politicians and business leaders alike have come to a postelection consensus that India must find a way to give its poor better prospects. "Having two Indias will not work," said Mr. Nilekani of Infosys. "Because of the democratic system, any strategy will have to involve getting more equitable growth. Politically, you will have to carry everyone on that journey."[43]

After Mr. Vajpayee's 2004 defeat, the next government was a coalition of various parties, led by the Congress Party. To appease the poor, one of the new government's earliest endeavors was the National Rural Employment Guarantee Act, passed in parliament in 2005, which guarantees a hundred days of work a year to every rural household that wants it at pay around the average minimum-wage level of $1.35 a day. Because of the sheer numbers of India's poor population, the cost is a staggering $9.1 billion, or 1.3 percent of India's GDP at a time when the government is already running a large deficit. The jobs program will function as a bare-bones safety net for the very poor, but the biggest economic lift would come from the creation of private-sector jobs. What has frustrated those who want to see India continue its economic gains is that the leftist parties in the coalition government—like Gandhi and Nehru decades before—have in the name of protecting the poor held up the very economic development likely to create jobs for them. Politicians have delayed the building of airports and new roads that could help attract new factory jobs. Sometimes the politicians side with illegal squatters who would otherwise be forced to move from areas where construction is planned. Sometimes they back local companies that object to airport and infrastructure building contracts' being given to experienced foreign companies. Either way, economic progress is slowed. In the summer of 2006, a modest government plan to sell off minority stakes in government-owned companies was scuttled when leftist parties threatened to pull out of the coalition and bring down the government if it were implemented. The new special economic zones being championed by the Indian Commerce Ministry are threatened by political infighting and the nation's on-again, off-again politics of reform. The Indian Finance Ministry has been grousing that lower tax rates in the zones will crimp government revenue, while Sonia Gandhi, the powerful leader of the Congress Party, complained in September 2006 that they are bad for farmers.

The political strains come in part because of India's past colonial history and in part because of the disparities between India's two worlds. Under billboards in Bombay touting the latest cell phones, credit cards, and insurance policies marketed to India's new yuppies, the old India endures: stray dogs hover as men dig through piles of trash, vendors at filthy roadside stalls sell glasses of sugarcane juice for a penny, men working like oxen push ten-foot-long wooden carts stacked high with building materials through city streets, heading for construction sites.

Without changes, job creation will stall, and the very poor—the ones politicians claim they are protecting—will continue to suffer. "We have to create this as an engine that pulls the whole economy. You need to create manufacturing jobs, service and farm jobs," said

Mr. Nilekani. India's IT industry "can't be the only game in town. It may only create jobs for a few million people. This is a terrific engine which is pulling the train, but we can't allow the engine to go ahead and let the rest of the train sit in the siding."

What China accomplishes by fiat, India must accomplish partly through persuasion. To move its economic development forward, India must come to grips with the nation's enduring postcolonial aversion to connecting to the world economy, and it must put in place policies that encourage Indian and foreign companies to hire in India. The Indian government must master the delicate politics of the poor. India has by far more poor people than those in the middle class; McKinsey calculates that 110 million Indian households—about 550 million people—make do on incomes between $1,500 and $4,000 a year, and an additional 40 million households are simply destitute, scraping by on less that $1,500 a year.[44] They may be poor, but they are not quite powerless: in India, the poor vote in great numbers, and the middle class often skips the voting booth[45]—almost the opposite of the pattern in the United States. The Indian government must convince voters that the changes it uses to spur economic development will bring them gains—something that is sometimes easier to see from a distance. It must make the case that building new roads will create hundreds of thousands of construction jobs for the poor even as it displaces some from their homes. It must argue that allowing foreign companies to build new factories will bring steady paychecks to hundreds of thousands more. It must argue that allowing new retail stores to compete with traditional mom-and-pop shops will result in both lower prices and more jobs created than lost. And if the government fails to carry those arguments—as it has so far—it must be content to let companies like Mr. Murthy's Infosys, Mr. Ambani's Reliance Industries, and Mr. Tata's Tata Group make the changes the government cannot. Unlike China, where the government spearheads change by championing big development projects, India may need to let private companies lead the way. If India is to avoid being left behind, economic development must have a charismatic political champion. The current prime minister, Manmohan Singh, is committed to development, but he is a technocrat no one would accuse of being charismatic.

If India fails to fully unleash its economy while it has the attention of investors from around the world, it will pay a heavy price in prosperity both today and when its young population becomes a working-age behemoth in need of jobs. India must move past the on-again, off-again reforms that slow its economic rise or risk missing a historic chance to propel hundreds of millions of people out of poverty.

CHAPTER SEVEN

REVOLUTION BY
DINNER PARTY

Hung Huang is China's answer to Oprah Winfrey. Ms. Hung publishes women's magazines, writes one of China's most popular blogs, penned a juicy, best-selling autobiography, and even had her own TV talk show. She—and her surroundings—captures just how much China has changed in a single generation. After growing up in Beijing and then graduating from Vassar College, she returned to her hometown to find China in the midst of a metamorphosis. Ms. Hung, currently the CEO of China Interactive Media Group, lives in a vast loft apartment that could have been plucked from downtown Manhattan and deposited in Beijing's art gallery neighborhood intact, complete with towering ceilings and contemporary artwork. The art doubles as political commentary: adorning the exposed brick wall in the dining room is a neon sign with foot-high, red Chinese characters. "Revolution is a dinner party," it proclaims. Indeed. Mao defended the hardship his hungry subjects faced by declaring, "Revolution is not a dinner party." Today, with China in the midst of another kind of Cultural Revolution, it is.

Mao's Cultural Revolution devastated the nation, crushing its intellectual, scientific, and artistic capabilities, eliminating China's educational system, and ruining its economy. When Mao died in 1976, he left behind a nation of penniless peasants. Now that his Communist Party has done an about-face, gradually rejoining the world economy, moving toward a market economy and taking the nation through an industrial revolution, incomes are rising and the once quashed spirit of the Chinese is reappearing. Already China's new approach has lifted more than 100 million people out of poverty, and average incomes have doubled in a decade. But China is changing in ways mere numbers cannot convey. Hundreds of millions of lives have been altered as China's economy modernizes. The world's big companies may have come to China to sell to a billion new customers or to search for low-pay laborers, but despite their motives, their presence has brought incalculable change to the everyday lives of the millions of Chinese who work for them.

China's new Cultural Revolution plays out day after day on a single road in a sprawling industrial park in Shanghai's Pudong region. There, tens of thousands of Chinese workers clock in at factories owned by Ricoh, NEC, Siemens, Sharp, and other foreign companies. Inside a building bearing the familiar yellow-and-red Kodak logo, Ye Lu, thirty-six, is one of two thousand Chinese workers paid $125 a month to build cameras. Each workday morning Ms. Lu dresses in the company uniform—yellow jacket and yellow hat—and assembles the circuit boards that go inside cameras. Her salary has already doubled in the four years she has worked for Kodak. As a result, she and her husband have managed to buy the bare-bones, two-bedroom apartment once owned by the Chinese company he works for. Ms. Lu dreams of one day being able to afford a three-bedroom home with both air-conditioning and heating. By never eating out and always buying Chinese brands, she saves a third of her $41-a-month salary—sacrifices that allow her to stash away $160 of her $500-a-year income. Ms. Lu, like many Chinese factory workers who are earning more money than ever before, pictures a bright future for herself and her fourteen-year-old daughter: "Life will become better and better."[1]

While Ms. Lu's life holds promise, her white-collar colleagues are already living the life she dreams her daughter will have someday. Not far from the factory is Kodak's Shanghai product development center, where sixty employees write computer code for cameras, including the sophisticated software that creates special effects for cameras used in Hollywood. Salaries there start at $12,500 a year, putting employees in the top 1 percent of China's earners and, with

China's lower cost of living, giving them the same buying power as Americans earning $40,000 a year.[2] Miles Mao, thirty-three, works in Kodak's quality-control department. Like almost all of his co-workers, he already owns two apartments, each larger than what Ms. Lu hopes one day to afford. He bought the first in 1999 and lives in it with his wife and their five-year-old daughter. That apartment doubled in value in five years. He hadn't even finished paying it off before buying another—a luxurious, three-bedroom apartment—as an investment he hopes will help pay for the family's retirement. Despite what they spend on apartments, Mr. Mao and his wife, who works for Lufthansa, manage to save more than $600 a month, $7,200 a year.[3]

The high monthly savings of factory workers and white-collar workers alike are typical in China. Even as many Chinese benefit from today's good times, they find reminders of China's bleak past close at hand in the form of relatives and friends who have not been so fortunate. Mr. Mao and his colleagues trade horror stories: one has relatives in Changsha who earn just $17 a month. They don't dare go to the doctor if they're sick, since they cannot afford the bill. Another resents the fact that his mother is expected to live on a government pension of just $28 a month after forty-five years of hard work. Like all of his white-collar colleagues, Mr. Mao sends money home each month to help. He gives $370 a month to his retired parents. A colleague sends $250 a month to her parents and another $125 to help her husband's grandmother.

China's younger generations have replaced the state's Iron Rice Bowl. Their monthly contributions are a constant reminder of how China's social safety net has frayed over the past decade. Just one of every four people in China has health insurance now, only 14 percent have pensions, and with 25 percent of education costs shifted to parents, school dropout rates are rising, particularly in lower-income rural areas.[4] So Chinese sock away savings in case they or their family members need to go to the hospital or lose their jobs with state-owned companies. Or in case the government reverses tack again, and the future clouds over. The high savings rate—30 percent on the average[5]—is not just a measure of the strong economic growth that has given many Chinese higher salaries. It is a reminder that ordinary Chinese, not just the Chinese government, fear political instability. It is very different from the pattern in the United States: Americans earn more than ten times as much as the Chinese on average, but spend more than they earn and have a negative savings rate.

Not that the Chinese aren't spending. Released from the prison of poverty, they are spending freely. Mr. Mao and his colleagues at Kodak talk about buying not just apartments but cars, expensive stereos and home theater systems, top-of-the-line Sony laptops, televisions and washing machines, overseas vacations, designer clothes. When they get raises, Chinese women switch cosmetics brands from Oil of Olay and Avon to Shiseido and Lancôme. Well-educated, middle-class Chinese have seen their incomes at least double in a decade. Most foreign companies are counting on this growing middle-class and upper-class group of Chinese to become customers. As Ying Yeh, chairman of Kodak's Greater China Region, put it, "We are seeing a growing middle class with very, very strong buying power. They believe, 'I have earned my right to spoil myself.'"

○

AS RECENTLY AS FIFTEEN YEARS AGO, nearly everyone in China was equally poor, but incomes are stratifying quickly. China already has 320,000 millionaires, according to Merrill Lynch.[6] Ms. Yeh took a break one Saturday[7] to explain that China now has blue-collar factory hands plus pink-collar secretaries, flight attendants, and other service workers. It also has white-collar office workers and the most recent addition, gold-collar workers, like her. Dressed for a weekend meeting in expensive, trendy casual clothes—a white T-shirt decorated with red sequined heart over designer blue jeans stretched tight, her ponytail topped with a red baseball cap—Ms. Yeh said China's gold-collar workers are executives in multinationals doing business in China. Their companies pay for a glamorous lifestyle that includes a luxury apartment, full-time car and driver, and extensive travel across the region and back and forth to company headquarters in the United States or Europe. They buy expensive clothes and art, take jet-setter vacations, play golf at China's mushrooming number of luxury country clubs, and think nothing of spending $8,000 on giant flat-panel televisions.

Once egalitarian China now has so many variations of rich citizens that they've been given special names. There are the *dan shen qui zu*, the "single aristocrats," usually women over thirty, working as managers or perhaps bankers for foreign companies and earning at least $24,000 a year, enough to buy luxury cosmetics and clothes and go on beach vacations with their friends. They are the kind of women who would have starred in *Sex and the City* if it had been set in Shanghai instead of Manhattan. Then there are the *bo pu zu*, the well-off intellectuals, whose tastes run more to books than to shopping. Those who earn middle-class salaries but spend money as fast as they earn it are known as *yue guang zu*, the tapped-out class. And there are the affectionately named *you pi*—yuppies—or *xiao zi*, the "little capitalists," workers like Mr. Mao and his Kodak colleagues, who own apartments and cars and spend time in cafés on weekend afternoons. Already there are 14 million Chinese like them earning more than $12,500 a year. The disposable income of that elite group stands at $61 billion a year.

However stratified, incomes are rising quickly across the board. Today 77 percent of urban Chinese live on less than $3,100 a year; by 2025, just 10 percent will earn that little. By then, urban Chinese will spend $2.5 trillion a year, almost as much as Japanese now spend in what is today one of the world's biggest consumer markets. By 2011, a large wave of 290 million Chinese is expected to reach the lower-middle class, earning between $3,100 and $5,000 a year. By 2025, about 520 million Chinese should have reached the upper-middle class, earning between $5,000 and $12,300 a year. The combined disposable income of that group is expected then to reach $1.6 trillion.[8] As incomes rise, China is emerging as a giant consumer market, and companies' attempts to reach it are changing core traditions in China. Tom Doctoroff, CEO of Greater China for the J.Walter Thompson advertising agency, has marketed some of America's most prominent brands to Chinese buyers.[9] He likens the setting to America in the 1950s, long before Tivo let TV viewers skip commercials. People in

China believe what they see on their new TVs. And commercials using the sophisticated production techniques common in the West can be far more eye-catching than the stuffy, censored programming of China's state-run television stations. China's TV viewers are more impressionable than jaded American and European viewers, and that naïveté is helping Western companies sell to the Chinese.

Some companies have made breathtaking inroads. Chinese wedding traditions from before the Cultural Revolution called for red dresses and gifts of jade or gold. During the Cultural Revolution, such extravagance was frowned upon. Now Chinese weddings resemble those in the United States: brides wear a white dress and expect a diamond ring. This remaking of Chinese traditions is all the audacious creation of the diamond marketer De Beers Group, which steadfastly advertised the Western approach as a means to sell more diamonds in a land of a billion people. Starting in 1993, De Beers planted plots in TV shows, advertised in magazines and on TV, and eventually organized mass wedding ceremonies for couples, making sure the main attraction was the moment the groom gives his bride a diamond ring.[10] Young, urban Chinese on their way toward marriage bought into DeBeers' message en masse. In just a few years, they began to believe, zuan shi heng jiu yuan, yi ke yong liu chuan—a diamond is forever.

China is now one of the world's largest markets for diamonds. De Beers spends about $6 million a year advertising diamonds, which produced sales of $1.4 billion worth of diamonds in 2005.[11] Eighty percent of grooms in Beijing gave a diamond ring, just trailing the 85 percent of American grooms giving diamonds. All this in just over a decade.

Ms. Hung, reading the tea leaves about the Chinese women who buy her magazines, said that foreign traditions like giving diamond rings find easy traction because so many Chinese habits were erased after Mao took power in 1949. The Cultural Revolution "interrupted and discontinued" many traditions, said Ms. Hung. "The discontinuity of everything Chinese has made it so easy for the younger generation to pick the Western version." Chinese consumers are a tabula rasa for Western advertisers. "It is like entering a huge market with no preconceptions."[12]

For example, Starbucks Coffee has captivated Chinese as it has

Americans. The first Starbucks in China opened in Beijing in 1999, and since then more than 220 Starbucks have opened across China. This is remarkable, of course, because for centuries China has been the land of tea. But for Chinese, going to Starbucks is not about drinking coffee. Chinese go to Starbucks to be seen, said Mr. Doctoroff, the adman. Starbucks is a status symbol in China because of its extravagant prices: a tall latte costs 22 renminbi, about $2.75. Spending that much on a single drink is deep into the realm of luxury, especially compared with prices at Chinese restaurants. "For that, somebody could buy a family a substantial lunch," said Claire Jackson, senior planner at Ogilvy & Mather in Shanghai. "It is about status and being able to show off."[13] There is a lot of showing off going on. Only fifteen years after ration coupons were in circulation, China now has more than four hundred shopping malls, including four that are bigger than the Mall of America in Minnesota.[14]

○

THE CONTRAST BETWEEN the China of a few decades ago and the China of today can be disconcerting. In Shanghai, there's a futuristic spot called Tomorrow Square. All the buildings in the area are new, and the architecture is striking—all cubes and triangles, the shapes of modernity. Rising from a grass plot is a glitzy skyscraper housing a J. W. Marriott hotel. Down the block is a Ferrari showroom. Another new glass skyscraper houses the Mercedes-Benz dealership. Near the luxury car showrooms is the most common sight in Shanghai: orange construction cranes erecting the next trophy building.[15]

Near Tomorrow Square is a small park where the elderly gather to sit, escaping their tiny apartments. Yuppies bustle past them—past yesterday's China—heading toward the Shanghai Art Museum. Inside the museum bookshop, a guard snoozes, head resting on his arms. The shop sells a number of Chinese-language primers on famous Western artists—Seurat, Klimt, Giotto, even Andy Warhol. Tucked away in a less prominent spot is a single copy of a book of photos documenting the Cultural Revolution.[16] One shows a sea of onlookers gathered in a city square to watch as "Capitalist Roaders" and "class enemies" are denounced and humiliated, made to wear tall paper dunce hats, to bow in front of the crowd, and to confess their crimes. The faces in the crowd are young, idealistic, righteous, and determined to right wrongs. A series of photos shows a group of eight people paraded through the streets of Harbin and then publicly shot in front of a crowd of hundreds, executed for being "counterrevolutionaries" and criminals. Another picture shows the "landlord mansion" of an accused "rich peasant" family. The riches consisted of one pair of silk stockings, two leather jackets, and a lone wristwatch, and the "mansion" was a one-room house. The family was sentenced to two years' hard labor. Most of the cadres who had gathered to denounce the Capitalist Roaders—to watch them be humiliated or even executed—would now be in their late fifties and sixties, the same age as the leaders of today's Communist Party. Whatever their communist credentials earned in decades gone by, the leaders of China today are living in surroundings far more comfortable than those the party condemned just a few decades ago. China's leaders have morphed into the very Capitalist Roaders the Communist Party once so severely punished.

However hypocritical, the Capitalist Roaders running today's Communist Party have brought the country prosperity, and most Chinese are better off under their leadership. In fact, China has risen so fast that the world's powerful nations sometimes fear it. It took England fifty-eight years to double its GDP starting in 1780; the United States needed forty-seven years starting in 1839; Japan doubled its GDP in thirty-four years starting in 1885; South Korea doubled the size of its economy in a remarkable eleven years starting in 1966; and then China came along to set a new record—it doubled its per capita GDP in just nine years starting in 1978, then doubled it again by 1996.[17]

In a single generation, China has gone from being economically backward to being the world's fourth-largest economy. The China of the present is not as strong as the stunning numbers suggest, in part because of its unusual history—namely the authoritarian system that took it through both the lows of the Cultural Revolution and the giddiness of the current economic advances.

O

FOR ORDINARY CHINESE, perhaps the biggest adjustments to the new China have come with the ongoing mass migration of peasants from the countryside to the cities. The mass movement was triggered by China's economic transformation: rural incomes that tripled when China began its reforms have since stagnated at levels far below city incomes. About 120 million peasants left their farms over the past decade—nearly 1 of every 10 people—and up to 70 million more will do so by 2010.[18] Imagine if two-thirds of all Americans suddenly moved halfway across the country; an equal number of Chinese have migrated from their homes to find jobs. Cities have become magnets for simple reasons: the average annual disposable income in rural areas was $488 in 2006, while urban disposable income averaged $1,600.[19] The former farmers are going to work on construction sites or in freshly built factories. These workers are the children of the countryside. According to a Ministry of Labor study, 75 percent of Chinese factories employ only women between eighteen and twenty-six years old. There are similar concentrations of young men working in construction jobs that have been created as China builds factories, highways, and skyscrapers.[20]

Walk through a Chinese factory making DVD players or shoes or televisions, and you'll see row after row of twenty-something workers on the assembly lines. Most have come from faraway farms. Migrant workers are housed in dormitories with up to a dozen workers per room, and children and spouses are not welcome. Just like the middle-class Kodak employees, the young factory and construction workers send money back to their parents in the villages and earn in a month what their parents earn in a year. Those new to the cities are introduced to all the trappings of modern life—cell phones, skyscrapers, electric rice cookers, even air-conditioning—and often have a hard time adjusting when they return to visit the relative deprivation of their parents' homes, which frequently lack electricity, telephones, and running water. In many rural Chinese towns, people are so poor that newspapers are hung up on the main street and shared with those who can't afford to buy one each day. Newspapers typically cost half a renminbi, which is about one-twentieth of one American cent.

Older workers, those over thirty, are not welcome in the newly built factories. Factory bosses found that older workers picked up hard-to-reform, bad working attitudes during the Maoist era when they toiled for state-owned companies. Those over thirty are simply considered unemployable by most of China's factory bosses. With the exception of a small number of managers, anyone older is considered obsolete. With limited options, those over thirty are mostly doomed to a life of poverty: they must stay on the farm, continue working at the same state-owned company and hope it doesn't close down, scrounge up enough cash to start a small business, or rely on a child for support. The exceptions are the politically well connected or the few who managed to get a good education despite the anti-education bent of the Cultural Revolution.

Not all of China's young people work in factories. Those who grew up in cities tend to be better educated than their rural counterparts; many of them have attended university. They work in the skyscrapers now sprouting up in Shanghai, Beijing, Guangzhou, Shenzhen, and other big Chinese cities. They not only work as secretaries, accountants, marketers, and administrators, but more and more write computer code and answer emails on behalf of foreign companies like Microsoft and HSBC that have moved work offshore to China. Young urban Chinese workers tend to live with their parents until they are married or in their thirties, saving three-quarters of their $5,000-a-year salaries to buy a home or a car. Delaying gratification is not a sacrifice for them; it is a marked improvement over the opportunities they would have had even five years before.

In Chinese cities most outsiders have never heard of, even Korean and Japanese workers are finding white-collar competition. Two million people in northeastern China speak Korean, and they are increasingly working in China for Korean companies. There are 500,000 Japanese-speakers in Dalian, China, where Japanese companies are opening call centers, paying just one-twentieth of the wages they would have to pay in Tokyo. Kenichi Ohmae, known in Japan as "Mr.

Strategy," said white-collar work from Japan is "migrating through the telephone lines and the Internet lines into China. This is where the new competition is."[21]

The Chinese equivalent of India's Infosys campus in Bangalore is the Pudong Software Park in Shanghai. It, too, looks like an American college campus, with sidewalks crossing grassy parkland between dozens of office buildings. Scores of foreign and Chinese technology companies are housed there, but they share a central cafeteria, where a sturdy lunch will set you back seventy-eight cents. Multinationals from around the world have offices there: GE, Citibank, IBM, Sun Microsystems, Sony, HP, and Intel as well as the Indian offshoring firm Satyam Computer Services. Jun Qian, twenty-eight, earns $7,500 a year working for a startup called Codex. Told that workers in Silicon Valley earn ten times as much for the same work he is doing in the Shanghai software park, he shrugs. Even if he were given the chance to move to America, he would stay in China. "I'm focusing on the future," he says. "We have a lot more opportunities here."[22]

The fact that a Chinese worker would reject the notion of going to America, or leaving China at all, marks a stunning evolution. Millions of people risked their lives to escape China for Hong Kong or Taiwan after the Communists took power in 1949.[23] China used to worry that anyone let out of the country would not come back. Even as recently as 1999, Hong Kong officials worried that if they allowed too many mainland Chinese to enter the city, the mainlanders would stay illegally. Now Hong Kong welcomes Chinese tourists because they boost the city's economy by shopping and dining out, then cross the border to go back home. To escape China's 17 percent value-added tax,[24] they buy $2,000 Louis Vuitton handbags or $200 Nike sneakers in Hong Kong, making it necessary for Hong Kong taxi drivers to learn Mandarin instead of relying on the hometown Cantonese dialect. Chinese entrepreneurs who once escaped to Hong Kong or Taiwan then moved to the United States or Europe to make their dreams a reality are now finding opportunity at home.

While ambitious Chinese usually want to stay in China today, many aspire to work for foreign companies, at least early in their careers, for two pragmatic reasons. First, Chinese companies tend to have top-down, command-and-control working cultures instead of the teamwork approach popular with most multinationals. Second, as many young Chinese are startlingly frank to admit, they plan to learn all they can from foreigners and then take that knowledge to Chinese companies. Robbie Yang, twenty-five, received three job offers when he graduated from college, but he chose to work in a Beijing call center run by Hewlett Packard. Between fielding calls from GE employees in New Zealand who had forgotten their computer passwords, he explained that he had worked with the Chinese computer company Legend (now known as Lenovo) during college. "The reason why I work in a foreign company is I really want to learn something from them—they are really advanced," said Mr. Yang, who spends just $1.50 a day on lunch and lives with his parents so that he can save 80 percent of his salary. "We should learn more from them, then we can start our own companies. Maybe in the future we will have some big Chinese companies like HP and IBM, and we will need to hire American workers," Mr. Yang said in 2003.[25] Within two years, he got his wish: his former company, China's Lenovo Group, bought IBM's PC operations, giving the Chinese company 2,500 former IBM employees in the United States.

In China, nationalism is always present, and it is usually close to the surface. It can be found in the harmless but ubiquitous adoration of Yao Ming, the Chinese basketball star who plays for the Houston Rockets. But it goes beyond ballgames. Almost all young, well-educated Chinese fervently believe that Taiwan is rightfully part of China and should not be allowed political independence. Many otherwise moderate Chinese yuppies believe that Taiwan should be invaded and taken by force if Taiwanese politicians declare independence. Anger at Japan, which brutalized China in the 1930s and 1940s, erupts regularly. Chinese authorities who quickly clamp down on other demonstrations allow Chinese crowds to smash Japanese restaurants and cars or demonstrate in large numbers at the Japanese embassy. The anti-Japanese sentiment stems from Japanese atrocities, like the rape of Nanking, during its occupation of much of China from 1937 to 1945. But today's technologies fan the protests through Internet blogs and angry SMS phone messages. The United States is sometimes a target, too, but that usually requires more provocation, such as the 2001 incident when a U.S. spy plane collided with a Chinese fighter jet, triggering outrage and a large protest at the U.S. embassy in Beijing.

○

BECAUSE CHINA—WITH ITS NEW highways and skyscrapers and factories—looks more and more like the West, because its economy is integrating so thoroughly with the world's as it moves toward a Western capitalist system, and because China is allowing foreign tourists and business leaders to visit, foreigners sometimes assume that China has changed more than it really has. Despite its people's growing incomes and opportunities, China's authoritarian regime has retained in practice much of the mind-set and many of the abusive practices of the past, most of them designed to preserve political stability.

China's seemingly perpetual economic growth of nearly 10 percent a year since reforms began in 1978,[26] and the resulting gains for most Chinese people, has masked some of the very strong undercurrents threatening to drown the nation. Some are social, some are political, and some are financial, but, coming all at once, they mean that a government that prizes political stability is having a tough time working behind the scenes at keeping the nation stable.

China's most pressing social problem is the fast-widening gap between rich and poor in a nation where a mere generation ago almost all comrades were equally poor. China's rural population, plus nearly everyone over thirty, are fast being left behind by more prosperous city dwellers, particularly those living in the booming cities along China's coasts.

The shockingly widespread corruption of government officials is sapping the incomes of ordinary Chinese and spawning dissent nationwide. The Communist Party punished 97,260 members for corruption in 2006, including the nation's chief statistician and the party boss of Shanghai.[27] Still, local officials remain very powerful and far too numerous to be policed from Beijing, despite the existence of a one-party, authoritarian government. China's bureaucracy, while extensive, is not unified; many local officials effectively preside over personal fiefdoms rather than efficiently carry out Beijing's declared policies. Sometimes the cause is simple corruption and in other instances the officials are catering to legitimate local needs. With 1.3 billion people, China is hardly monolithic; its people speak more than fifty dialects, and residents of the thriving cities along China's coasts have little in common with their compatriots in the countryside, or even in China's Western cities. In other words, in a nation that fears political instability, the central government and local governments are often at odds.

There are many other nationwide problems: Chinese banks, where most Chinese keep their savings, remain fragile; China's environment is being destroyed, with dire shortages of drinkable water in some places; the system of state-owned enterprises is just half restructured, with many still churning out goods no one wants to buy with work-forces far larger than necessary, despite tens of millions of layoffs in recent years. In an effort to provide jobs for those laid off or leaving the farms, the government has invested stunning amounts of money—half of the nation's GDP in 2005—into the construction of large-scale projects. That money is often spent inefficiently both because of corruption and because the government is building the projects ahead of demand for them.

Even as China's relations with the outside world have dramatically thawed since the end of the Cold War, China remains in the midst of a Cold War with its own people. China's citizens have few rights and little protection from government abuses. Fair trials remain rare. Prisoners are still tortured. Religious activity is curtailed, particularly that of Falun Gong, but also that of Christian and Muslim worshipers. The most vulnerable easily fall through the nation's safety net. In Henan Province, hundreds of thousands of peasants contracted the human immunodeficiency virus in the 1990s after selling their blood in government-sponsored schemes. Infection rates have reached 80 percent in some villages. Since 2004, Henan's provincial government policy has called for subsidies to children who lost their parents to AIDS. Those who lost one parent are due $6.15 a month, and those who lost both mother and father are awarded $15 a month—fifty cents a day if both parents died because of the government. Often the orphans get nothing, or get far less: just $1.50 a month in one prefecture, according to charity workers—five cents a day.[28]

China has more than four hundred daily newspapers—more than any other nation—but lacks a free press. Chinese journalists are regularly banned from reporting "sensitive" stories, including the breakout of SARS and cases of bird flu. They can still be jailed when they offend the government or publish what the government decides are "state secrets." For eight years in a row, China has been the world's leading jailer of journalists, according to the Committee to Protect Journalists. There's no such thing as free speech—mouthing off on an Internet blog can result in arrest—sometimes with cooperation from Yahoo and other Western Internet companies. China employs between 30,000 and 40,000 cyber police to monitor the Internet and help with censorship.[29] Sometimes the government's efforts are unnecessary: Google admits that it censors itself in China, despite its corporate feel-good motto, "Don't be evil."

The list of China's abuses of human rights goes on and on. There have been many cases of arbitrary arrest, which sometimes leads to prisoners' being held incommunicado. Forced confessions and torture or less severe mistreatment of prisoners is not unusual. A renewed crackdown on journalists began in 2005, along with continued imprisonment or harassment of lawyers and rights activists. Amnesty International estimated that at least 1,010 people were executed and 2,790 sentenced to death during 2006 for both violent and nonviolent crimes—a particularly problematic number because of the paucity of fair trials in Chinese courts.[30]

But shockingly, despite the plethora of abuses, the political atmosphere has improved. Some of those abuses remain official policy, but some have been declared illegal—in word if not in practice. Back in 1996, China changed its laws to presume innocence for those arrested and to guarantee them the right to a lawyer, promises that a decade later are only occasionally carried out. Although police abuse of those detained reportedly remains rampant, torture of those in custody is now illegal and arbitrary detention has been abolished—on paper. In

2004, the Chinese constitution was amended to recognize private property, which was banned in Communist China as recently as 1978. China has been adding other new laws to its books: in July 2005, China enacted a law banning the buying or selling of human organs and requiring written consent from organ donors. International lawyers say that China has made incredible progress by passing these laws, but does not yet enforce them. A good example of the one-step-forward, two-steps-back progress China has made can be seen in the mushrooming number of public protests nationwide—an average of two hundred a day. Typically, demonstrators are peasants whose land was confiscated by corrupt local government officials and sold to developers, who leave the peasants with little. Local police or hired thugs often beat or even kill the demonstrators. A decade ago, with memories of the Tiananmen Square massacre of peaceful protesters still fresh, no one would have had the nerve to protest, and the fact that so many dare stage demonstrations shows progress as well as fury. The sheer numbers of protests have alarmed the central government, which in response plans to devote more resources to rural economic development.

Some of China's challenges are demographic, and some of them are man-made. The Chinese government still determines how many children families are allowed to have, generally permitting one child for city residents and two children in rural areas if the firstborn is a girl. Without this one-child policy begun in 1979, China estimates its population would be 1.7 billion as opposed to 1.3 billion, a difference greater than the entire population of the United States. However, because of Chinese society's preference for boys, there have been many cases of infanticide and, more recently, sex-selective abortion that has left a severe imbalance in the gender ratio. Within the next decade, there will be 40 million more men than women in China.[31] In addition, the one-child policy has created a demographic time bomb. Chinese call it the 1:2:4 problem: China's soon-to-be retirees tend to have one working-age person supporting two parents and four grandparents. By 2025, some 200 million Chinese will be at least sixty-five years old.[32] If the government fails to create enough jobs for those of working age, it faces a stark choice: it must spend far more to support retirees or be prepared to face a dramatic increase in poverty.

Meanwhile, China's population is beginning to age even as India's explodes with youth. Projections show that China's working-age population will peak in 2015, and then steadily shrink as the population grows gray. Some experts believe that India's economy will overtake China's because of these demographic trends. China has proved so much more efficient than India at developing and managing its economy that this scenario is unlikely unless China falls into political turmoil.

Despite China's steady advances in the past two decades, a government implosion is not out of the question. China's authoritarian political system has many fault lines and could collapse. The Communist Party could hang on to power for decades, or it could be overthrown in a matter of years. One possible outcome taps the party's greatest fear: like the Soviet Union, the nation could break apart, particularly if China's economically strong coastal provinces insist on political and economic autonomy. Some academics say that the government will likely fall, crippled by internal strife—whether rivalries between provinces, rage boiling over from peasants who feel victimized by corrupt officials, or democracy advocates who, against the odds, demand and win some measure of political freedom of choice. More likely, the fear of a Soviet-style collapse may lead Chinese leaders to take an even stronger grip on the country, with Beijing swinging toward ever-stronger authoritarianism much as Putin has taken a hard line in Russia. Despite its outward invincibility, the future of China's current political system is not assured.

○

WHAT IS CLEAR IS THAT CHINA'S political system is far more likely than India's to face great turbulence, even the possibility of collapse. Diplomats and scholars find India's future easier to predict. They say its central question is whether it can stay on its current reform path. If the Indian economy fails to take advantage of the tailwinds it now finds, the nation's powerful demographic trends could saddle it with far more working-age residents than jobs for them, which could doom another generation to poverty. But the consensus is that India will trudge on, slowly and heavily, elephantlike, along the path of economic growth.

Business leaders, both Chinese and Western, usually insist that China can thrive economically under the leadership of the authoritarian Communist Party for decades to come. After the Tiananmen Square massacre, many Chinese people crave stability and economic progress more than they long for a voice in politics—they have bought into the Singapore model. As they grow wealthier, Chinese crave more personal freedoms and rights, particularly property rights, but they do not long for democracy.[33]

Yet one of the most commonly held Western hopes for China's future is also one of the least likely outcomes for China, at least in the near future. The West presumes that "democratic capitalism" is a phrase whose words belong together. Democratic capitalism is finally becoming a reality in India as it leaves decades of socialism behind. For China, however, it is simply wishful thinking. China will not become a democracy anytime soon. Chinese people do not celebrate Taiwan's democracy and dream of sharing Taiwan's political freedom. Most mainland Chinese concern themselves with making money rather than the prospect of voting. Chinese political leaders claim occasionally that China will transition to democracy once it is well educated and rich enough, and they have indeed allowed limited village elections already. Alas, China's literacy rate is already 91 percent,[34] and the nation's income has been rising steadily. China's treatment of Hong Kong is a proxy: Hong Kong has not only the education levels and standard of living of a developed country but also the popular demand for democracy. The mainland government, however, has taken steps to keep Hong Kong from becoming democratic. Such a policy suggests that China's promises to allow democracy in Mainland China are empty. Thus there is no push for democracy from either the Chinese citizenry or the government. Indeed, the Communist Party counts on attracting foreign investors from the West to create the new jobs and growing incomes that keep political opposition at bay in China.

Another myth, commonly held in the West, credits China's rapid economic rise to its authoritarian political system. Many people believe that India's growth has been hindered by democracy. In fact, India's slow rise stems from more basic differences with China. First, the order in which reforms occurred matters: China focused first on improving rural incomes, whereas India waited until there was a crisis and then adopted the technocrat's recipe—the prescription of the International Monetary Fund and international business—to reform its global business systems. The majority of Indians—rural Indians—did not find immediate economic gains from the new policies, but instead watched others prosper. Second, China was much better educated by the time it began reforms. In 1979, China's literacy rate was nearly 70 percent and rising. By 1982, China's literacy rate for girls aged 15–19 was 85 percent, and for boys aged 15–19 it was 96 percent. By contrast, half of India was illiterate until the 1990s, and 35 percent of Indians remain illiterate today. When reforms began in 1991, half of Indian girls aged 15–19 were illiterate, while 25 percent of Indian boys aged 15–19 remained illiterate.[35] With the exception of India's well-educated elite, India's workforce was less prepared than China's, and it still is. As Arthur Kroeber has pointed out in the *China Economic Quarterly*, China's extremely high savings rate gave its government an advantage. It allowed the government to fund expensive infrastructure projects that most developing nations cannot afford. Counting government savings, not just household savings, China's savings rate is 40 percent, while India's is 26 percent.[36]

Most Indians would not trade their political freedom for economic gains, but, as it happens, the discrepancy in growth rates seems to be unrelated to politics. It is fashionable, especially in Asia, to justify China's authoritarianism with the "Singapore excuse," to argue that Lee Kwan Yew could not have so dramatically taken Singapore from a third-world backwater into a first-world economic powerhouse in a single generation without employing authoritarianism. In fact, other social and economic data explain why China was able to move forward faster than India. And, of course, as everywhere, a nation's prospects often depend on its leaders. China's authoritarianism in past decades, when Chairman Mao was its leader rather than the more progressive Deng Xiaoping, led to poverty instead of riches, backwardness instead of advancement, fear instead of hope.

○

WHATEVER CHINA'S FUTURE, the world's view of China is likely to be dramatically shaped by Beijing's role as host of the 2008 Olympics. Culturally, the Olympics will launch present-day China on the world's stage. The worst-case scenario is that Chinese audiences will engage in ugly displays of nationalism, or that Chinese teams will be caught engaging in the bad sportsmanship of rampant doping. If all goes smoothly, the Olympics will likely reconstruct the West's image of China from that of a bicycle-riding, human-rights-violating third-world country to that of a powerful equal in the first world. Beijing has hired none other than Steven Spielberg to work on the opening ceremony, which will feature a staggering one million performers.

The nation is sparing no expense to make the Olympics go smoothly. China is building a dozen new sporting-event venues, including the captivating Beijing National Stadium, nicknamed the "bird's nest" because of the gigantic, twisted steel beams curving gracefully around the exterior like twigs woven into a bird's nest. New roads, subway lines, and hotels are under construction, too. At the same time, the nation is in full control-freak China mode. It has vowed to clean the filthy air, by shutting down factories near Olympic events if necessary. In an attempt to keep visitors from getting food poisoning, Beijing plans to inspect vegetables, fish, and meat during the Olympics, and trace the movement of all food from farm to Beijing plates. Two years before the opening ceremonies, the Chinese government was already testing cannons filled with cloud-seeding chemicals that it can fire into the sky to dissolve clouds before rain threatens sporting events.[37] Already a master at stifling political dissent, the Communist Party is now poised to crush even the dissent of the sky.

For Chinese leaders, the 2008 Olympics amount to China's

coming-out party, so the stakes are high. As the world's flags flutter in Beijing during the opening ceremony, China will mark its reemergence on the world scene—not just in sports but in business and culture and politics as well. Watching on television, people around the world will find a China that has remade itself into a nation that is a powerful force to be reckoned with, and not just on the sports field.

CHAPTER EIGHT

GEOPOLITICS MIXED
WITH OIL AND WATER

Wandering through the galleries of the Metropolitan Museum in New York, you'll come upon a room that houses Louis XV's desk. The room is decorated in ornate eighteenth-century French style—complete with Asian accents. Blue-and-white porcelain bowls from China adorn a fireplace, and the writing table the king used at Versailles starting in 1759 is replete with painted pagodas. This decoration was not unique to royalty; as a result of vigorous global trade in the sixteenth through nineteenth centuries, Europe had developed a taste for Asian design. From India, Europeans imported textiles along with wooden boxes and furniture intricately inlaid with ivory. Chinese designs inspired imitations throughout the Continent. In 1664 alone, the Dutch East India Company imported 45,000 pieces of blue-and-white porcelain from China. The dishes were originally carried as ballast for ships bringing tea to Europe, but proved so popular that they came to be known as "China."[1]

After a centurylong hiatus, India and China are moving back toward their historic equilibrium in the global economy, and that is producing tectonic shifts in economics as well as in geopolitics. It seems unlikely that 250 years from now, Chinese-made items sold in today's Wal-Marts will make their way to museums, but the prevalence of made-in-China goods on American store shelves is evidence that truly global trade is again flourishing. India's service exports are

not as visible, but India, too, is clearly returning to its former important role. "Both countries are on the way to reclaiming their rightful
places in the world economy," India's prime minister, Manmohan
Singh, stated in 2006.

In 1600, India and China combined accounted for more than half
the globe's economic output, sending everything from silk, porcelain,
tea, furniture, spices, and wallpaper—a Chinese invention—overland
via the Silk Road or via ship on the Spice Route. Until the late nineteenth century, China and India remained the world's two largest
economies, according to Angus Maddison, the distinguished economic historian. But protectionism and world wars intervened, then
India and China shut themselves off from the world, and by 2003
India and China together accounted for just 20 percent of the global
economy, despite their vast populations. When looked at with a
centuries-long time horizon, the twentieth century was just an historical aberration for these two economic giants. China's economy
will grow larger than the long-reigning United States' again by 2020,
and by 2030 India will have the third-largest economy, Mr. Maddison
predicts.[2] In 2030, India and China combined will account for 28 percent of the world's economic output, up from 18 percent in 2001.
Although Americans will remain far richer per person, the U.S. economy by 2030 will have declined in relative terms from 21 percent of
the global economy to 18 percent.[3]

But as India and China rejoin the global economy, three big issues,
besides jobs, are coming to the forefront. First, as the two giant
nations go through industrial revolutions, their appetites for natural
resources are skyrocketing. The new demand is leading to higher
world prices. Their growing thirst for petroleum, along with newfound economic strength, is causing shifts in political alliances
around the world. In addition, now that both nations are richer and
have new technology, both are quickly modernizing their militaries,
causing powerful shifts in geopolitics not seen since the end of the
Cold War. Finally, as India and China industrialize, their already dire
pollution is worsening. The result is blackened air and water for
them, along with danger for the world's environment.

○

FROM AN AIRPLANE SKIMMING over northeastern India's Jhark-hand State, the wild elephants, tigers, monkeys, and leopards in the hills and jungle below are impossible to see amid the bright green rice paddies and farmland where cashew bushes grow. But what is under the soil vitally connects this remote, wild region to the global econ-omy and links jungle to city: iron ore, vital for making the steel nec-essary for the production of cars, skyscrapers, and subways. India has one of the world's largest deposits of iron ore, and a vast amount can be found near the town of Noamundi, just eighty miles from where Tata built India's first steelworks in its historic drive to help the nation achieve self-sufficiency.

To mine the ore, Tata Steel packs forty-two tons of explosives down holes drilled in the hills of its Noamundi Iron Mine. Each blast knocks down a pile of dusty rubble that contains 300,000 tons of iron ore. Oversized yellow dump trucks coated in red dust drive back and forth on the dirt roads crossing the mine, which looks like a giant, red earth terrace carved into a hillside. From the top of the ever-deepening hole being blasted in the earth, the enormous mining trucks resemble toys as they cart away load after load of lumpy, ore-rich rocks loosed by the blasts. Global demand for steel has soared in recent years, propelled by China's drive to build infrastructure and skyscrapers and both India's and China's newfound love of cars. The fast-paced economic growth in India and China has thus dramatically increased demand for the iron ore needed to make steel—to such an extent that the mine runs twenty-four hours a day, producing six train-loads of iron ore daily for Tata and its customers around the globe.

The frantic production at a single mine in off-the-beaten-track India isn't notable in itself. But similar round-the-clock pushes are occurring at mines and wells all over the world, to acquire a variety of natural resources, ranging from iron ore to oil, coal to natural gas. The impact of rising worldwide demand fueled by economic growth in India and China is felt in off-the-beaten-track towns in the United States, too.

The yin and yang of the rise of India and China can be dramatically seen half a world away in southwestern Wyoming. Most days, a clear blue sky stretches over the sagebrush to the horizon. Unseen beneath the sage is a deep pool of natural gas called the Jonah Field. Companies have drilled hundreds of new natural-gas wells in the area as prices have skyrocketed, and the effects are diverse: smoke from gas flares drifts into the pristine air, the county's unemployment rate has dropped to an all-time low of 1.7 percent, and roughnecks instead of cowboys and hikers stroll the streets of Pinedale, Wyoming.

Two hours' drive away in Green River, Wyoming, the story is completely different, again because of what's happening half a world away. That stretch of Wyoming has the world's largest deposit of a mineral called trona, which is processed into a chemical called soda ash, an essential component of glass, certain chemicals, detergents, and paper. Mining trona underpins the city's economy, as it has for decades. However, after China's economy started to boom, it began to import more and more trona. Then China raced to manufacture synthetic trona and began exporting what it did not use domestically, overtaking the United States, primarily Wyoming, as the world's leading producer of soda ash in 2003. As world prices plunged from $77 a ton in 1997 to $60 a ton in 2005 with the new supply from China, more than 800 Wyoming miners lost their jobs—which had a big impact in Green River, a city of 12,000 people.[4]

○

WESTERNERS FEAR JOB LOSSES as China and India ascend, but the most troubling element of their industrial revolutions may instead lie in their soaring energy needs. The rise in the consumption of natural resources in Asia is significant because of the sheer numbers of people involved: there are a combined 600 million Americans and Europeans but more than a billion Chinese *and* a billion Indians. India's oil consumption has doubled since 1992, and China's has doubled since 1994. China already consumes more coal and steel than any other nation, including the United States. Demand has dramatically driven up the world prices of a range of commodities, from aluminum to oil to zinc.[5] As India and China race back toward their former prominent roles in the global economy, their economic successes don't just create and destroy jobs around the world; they impact the natural world, too.

Consider petroleum. To be sure, the world's biggest consumer of oil by far remains the United States. It uses 20.6 million barrels of oil each day, while second-place China, even with a billion more people, uses 7.3 million barrels daily. India uses about the same as Germany, 2.5 million barrels a day.[6] Per capita, Americans today use twelve times more oil than Chinese and thirty times more than Indians.

Nonetheless, as Indian and Chinese incomes rise, Asians are buying more cars and thus consuming more gas, and that is helping drive up prices all around the world. In 2005, China slipped past Japan to become the world's second-largest auto market, after the car-crazy United States. By 2007, Americans bought 16.1 million new cars and trucks, while Chinese bought 5.2 million and Japanese bought 2.95 million. Car sales in India have more than doubled since 2002, reaching 1.5 million in 2007.[7] One reason—though certainly not the only one—that American gas prices sometimes hit $3 a gallon[8] is that Indians and Chinese are learning to drive. Another big reason is that these countries are lighting up new homes and factories with petroleum-fueled electricity plants.

If India and China used as much oil per person as Japan does today—and Japan is considered a model of energy conservation—the two nations would use more oil than is currently sold worldwide each year, according to the Worldwatch Institute. China currently imports 3 million barrels a day, but that should rise to the current American level, 10 million barrels a day, by 2020.[9] If the two nations used as much oil as the United States, there wouldn't be enough oil for the world. Demand around the world seems unlikely to fall soon, and that means prices are also unlikely to fall too far.

India and China are not the only ones to blame. Even as America frets about India's and China's growing thirst for oil, the United States not only gulps far more than any other nation, but its oil demand is also increasing fast. Thus, part of the jump in oil prices can be traced to higher American consumption. Between 1980 and 2006, China increased its oil usage by 5 million barrels, but the United States increased its use by 3.75 million barrels.

○

THE RACE FOR RESOURCES, especially oil, can put countries at loggerheads. That is producing tectonic political shifts as sizzling economic growth in India and China propels the two nations back toward their historically mammoth roles in the world economy. This global rebalancing of political power means that both are also taking their rightful places at the table of international diplomacy, and marks a new post–Cold War era, one that has decisively moved past the ideological battle of communism versus capitalism.

The rise of the two Asian giants comes at an already turbulent time. Within a few short years, the world has seen not only the end of Cold War détente and decades of division between East and West. It has also experienced the emergence of deadly threats from stateless terrorists. It has witnessed the opening of a schism between continental Europe and the United States—one stemming mostly from America's conduct after the September 11 terror attacks, particularly during the Iraq War. With the advent of high petroleum prices, oil-rich nations from Russia to Venezuela to Iran have been reasserting political and military power. And as religious fundamentalists flex their power both in the United States and in Muslim nations, the world has what on a bad news day seems an emerging clash of rigid religious beliefs and a decline of secular politics in the United States as well as the Mideast. This emerging diversity of views along with shifts in geopolitical power is rendering the United Nations nearly impotent in resolving urgent disputes because of the lack of consensus—just at a time when more and more disputes between nations seem to be arising. That makes the early twenty-first century one of the most unstable times in decades.

Amid the backdrop of shifting political sands, India and China are engaged in a desperate race for the resources they need to continue to grow, and that is driving their foreign policy agendas. Both countries have been cutting deals around the world to buy oil, natural gas, and even nuclear reactors. India, whose petroleum needs were met by the Soviet Union before the end of the Cold War and the Indian financial crisis in 1991, has been in petroleum talks with Iran and Venezuela, and has even proposed a natural gas pipeline across its arch-enemy Pakistan. To build its oil reserves and to guarantee oil access for the future, China's state-controlled oil companies spent more than $15 billion between 2000 and 2005 to buy stakes in one hundred foreign oil companies and exploration rights in foreign oil fields, devotedly courting South American, African, and Middle Eastern governments. And both India and China have talked with the United States about buying civilian nuclear power plant technology so that they can produce electricity with less pollution. Those discussions were inconceivable when China was America's Cold War enemy and, until recently, were unthinkable for India, after its 1998 test of nuclear devices in defiance of international proliferation controls.

Most troublesome for the rest of the world, both India and China have been making deals with pariah states—from Sudan to Iran to Myanmar—to secure supplies of oil and other resources they desperately need to ensure growth. As a result, the foreign policies of India and China are increasingly dictated by their energy needs. This drive has caused them to make up with historical enemies and, more alarmingly, to cozy up to nations led by despots or in otherwise unsavory states of affairs.

China has most frequently put its need to secure energy supplies ahead of other concerns. Consider Iran. China already buys much of its oil from Iran: 13 percent in 2003. But in 2004, China's state-owned Sinopec signed a $70 billion, thirty-year deal to buy liquefied natural gas from Iran and to develop an oil field there, bringing China's total deals for Iranian petroleum to nearly $100 billion. Two years later, Iran was in the midst of a nuclear standoff with the West, which accused Tehran of violating nuclear nonproliferation agreements. China, a permanent member of the UN Security Council, initially joined Russia to block the UN from considering imposing sanctions against Iran. Later, after much behind-the-scenes diplomacy, China agreed to join the West in imposing limited sanctions on Iran. Given Russia's and China's hesitation to support enforcement of sanctions,

China's thirst for oil could ultimately prove partly responsible for Iran's becoming a nuclear state.

China is already responsible for facilitating the genocide in Darfur, Sudan. Sixty percent of Sudan's oil is exported to China with the proceeds helping pay for Sudanese terror. Not only has China, with Russia, blocked any UN action to stop a genocide that has killed 300,000 Sudanese;[10] China has built arms factories in Sudan and sold the war-torn nation guns, rocket-propelled grenades, tanks, helicopters, and ammunition. "Chinese oil purchases have financed Sudan's pillage of Darfur, Chinese-made AK-47s have been the main weapons used to slaughter several hundred thousand people in Darfur so far, and China has protected Sudan in the U.N. Security Council," charged the *New York Times* columnist Nicholas D. Kristof.[11]

Chinese leaders have raced across Africa inking deals with Nigeria, Angola, even Equatorial Guinea. Indeed, Angola was China's largest oil supplier during the first half of 2006, followed by Saudi Arabia, Iran, and Russia. In November 2006, China hosted a summit that brought leaders from forty-eight African countries to Beijing, where they proclaimed "a new type of strategic partnership," signed $1.9 billion worth of trade deals, and were given $5 billion in Chinese aid. In February 2007, Chinese President Hu Jintao visited eight African nations, offering development aid and cementing ties.

China has also aggressively courted Latin American nations and is developing a sphere of influence halfway around the world. Often overlooked, trade between China and Latin America has grown from $200 million a year in 1975 to $400 billion annually in 2004, as China rushes to import natural resources and food. Anti-American Venezuela sells oil to China. Argentina sends 9 percent of its total exports to China. Chile, the world's largest copper producer, supplies a fifth of China's imports of the metal. Brazil sells China soybeans and coffee, and China has promised to invest $100 billion in Brazil over a decade. Indeed, a third of China's food imports come from Latin America, mostly soybeans. This shift has allowed the soybean trade to achieve historical symmetry. In the 1930s, a Brazilian friend of the last Chinese emperor, Pu Yi, asked for some soybeans, a staple of the Manchurian diet. The beans quickly made their way to the Brazilian ambassador in Tokyo, who put them in the next diplomatic pouch to Rio de Janeiro. Soybeans, then unknown to Brazil, have become Brazil's biggest export. Today China's tofu comes from the opposite side of the earth,[12] and so do much of the oil, copper, and other commodities for which the nation hungers.

India is also putting its energy needs first, but closer to home. Both India and China have stepped up ties to Myanmar (formerly Burma), the nation sandwiched between India to the west and China to the east. Myanmar has been a pariah state since the 1988 military crackdown on the nation's prodemocracy movement that led to Myanmar's long-term house arrest of opposition leader Aung San Suu Kyi, the dignified, stubborn, and very, very brave daughter of independent Burma's founding father. In 1989, Suu Kyi led a group of democracy activists touring Burmese villages when a line of soldiers, kneeling and pointing automatic rifles at her, ordered her to stop. She walked on, inspiring the U2 song "Walk On." The following year, Suu Kyi led her prodemocracy party to a landslide victory in Burmese elections, which the country's military government refused to honor. When Suu Kyi won the Nobel Peace Prize in 1991, she was under house arrest in the very country her father had helped win freedom from Britain. Her two teenaged boys accepted on her behalf, having been raised in Britain by their father since her arrest. She remained under guard in Burma, knowing that if she left her country she would not be allowed to return.

Beijing would surely have imprisoned her, too, if she had been pushing for democracy in China, but India used to be a vocal supporter of Suu Kyi, who lived in Delhi as a teenager, then returned to India as a scholar with her own family years later.[13] India's president, A. P. J. Abdul Kalam, leader of the world's largest democracy, visited Myanmar in March 2006, but he did not meet with the detained democracy leader, who with her patient, nonviolent protest was following in the footsteps of India's Gandhi. His visit came weeks after Beijing welcomed Myanmar's prime minister, Soe Win, to China, where Soe Win met with President Hu Jintao and Premier Wen Jiabao.

China has military ties to Burma, particularly with the Burmese navy, and both nations have cut deals to buy natural gas from Burma.[14]

Of course, India and China are hardly the first nations to put their economic interests ahead of diplomatic and human rights concerns. Americans eager to criticize the Asian nations can consider President George Bush's decision in 2006 to share civilian nuclear fuel and technology with India. Diplomats were shocked that he would abandon the long tradition forbidding nuclear powers from sharing nuclear technology with countries that refuse to sign the Nuclear Nonproliferation Treaty. Just eight years before, Washington had imposed sanctions on India for developing and testing nuclear weapons. Critics say President Bush's realpolitik regarding India made America inconsistent in demanding that North Korea and Iran stop producing nuclear fuel.[15] The ever powerful American business lobby was unlikely to protest President Bush's move, because the closer ties mean that American companies will likely end up selling India billions of dollars worth of nuclear technology, along with fighter jets and other equipment.

And in 1989, when the Chinese government ordered a crackdown on student democracy advocates, quashing protests in Tiananmen Square and across the country, China became the world's pariah state. But it didn't take Washington long to stop protesting the killing of innocents—innocent advocates of democracy, no less—so that American businesses could be among the first to sell to a billion Chinese in the early 1990s. After the horror of the Tiananmen Square massacre, the United States argued that engaging China in commerce would prompt China eventually to forgo authoritarianism for democracy just as it was moving from communism to capitalism—an assumption that has been proven wrong.

Viewed from abroad, America shows breathtaking inconsistencies: consuming far more oil than any other nation while complaining about China's and India's increasing consumption, pushing free trade while grumbling about job losses, and, of course, decrying human rights abuses in China even as it defies the United Nations by holding terror suspects without trial for years in its offshore prison in Guantanamo Bay. The United States complains about China's arms buildup, yet has by far the world's most powerful army, with greater military spending than almost all other nations *combined*. Moreover, while the United States wonders why China and India are building their militaries, it is the United States that has acted as the world's opportunistic military aggressor, particularly in Iraq, since the September 11 terrorist attacks, as if it were unconscious of the fact that its own actions frighten the rest of the world. Because it has acted as an irresponsible invader in Iraq, it has destabilized the Middle East and alienated traditional allies, like Europe and Korea.

With the self-inflicted injury to its moral authority, the United States is losing some of its diplomatic clout. This happens to come just as India and China are reemerging on the world stage, flexing economic and military muscles. The early twenty-first century may mark the time when America's reign as the world's lone superpower in the immediate post–Cold War era begins a slow slide that, a few decades from now, will result in a world with three strong powers: the United States, India, and China.

○

THAT WAS HARD TO IMAGINE just a generation ago, when India hadn't yet begun its economic reforms, and China was struggling to bring a nation of hungry peasants into modern times. In fact, when China began its reforms, Deng Xiaoping put the military last on the list for modernization. He stunned Chinese leaders—and the world—on June 4, 1985, when he addressed China's powerful Central Military Commission. He sat before the generals in his light gray Mao suit, held up his forefinger for emphasis, and dictated China's course: "We are determined to reduce the People's Liberation Army by one million men," Deng told his country's military leadership. "The party, government, army and people are all supposed to focus on domestic construction. On this issue, the army has its responsibility. No one is supposed to do anything that hinders development. Everyone should go all out for development."[16]

Indeed, when Deng insisted on the demilitarization, China's military was as obsolete as its economy. Its army was enormous—more than 4.2 million men,[17] compared with half a million in the powerful

U.S. forces—but consisted mostly of nearly illiterate peasants and obsolete equipment acquired decades before from its former ally, the USSR. In 1985, China couldn't build modern tanks; its factories couldn't even build a modern car. Deng's disarmament and reduction in military spending left the nation with more money to spend modernizing the rest of its economy and raising living standards.

Just two decades later, the picture could hardly be more different. China has soothed the rest of the world by saying it is concentrating on what it calls its *heping jueqi*, or "peaceful rise," bringing its factories into the modern era. But in reality, since the late 1990s, China has spent billions building up its military during peacetime. China would not have had the know-how to build modern military equipment before foreign auto and electronics factories dotted the Chinese landscape. Now China has the manufacturing know-how to build much of its own gear. Because its economy is so strong, it can also now afford to buy modern weapons and equipment. Between 2000 and 2003, China increased its weapons procurement budget by more than 18 percent annually, much of which was spent buying new Russian equipment. Military experts around the world see China laying the groundwork for a shift in military power. Chinese military equipment today is not as advanced as the latest equipment the United States military is buying, but is "comparable in capability to the systems we fielded in the 1970s and 1980s that still make up the bulk of our forces," according to a recent assessment by Roger Cliff of the RAND Corporation.[18] By 2025, China should have defense resources comparable to those in use today by the U.S. military. Thus the United States must upgrade its military capabilities if it wants to stay ahead of China's.

At stake most immediately is American dominance of East Asia, and eventually American military hegemony worldwide. Western as well as Japanese and Australian military experts are concerned about China's fast-growing military power, the resulting regional security shifts already happening, and the implications a generation from now, when the world will likely have several very strong powers instead of a lone superpower. Today the American military remains by far the world's most powerful. It comprises half a million soldiers and another half a million reservists, and its annual budget of nearly $500 billion is nearly as large as the rest of the world's military budgets combined. But China has the world's largest standing army—2.3 million soldiers in 2006—and spends an estimated $45 billion–$70 billion annually on its military.[19]

"Of the major and emerging powers, China has the greatest potential to compete militarily with the United States," the United States declared in its latest Quadrennial Defense Review Report.[20] China, for its part, counters that while it has increased its military spending, the United States spends far more, no matter how you count it. "In 2005, military spending as a share of GDP was 1.3 percent in China and 3.6 percent in the U.S.," said Xie Xiaoyan, deputy commissioner of China's Ministry of Foreign Affairs in Hong Kong. "Military spending as a percentage of total budget spending was 7.4 percent in China and 17.8 percent in the U.S.," he said. China has increased its military spending because "China has the world's largest military, so it has focused on raising salaries and improving living conditions for those in the armed forces. The increase is there, but it is not as big as some of the other big powers."[21]

Why has China changed tack from sizing down to building up its military? The U.S. Navy controls the world's oceans just as the British navy once controlled the world's seas, back when nations denominated their trade in pounds sterling instead of dollars. China's economy is underpinned by exports of Chinese factory-made goods and imports of oil and other natural resources, most of which are carried into and out of China on ships sailing seas controlled by America's navy. This fact provides both an incentive for China to maintain peace with the United States and a motivation for China to develop the weapons and ships needed to prevent the United States from shutting down the Chinese economy with a blockade, which it could do if so inclined.[22] This is true for other Asian nations, but only Japan is powerful enough to put up meaningful military resistance today, and Japan is a longtime American ally. Oil imports would be particularly easy for the United States to stop: almost all oil from the Middle East to Asia sails through the Strait of Malacca, which the United States controls. If it and China ever went to war, America could almost immediately block 40 percent of China's oil supplies, the portion imported by sea. Because of the vulnerability of its oil tankers, China has been keen to cut deals to build petroleum pipelines to bring oil and natural gas overland. China has already reached pipeline deals with Burma, Russia, and Kazakhstan. It is also one reason China is building nuclear power plants at a rapid clip.

Both China and the United States recognize that any future war between them might well be fought on the waves, and China is upgrading its fleet of submarines and is working to develop a ballistic missile that would be able to hit a moving ship. If China succeeds with the missile, it "would provide China with a unique and unprecedented military capacity," according to Mr. Cliff of RAND.[23]

Despite its increased military spending and its attempts to develop sophisticated missiles, China still stresses its "peaceful rise." During the 2004 tsunami disaster, the United States used one of its aircraft carriers stationed in Asia to quickly deliver supplies to Indonesian victims. Two years later, participants in an academic discussion among military experts in Hong Kong were surprised when a Chinese military expert brought the matter up. He argued that China needs an aircraft carrier, which costs $4 billion to build and $2 billion a year to operate,[24] so that it, too, can offer humanitarian aid during disasters in the region.

Eyebrows rose all around.

Despite the humanitarian pretense, it seemed more likely to American, Japanese, and Australian participants that China might—legitimately—rather have an expensive aircraft carrier of its own to protect the vast tide of exported Chinese factory goods carried across the open sea on container ships. Or China might want an aircraft carrier to help it protect the oil imports flowing through the Strait of Malacca. When academic participants asked about China's need for an expensive aircraft carrier, the Chinese military man conceded that China wanted to be a "sea transportation" power, but insisted there was no need for China to be a "naval power." Perhaps that sounds more palatable for a country in the midst of a "peaceful rise."[25]

What is really underway is a geopolitical shift from the post–Cold

War era of American hegemony to what will be the next epoch: permafrost peacetime.

A quiet arms race between the United States and China has already begun during this permafrost peacetime era. It is less overt than that between the United States and the USSR during the Cold War. The United States is racing to maintain its sizable lead, looking over its shoulder because it sees China as a potential future military threat. "The United States' goal is for China to continue as an economic partner and emerge as a responsible stakeholder and force for good in the world," according to the 2006 U.S. Quadrennial Defense Review Report. It "will attempt to dissuade any military competitor from developing disruptive or other capabilities that could enable regional hegemony or hostile action against the United States or other friendly countries, and it will seek to deter aggression or coercion. Should deterrence fail, the United States would deny a hostile power its strategic and operational objectives," the report concluded.

The newest front in this permafrost peace is no less than a new weapons frontier: space. The United States economy relies heavily on satellites for communications and all kinds of other commercial purposes. And the high-technology U.S. military is particularly dependent on space—for navigation, for espionage, for detection of incoming conventional or nuclear attacks, for weapons guidance systems and even for directing troops on the ground. But in January 2007, China shot down a past-its-prime Chinese weather satellite orbiting 530 miles above the earth, and with that it shot down the notion that the United States would be allowed, uncontested, to continue to dominate space the way it now commands the seas. With the ability to shoot moving satellites and ships, China could rather inexpensively constrain American dominance of both space and sea.[26]

The United States is determined to contain China, and China is resisting now that it has the capability to rearm. During this century, we'll see a complex dance of containment and countercontainment. The United States and China are not enemies, but it is hard to imagine they will be allies when both nations see their strategic interests to be in conflict.

Deng Xiaoping, the man who did more than any other to put China on the path to modernization, predicted it would take China half a century to modernize. That milestone will come in 2028, not so far in the future. Chinese leaders, as usual, are wary of the Soviet Union's example of engaging in an expensive arms race then collapsing under the weight of heavy defense spending. Even military leaders say China cannot support a strong military without first rebuilding its economy.[27] So far, China's economy has blossomed faster than anyone predicted. Indeed, advisers to China's current president, Hu Jintao, argue that today China needs the United States economically more than America needs China. Beijing needs American exports of technology and needs American consumers to keep buying Chinese-made goods. But the two nations should reach economic parity around 2015, less than a decade from now, and then the United States will need China economically as much as China needs the United States. At that point, China will have much more economic and military clout than it has today.[28] That will mark a decisive shift in the global balance of power.

○

DENG ALWAYS ADVISED that as China reformed its economy, it should keep a low profile diplomatically. In the mid-1990s, as the economy thrived, this began to change. Chinese leaders sought a bigger role in foreign policy by exercising soft power. China wooed the United States, even stripping anti-American books from bookstores in Beijing ahead of President Clinton's visit in 1998. Later, it concluded generous trade deals with its neighborhood nations, themselves unnerved by China's growing economic power. China is currently wooing Africa. Militarily, China's countercontainment efforts center on the Shanghai Cooperation Organization, a quasi-military alliance that gathers China, Russia, and some neighborhood "stans"—Kazakhstan, Kyrgyzstan, Tajikistan, and Uzbekistan—plus the observer countries of India, Iran, Mongolia, and Pakistan, moves detailed in the Sinologist Willy Wo-Lap Lam's book *Chinese Politics in the Hu Jintao Era*.

Much as America used financial clout to extend its influence with dollar diplomacy, China has been practicing currency diplomacy too—call it renminbi relations. China has dispensed foreign aid across Asia and Africa in an attempt to win political allies. "What you are seeing is a new game in Asia," says Manu Bhaskaran, adjunct senior research fellow at the Institute of Policy Studies in Singapore. China has changed its global game as well. As China cuts petroleum deals in Africa, Latin America, and the Mideast, it often agrees to take charge of building roads, bridges, and other infrastructure—a Chinese specialty.

But China's more hard-edged moves came after September 11, 2001. The handful of terrorists who launched an attack on the mighty United States that cost just a few hundred thousand dollars triggered unapologetic aggression on the part of the United States and geopolitical repercussions heard around the world. North Korea tested a nuclear weapon, and Iran worked on nuclear technology, perhaps in pursuit of the same, according to the West. Russia, with China, flexed its diplomatic muscles to counter what it viewed as American bullying of the UN Security Council, particularly regarding Iran. Anti-American Venezuela reacted with fiery rhetoric and even longtime ally France launched vigorous objections to American actions. Soon the United States, stretched thin diplomatically and militarily, pushed China to negotiate nuclear policy with North Korea. China called for trade-offs: in exchange for its efforts to dissuade North Korea from developing nuclear weapons, the United States should lean on Taiwan to quell a pro-independence movement there. When American wanted support for its global war on terrorism, China pressured it to look the other way as China pursued repressive policies in majority Muslim Xinjiang Province and in Tibet.[29] And the United States leaned on both China and India not to allow Iran to develop nuclear technology unchecked by the UN.

○

INDIA, FOR ITS PART, is caught in between the United States and China and resolving, as usual, to maintain its independence. Both the United States and China have tried to draw India into their sphere, given that it is likely to emerge as a third great power within decades of China. The United States is courting India, hoping it will serve as a pro-American counterweight to China's growing power. The realpolitick of military strategy is one reason—in addition to furthering American business interests—that President Bush offered to share nuclear technology and fuel with India. The United States would like to make India its global swing vote in military power, part of its ongoing effort to contain China.

While India was happy to accept a nuclear upgrade from America, it prizes its independence and has been reluctant to get involved in the complicated relationship between the United States and China. India is instead preserving its ties with China by cooperating on a number of fronts. They have jointly bid for overseas oil fields, agreed to partner on petroleum research and development, and even held their first-ever joint military exercises in December 2007.

Like China, India is a nuclear-armed regional military power that wants to be recognized as a global power. With 1.3 million soldiers and the eleventh-largest military budget in the world, at $17 billion and growing, it is buying helicopters, fighter jets, missiles, and submarine parts to replace its aging, Soviet-era stocks. Like China, India has an army larger than that of the United States and is now able to build or buy near state-of-the-art equipment.[30] India is building Asia's biggest aircraft carrier and ordered 126 sophisticated combat planes for its air force. Its economy lags China's, but it is strong in military technology.

At the same time, India seems less of a worry for the West because it wasn't an enemy during the Cold War, and because the West has few quarrels today with India. Yet India's ongoing tensions with Pakistan, the nuclear-armed neighbor it routinely quarrels with over the fence, means that India's military expansion cannot be ignored.

○

WHILE RELATIVE PEACE in recent decades in Asia has helped the entire region concentrate on economic development, the prospect of terrorism, as well as a number of potential volatile flash points, could threaten the *butter-not-guns* era. Any that go the wrong way could slow economic growth and thus India's or China's return to global prominence.

India's biggest potential military problem is Pakistan, the majority-Muslim territory cleaved from India and created by the British when India won its independence in 1947. India and Pakistan have fought three wars since then—two over the disputed region of Kashmir—and both are now nuclear armed. Renewed Hindu-Muslim violence and terrorist episodes like the Bombay train bombings that killed two hundred people in July 2006 could thrust India and Pakistan into renewed conflict with grave consequences for both sides.

Trouble in Nepal could provoke tensions between India and China. Nepal's politics are unstable. Yet India feels it cannot let Nepal become a failed state, because the nation, albeit famed for its peaceful temples and soaring mountains, also serves as a base for violent groups that could attack India. Military experts say China would likely react if India interfered in Nepal. Neither China nor India wants to be pushed into conflict, but they could end up butting heads.

Two important American allies face periodic threats from China, which could draw the United States into military conflict with China. Many Chinese hate Japanese, who are vilified in Chinese textbooks and on Internet discussion boards for their horrific treatment of the Chinese during the Japanese occupation of China. Junichiro Koizumi, the former Japanese prime minister, repeatedly antagonized China with his defiant visits to the Yasukuni shrine, which honors Japan's war dead, including war criminals who participated in atrocities during the occupation. Japan, wary of China's growing power, is rethinking its defense strategy and cozying up to the United States, its powerful military ally.

By far the most likely military skirmish—even war—involving China would be prompted by disputes with Taiwan. China keeps six hundred missiles pointed at the island, and Chinese generals estimated in late 2004 that China could take out Taiwan's military installations within a few days.[31] Such a war could halt the massive trade between China and the West and even, in an extreme scenario, lead to World War III by drawing the United States and Japan into war against China.

Few Westerners are aware of the depth of Chinese people's feelings toward Taiwan. Americans, in particular, assume that mainland Chinese might long for Taiwan's democracy and support the island's independence. Not so. There is remarkable unanimity among Chinese—from government officials to peasants to well-educated Chinese yuppies—that Taiwan is a renegade province that is rightfully part of mainland China. If Taiwan declared its independence, support for the use of military force against the island would be widespread among the mainland Chinese public. The stakes are high: America and Japan have pledged to defend the island militarily if China attacks Taiwan unprovoked. However, the United States, mainland China, and Taiwanese business leaders and moderate political leaders are eager to preserve the status quo as long as possible. American diplomats give Taiwanese politicians stern lectures behind closed doors that raise questions about whether the United States would back its longtime ally militarily—as it has pledged to do—if Taiwan provokes a Chinese attack by declaring independence. Japan is wary of any Chinese aggression in the region, given the animosity Chinese feel toward Japan. Either a confrontational move by Taiwanese leaders or an eruption of nationalism on the Chinese mainland could quickly escalate into a war that draws in Japan and the United States. If an unprovoked China attempts to take Taiwan by force, China risks becoming a villain to the world, with grave political and economic repercussions. For now, China has a more unmistakable problem.

○

NOTHING CAN PREPARE VISITORS for the pollution in China. In various cities, if you are indoors and open a window, a strong, foul odor confronts you immediately. It isn't that there is a bad smell in the outside air; it is that the air *is* the bad smell. The water in many rivers stinks of sewage, and lakes are blackened by waste from chemicals pouring out of nearby factories.

One of the worst places to breathe on the planet is the world's biggest city: Chongqing, China, with a population of 30 million people counting the exurbs, about the same number of people as live in the entire state of California. There the New China coexists with the Old China: skyscrapers and construction sites decorate downtown, but scrawny bong-bong men wait for work on streetcorners. Bong-bong men are paid sixty cents an hour to ferry heavy loads—from building materials to groceries—up and down the city's hilly streets using bamboo poles slung over their shoulders. They must have powerful lungs, not just strong legs: the city is half dark most days. Sunlight barely reaches the ground, dimmed by thick, gray smog. Skyscrapers just three blocks away are mere outlines because of air pollution. Emerging from the inside of a building onto the streets prompts one's eyes to water. The air is filthy, but that is not all. The raw sewage produced by 30 million people—30 *million*—is dumped straight into the Yangtze River as it flows past. The countryside nearby is not the place to go for fresh air: there you notice that the leaves of trees—along with everything else—are coated with black dust from the coal mines and factories in the region. More acid rain falls on Chongqing than anywhere else on earth.

Sadly, Chongqing is not an isolated example. About two hundred Chinese cities fail to meet World Health Organization standards for airborne particulates that cause respiratory diseases. All but three of the world's twenty most-polluted cities are in India or China, according to pollution data collected by the World Bank. Chongqing's apocalyptic conditions rank fifth.[32]

Both India and China rely on coal for much of their energy needs, from fuel for home-cooking fires to electricity grids. Unfortunately, coal burns with particularly high pollution levels. Half of India's energy comes from coal, as does two-thirds of China's,[33] because both nations have large deposits of coal. The creation of millions of jobs in India and China has had a dangerous side effect: Each new factory, office building, or apartment requires more electricity. The result is choking air pollution in both countries on a scale not witnessed since Britain's Industrial Revolution.

In Beijing (number 13 on the pollution list), authorities are already worried about how Olympic athletes will be able to compete at top form in 2008 while breathing the city's filthy air, and have vowed to improve it. Some of the capital's worst pollution is caused by dramatic sandstorms that blow in from the nearby Gobi Desert and regularly turn the city yellow, forcing bicyclists and pedestrians to tie scarves over their mouths and noses to keep from inhaling the blowing dust. Beijing keeps track: it counts "blue sky days," or days in which the air quality measures "good" or "moderate." During a particularly bad stretch in early 2006, Beijing had just nine blue-sky days in a month.[34] On the average, Beijing has air pollution levels up to four times higher than U.S. safety levels would allow.[35]

The World Bank estimates that pollution and pollution-related health problems cost China $54 billion annually and already shorten the lives of 178,000 people a year.[36] It predicts those numbers will grow: between 2001 and 2020, premature deaths will more than double, to 590,000 a year dying early because of the air pollution in their cities. In China, breathing is hazardous to health—not that there is much alternative.

Delhi and Calcutta are more polluted than any Chinese cities, according to the World Bank. Indeed, most of India's big cities are eight to ten times more polluted than the worst-polluted American cities. The environmental price of increased development has been high for India: the nation's carbon emissions jumped 103 percent between 1990 and 2005 (only China's increase of 137 percent was higher). India's energy consumption has skyrocketed—up 301 percent between 1980 and 2005, even faster than China's 283 percent growth—and that triggered higher pollution levels.[37] The nation's greenhouse gas emissions are expected to jump 70 percent by 2025.[38] Each year between 2001 and 2020, some 460,000 Indians will die early because of the air pollution in its cities, according to World Bank predictions. Many Indians will die because of severe indoor air pollution, largely coming from home cooking fires that lack proper ventilation. Indoor pollution causes 4–6 percent of sickness in India, according to the World Health Organization, particularly deadly respiratory illnesses in children and pulmonary diseases and lung cancer in adults.

As if the air weren't dirty enough, China also has problems with water: there isn't enough of it, and most of it is undrinkable. Nearly a third of China's rivers are so polluted that they aren't even fit for agricultural or industrial use, according to Chinese government statistics. Village doctors have documented increased cancer rates near polluting factories and chemical plants.[39] Untreated waste water dumped into China's famed Yangtze River is killing marine life and turning its water "cancerous," according to Xinhua, the state-controlled media outlet.[40]

"If you have to give a one-word answer to what will shape China's future, it is water," said Kenneth Lieberthal, the former U.S. National Security Council aide and China expert from the University of Michigan.[41] Part of the strain comes from the nation's huge population: China has 8 percent of the world's fresh water, but 22 percent of the world's people. China faces such dramatic water shortages in certain regions that economic development and growth may soon be held back. As cities and factories suck up more and more of the nation's scarce water, entire regions dry up and farmland is lost to erosion and desertification. Water shortages cut the nation's grain output by 8 percent in 2004, according to the National Bureau of Statistics.[42]

The problem of pollution looms so large that it will be easier for China to get the oil it needs than the water it needs. Chinese leaders are already planning how they will go about rationing water in the future, planning huge engineering projects intended to move water from the rainier South to the drier North, and from western China to the nation's thirsty cities in the East. Already, deserts are expanding, farmland is drying up, and cancer rates are soaring near lakes and rivers filled with water poisoned by industrial pollution. Some Chinese cities, like Tianjin, now survive with just a third of the water used per person globally.

Beijing is belatedly alarmed, and in 2006 named access to clean water a national priority, in part because more and more public demonstrations reportedly revolve around anger at pollution. Since the mid-1990s, China has closed 80,000 highly polluting small enterprises, many of which were inefficient factories. China passed a landmark renewable energy law that took effect in January 2006 and encouraged the use of wind power, biofuels, and other low-pollution energy sources. "We are resolved to change the practice of polluting first and cleaning up later," said Xie Zhenhua, director of China's State Environmental Protection Administration.

○

WHILE THE CHANGES SHOULD HELP, it is remarkable to consider how different the situation could have been—for China and for the world—in a country whose government strictly planned development in what amounted to essentially a clean slate for modern industry, homes, and cars. China has leapfrogged ahead of other nations in adopting certain technologies—in developing cell phone networks, for instance. It is a pity that China was not wiser than the United States, Europe, Japan, and other nations that also failed to make the environment a priority during their industrial development. Had the Chinese government insisted that all new factories be built using cutting-edge environmental practices—solar panels providing some of their electricity needs, for instance—most of the massive amounts of foreign investment would still have come to China. Foreign companies would still have salivated over the billion-plus Chinese consumer market, and would still have built skyscrapers in Shanghai and Beijing and Guangzhou, but they would have been visible from miles away, not just from a few blocks' distance on a bad-air day.

Similarly, before the Chinese car market took off, China could have mandated that all its cars and trucks run on cleaner fuels like ethanol, or that all the cars have hybrid-electric engines. That might have slightly slowed down the sales of the world's automakers in China by increasing costs, but would have kept China's air cleaner and could have created worldwide economies of scale in green car technology that would have driven down the otherwise higher price of hybrid cars in China as well as the United States, Europe, and the rest of the world. India still has a relatively clean slate to work with, and if India, unlike China, made taking care of the environment a priority now, it could reshape its future. Perhaps that is utopian: rampant corruption in both nations currently leaves existing environmental rules unenforced.

China already has environmental regulations on its books. But it is less zealous about protecting its air and water than about protecting economic growth. The same government that obsessively monitors the Internet, that imprisons human rights activists and their lawyers on vague pretexts, that detects and terminates pregnancies that violate China's one-child policy, routinely ignores flagrant, deadly violations of its laws on pollution. China's environmental control agency acknowledges that half the nation's coal-fired power plants violate its regulations. Even as it goes on tightening environmental rules, China has not stopped those who openly flaunt current rules—many of whom are corrupt local government officials.

Lack of enforcement of environmental laws is also a big problem in India. Its capital city, Delhi, used to have pollution levels ten times higher than the nation's legal limit, mostly because of the high-pollution taxis, trucks, and buses on its roads. Delhi had the world's worst air pollution in 2002,[43] but managed to clean up its filthy air after being taken to task by India's Supreme Court. The overhaul began in 1997. Some steps were long overdue: the city finally banned leaded gas. However belatedly, the city reduced pollution from Delhi's power plants by installing scrubbers to clean up smokestack emissions and requiring them to burn cleaner coal. It banished motorized rickshaws and buses built before 1990 from the roads. In 1998, the court required all city buses to run on compressed natural gas—a cleaner fuel than gasoline—by 2001. Less than 2 percent of buses met the court's requirement on time, but a gradual phase-out worked. Like seemingly everything in India, progress was one step forward, two steps back. After a meandering path toward progress, Delhi's air improved.

The Indian government is still concerned. It is pushing solar power as an inexpensive solution for the countryside, much of which still lacks electricity. It is tripling hydropower capacity by building large-scale hydroelectric plants. Auto emissions rules have now been tightened, and motorcycles have been required to convert to cleaner-burning engines. India's water, like China's, is filthy. Just 10 percent of sewage is treated in India, with the rest dumped into waterways, along with industrial pollution. India's rivers—even the holy Ganges—have become sewers.

Both India and China will be making big investments in pollution control, an opportunity for Western companies with sophisticated technology. Both are setting up windmills in an effort to vastly expand wind-driven power. India already has the fourth-largest wind power market, with 4.4 gigawatts of capacity, and China set a goal of creating 30 gigawatts of renewable energy capacity by 2020, up from the present 1.3 gigawatts.[44]

Nuclear power is next. India has struck a deal with the United States to cooperate on civilian nuclear power. China is racing to build 30 nuclear power stations by 2020 to boost its power supply without worsening its existing pollution catastrophe.[45] While it is crucial that China generate more power as cleanly as possible, its regulatory record is terrifying when extrapolated to nuclear energy. Local officials have a pattern of overlooking environmental rules in exchange for enough renminbi at coal-fired electricity plants. If they prove willing to continue that habit at nuclear plants, China—and the world—would risk disasters like the one that the former Soviet Union faced at Chernobyl in 1986.

In an attempt to take advantage of the large deposits of coal, both nations are experimenting with a technology pioneered in South Africa that, rather expensively, converts coal into a liquid that is then turned into oil. China is building one such plant in Inner Mongolia and is planning to build twenty-seven more.[46] General Electric has already set its sights on India and China, hoping to sell the developing nations windmills as well as water treatment plants and other environmental cleanup infrastructure. The Chinese government has laid out its priorities, and, as usual, there is money to be made for state-of-the-art Western products.

Cleaner air in Asia can't come soon enough. The dirty air is a problem not just for India and China but also for the world. "The pollution produced in China doesn't stay in China," says Mr. Lieberthal.[47] American scientists have found dust and soot from coal burned in China, as well as mercury, at monitoring stations halfway across the world. Chinese pollution has been detected in Oregon and Washington State and in northern California, near Lake Tahoe, Nevada. The U.S. Environmental Protection Agency estimated that a quarter of Los Angeles' particulate pollution blows over from China when the wind conditions are just wrong.[48]

Not only does pollution flow across borders; greenhouse gas pollution causes global warming. "With coal as the main source of energy and the rapid growth of motorized vehicles, both China and India are likely to grow into polluting giants unless effective environmental regulation is put in place," concluded a 2006 paper prepared by academics from the London School of Economics. China accounted for 14 percent of the world's carbon emissions and India for 5 percent, placing both in the top six countries for emissions even though the per capita pollution levels were low.[49] As the two nations' energy needs approach the per capita levels in the developed world, emissions will likely rise dramatically. Asia will be the largest single source of greenhouse gases by 2015, according to the Asian Development Bank. China's vice minister of the State Environmental Protection Administration said China's growing population and economy would at least quadruple pollution levels by 2020 unless changes are made.[50]

○

CHINA WILL FACE far more than environmental challenges in the future. Also around 2015, Chinese demographics turn less favorable, with fewer working-age Chinese to support retirees. If China cannot bring rural incomes up closer to those of its thriving cities, powerful social tensions could erupt. After years of soapbox campaigns, Beijing seems no closer to reining in China's rampant corruption, a major source of potential political unrest. The Soviet Union had its powerful oligarchs influencing government policy, and China has indeed avoided that. What China has instead are multigarchs—an incalculable number of corrupt local officials and former officials frequently engaging in the same kind of resource and land grabs as the oligarchs, albeit on a much smaller, more localized scale. The pollution and demographic and social issues may soon reach problem levels for China all at once. "There's a lot of indicators that they can sustain growth until 2015," said Mr. Lieberthal. "After ten years, these other problems come back to bite in such a way that if they don't make some very, very good decisions leading up to that, they'll be in big trouble."[51]

○

THE CHALLENGE FOR ALL NATIONS is to negotiate the new terrain of a globe that again contains a powerful India and China. "There will be a big security shift centering on oil and natural resources, especially as the United States makes itself unpopular," said Mr. Bhaskaran of Singapore's Institute of Policy Studies. The political lurch at the end of the Cold War was benign for the United States because its longtime political adversaries, the USSR and China, emerged with weak economies and concentrated on moving to capitalism. During intervening decades, China and India have begun moving back toward their historically larger role in the global economy, and the USSR broke apart. Meanwhile, the era of America as the world's unchallenged, hegemonic power could be truncated if the United States, through its own acts, further alienates much of the world or prompts further militarization from its enemies large and small.[52] No other hegemon is standing in the wings ready to replace it. Instead, the world is slowly shifting from an era of clear American dominance and leadership to one in which less powerful nations and even global religious ideologies are jockeying for a piece of power. In mere decades, we may have a tripolar world, with the United States, India, and China sharing superpower status. Before our eyes, post–Cold War political alliances are shifting once again. At stake is nothing less than peace and prosperity for the world.

The permafrost peace could end badly. The last two political and economic powers to emerge on the global scene were Germany and Japan. Catastrophic wars followed. Now the nations of the world face the rise of India and China, with more than ten times as many residents as Germany and Japan.

For now, as the Indian and Chinese economies grow and take hold of a larger slice of the global economic pie, both are growing more connected to the rest of the world, not more estranged from it. Disagreements between nations are no longer disputes about economic models—communism versus capitalism. Capitalism decisively won the Cold War debate, and that has helped hundreds of millions of Indians and Chinese prosper by ushering in the globalization era that has created so many jobs and bettered so many lives in developing countries. So far, the increased trade has drawn nations closer together, even to the point of answering each other's emails and phone calls. The whole world has a stake in keeping vibrant worldwide trade going, rather than giving in to the temptation to try to protect jobs at home instead of letting them flow freely around the world. The geopolitical shifts are enormous, but the economic developments may force even bigger adjustments—not only for India and China but also for the West.

CHAPTER NINE

A CATALYST FOR COMPETITIVENESS

Robert Rubin, the former U.S. treasury secretary, is sitting in his stately office overlooking Park Avenue, thinking about what the rise of India and China means to America. He spends a long time pondering, flicking a multicolored yo-yo up and down, up and down. His brow is furrowed, his lanky frame draped over a chair, the yo-yo spinning on its string, and finally he answers, "This is going to be enormous. People feel uneasy about the future, and they should."[1]

He's not the only one worried. From the opposite side of the country and the other end of the political spectrum, John Chen, a Republican, thinks about the same question a lot. Mr. Chen is on the front lines of the world's economic transformation because he is one of the "Benedict Arnold CEOs" Senator Kerry blasted during the last presidential campaign. During the past few years, Mr. Chen has hired hundreds of workers in India and China for his California software company, Sybase, but he says that doing so has pained him. Mr. Chen says that he has to hire overseas because the other American companies in his industry are doing the same and that he can't compete with them without lowering his payroll costs the way they are lowering theirs.

Mr. Chen is a proud American immigrant whose parents fled Shanghai for Hong Kong when the Communist Party came to power in China, and he is frustrated by the job migration. When he was a child, his family lived for several years in a single bedroom they rented in a larger apartment whose other tenants were strangers. In place of a dinner table, his mother covered some suitcases in cloth. Mr. Chen's father had graduated from college in Shanghai, but in Hong Kong he worked overtime at odd jobs in factories and shipping warehouses in order to feed his family and finally to allow them to move to a neighborhood with better schools. Mr. Chen's sweet tooth drove him to spend Saturdays learning Latin at his church—he became an altar boy because the priests handed out Life Savers and that was the only candy he got as a kid. Mr. Chen worked hard in school and dreamed of attending an Ivy League college in the United States, a dream he realized by attending Brown University. He eventually worked his way up through a series of jobs at technology companies until he became chief executive of Sybase in 1998, at just forty-three years old. As he expands Sybase's workforce in China and India, it troubles him to admit that he—an embodiment of the American Dream—may not be hiring more Americans anytime soon. He has hired about four hundred employees so far in the country his parents ran away from and is ramping up the workforce faster than planned in India, where he has hired nearly two hundred. "This is a shame," Mr. Chen said. "They were high-paying jobs in the United States."[2]

Both Mr. Rubin and Mr. Chen know that conventional economic theory holds that all nations benefit when global trade increases. While Mr. Rubin thinks this is still true, he says that predicting the full effects on incomes, economic security, and economic growth has become a lot more complicated as India and China quickly inject more than a billion new workers into the global economy. "These are tectonic shifts, and I don't think we fully understand them," says Mr. Rubin, the man renowned for talking a Democratic president into making unpopular choices that balanced the federal budget and cut the trade deficit, then for steering the American economy through the golden age of the booming 1990s. "Economists say that the result will be that their GDP goes up and ours goes up more slowly," notes Mr. Rubin, his yo-yo continuing its rhythmic movement. "I say that should be right, but the situation is complicated."

Mr. Chen, the immigrant turned American corporate executive, says Westerners got "a free pass" when India and China walled themselves off from the world in the twentieth century. During that time, "we got a false sense of security" about Western nations' and workers' competitiveness, Mr. Chen adds. No more. Suddenly, Americans must compete for their jobs with much of the rest of the world and are learning the hard way that they have no automatic right to earn ten times more than everyone else on the planet for the same work. With both China and India now open for business with the West, more than a billion workers earning dramatically less than Westerners have suddenly been added to the world's labor pool, including those 6.8 million college graduates a year. India and China are rising so breathtakingly fast that they inspire fear—fear of the unknown. And as they alter their destinies, India and China are changing fortunes in the West, too.

The United States cannot afford complacency. "Americans have to get more competitive," says Mr. Chen. "We know how to do this; we just need to get it done." Mr. Rubin agrees that the United States must urgently prepare for the increased competition from the East. "It is the greatest challenge since the emergence of the United States over a hundred years ago," he says.

Mr. Rubin and Mr. Chen are hardly alarmists, but they see the United States sailing blithely into the big waves of new competition almost entirely unprepared. Everyday families, as well as the U.S. government, have been spending well beyond their means. Just when the United States should be beefing up its educational system, voters have tolerated—and federal, state, and local governments have allowed—the failure of many public school systems to educate students even at a basic level year after year after year. Companies have become more and more focused on the next quarter's results instead of long-term strategy during the very time that the reemergence of India and China is roiling the global business landscape. Like the federal government, companies have cut back on basic-research spending at a moment when innovation may be the only means for staying ahead. Europe and Japan face many of the same challenges as the United States, but have so far proved even more resistant to change. Western Europe has tried to safeguard jobs, but the unintended result has been slow-moving economies and rising unemployment rates.

Stephen Roach, chief economist of Morgan Stanley, works in New York but has spent much of his time during the past few years traveling in India or China because the changes there are triggering such tectonic economic shifts worldwide. The man from Wall Street has learned to pack granola bars and Cup-a-Soup envelopes to fend off food poisoning in five-star hotels, but he still marvels at the readily available, cheap talent his own company and many others are able to connect with in Asia. His travels have shown him there is just one way forward for the United States. "We've got to reinvent ourselves again," Mr. Roach says. "The middle-aged, highly skilled white-collar workers are realizing, 'My job is gone and I'm not going to get it back.'" The rise of India and China is transforming the global economy, and neither America nor Americans are ready for the changes at hand.

○

ARE INDIANS AND CHINESE FRIENDS OR FOES? Is the rise of India and China good or bad for the West? For workers and consumers, there are paradoxes, contradictions, and even myths about who is causing the turmoil and what could alleviate the new competition. The broad changes underway in the U.S. and global economy have unexpected roots and invisible interconnections, and as Mr. Rubin points out, the effects of today's tectonic economic shifts are dramatic, but very complicated. Some individual Americans are feeling the squeeze from India and China, but collectively, Americans are benefiting.

The reemergence of these Asian giants and the vast increase in global trade that has ensued mean that ever-lower prices are offsetting what could otherwise feel like a falling standard of living for middle-class Americans. Consumers are the big winners. Call it the Wal-Mart paradox. By buying from factories in China, India, and other low-wage countries, Wal-Mart has brought Americans almost irresistibly low prices—sometimes for goods no one knew were needed. It is hard to walk out of a Wal-Mart without an overflowing shopping cart, in part because so many cheap goods have been put under a single roof. Wal-Mart and stores like it have allowed Americans to keep their closets—sometimes even their garages—overflowing, encouraging Americans to spend and spend on mostly foreign-made goods.

For those with stable jobs, the widespread availability of ever-shrinking prices lessens the pain of paychecks that have stagnated. Wal-Mart has become such a big player nationwide that it has helped set a "China price" for goods supplied to its stores (and their competitors), and that pressure has helped push companies to close factories in the United States and buy from low-wage factories overseas. The paradox is that Wal-Mart's success, and its eager shoppers, has led to job losses in the United States, even as it has eased the pain of adjustment for American factory workers who lose their jobs.

Just as a flood of cheap factory goods appeared at Wal-Marts, Woolworth's, and Japan's 100-Yen stores after factories moved en masse to China, costs are already dropping for some service-related work, and are likely to drop further in the future as more and more white-collar work is moved overseas. Potential for savings abounds even as middle-class jobs are threatened. For instance, Americans still employed with health benefits may see medical cost increases slow as the vast processing of health insurance claims is moved offshore. Nearly a third of America's ballooning health care spending is tied up in paperwork-processing costs, and potential savings from streamlining that process are in the hundreds of billions of dollars.[3]

Whatever the benefits to society as a whole, Americans who lose their jobs are the ones feeling the pain, and they want someone to blame for globalization's rough-elbowed economics. There are many culprits, including new technology and globalization itself. Americans could even glance in the mirror to discover one of the perpetrators.

For instance, some Americans demonize corporations for their endless cost cuts, which boost profits but often spell layoffs in the United States and hiring abroad. Not all benefits go to consumers in the form of lower prices, of course. Some are spent on $6,000 shower curtains in the subsidized homes of greedy chief executives.[4] But many of the benefits go directly to companies' bottom lines, and those profits can trigger higher stock prices. Some profits are passed on to investors in the form of higher dividends. Why are companies not satisfied with the profits they could earn without ongoing cost cuts? Because their stockholders compare them to other companies racing to cut costs. Who are those evil investors forcing companies to constantly lower costs to improve their profits and try to boost their stock prices? "They" are not just high-powered hedge funds but also everyday Americans, some of the same ones at risk of losing their jobs to offshoring.

Since Americans began managing their own 401(k) retirement plans, they—or their mutual fund managers—have been putting relentless pressure on American companies to turn in ever-higher quarterly profits and thus stock price increases, even if it means nearly endless restructuring and corporate cost-cutting drives that produce waves of early retirements, layoffs, and jobs moving overseas. Strong pressure for higher profits in the United States forced many European and even Japanese companies to improve their results to keep up, which in turn pressured American companies to begin a new round of cost cuts whatever the cost to American workforces. The demands from the world's investors—the everyday Main Street investors seen in the mirror as well as sophisticated Wall Street money managers—have led to unprecedented and unending corporate fat-trimming drives. Now, thanks in no small part to cheap overseas labor, investing profits are up along with corporate profits, but employment in America hasn't kept up the strong pace. The American middle class has become an army of investors whose tough demands are translating into more layoffs among their own ranks. Collectively, investors are better off in the short term as companies cut their costs, so the same company that lays off Americans in favor of Chinese or Indian employees might be a better investment than a company that keeps these jobs in America. But because all except the wealthiest Americans depend more on their salaries than on their investment incomes, layoffs are a much greater personal risk than subpar returns in the stock market.

Even as pressure from American investors prompts U.S. companies to hire overseas, crimping wages in the United States, there's a different invisible interconnection between China and the United States which dramatically helps Americans. Trade with China indirectly but powerfully holds down U.S. interest rates and inflation, benefitting consumers every time they use a credit card or buy a car or a home.

Because Americans buy more from China than China buys from the United States, the Chinese government has the world's largest dollar reserves. It buys those dollars, largely in the form of U.S. Treasury bonds, to keep its exchange rate steady against the dollar. At the end of 2006, China held $1.1 trillion in foreign-currency reserves, more than any other nation. China's total dollar reserves have more than quadrupled since 2002. Because bond prices move in the opposite direction of interest rates, when Chinese bond purchases drive up demand—and thus prices—for the bonds, they also put pressure on interest rates to stay low. Americans feel the impact of thanks-to-China lower interest rates in lower monthly credit card bills, lower car payments, and lower mortgage payments. Lower interest rates even helped keep America's housing boom in motion; it would otherwise have been braked sooner by higher interest rates. Lower monthly house, car, and credit card payments leave more pocket money, and many Americans have responded by buying more of everything— including lots of Chinese-made goods.

To see how interconnected the global economy has become, consider a typical homebuyer in Kansas City. She buys a house that costs $225,000, taking out a loan for $150,000 with an interest rate of 6.5 percent. Her mortgage payment is $950 a month. Economists estimate her interest rate would be 7.5 percent without China's downward pressure on interest rates; if it were, her monthly payment would be $100 more. She thus has $1,200 more to spend each year, thanks to China.

But the low interest rates also prompt more and more Americans to buy homes, driving prices up. After five years, her house is worth $350,000. So she takes out a $50,000 home-equity loan to borrow against the rise in value of her home, using it to build a garage and buy an SUV for additional payments of $500 a month for a few years. Even though she hasn't gotten a raise since buying the house, she can afford the new set of wheels because she can borrow against the increased value of her home. China has been integral to pressing U.S. housing rates skyward, and thus making American homeowners feel richer than they otherwise would with wages that have nearly stagnated.

In China's big cities today, automated teller machines spit out 100-renminbi notes even for bank cards belonging to foreigners—a convenience rarely found in China during the 1990s. The pink bills, each worth about $12, are a potent symbol of China's modern capitalism, despite featuring Mao's serene gaze on every printed denomination of renminbi, or "people's money."

Perhaps the most consistent complaint American politicians level against China concerns its currency—and not that it is still adorned with the face of Chinese communism. They contend that China manipulates its exchange rates to hold down the renminbi's value, which gives an unfair price advantage to Chinese exports. They are absolutely right, but they should pipe down if they want to protect American jobs in the long run.

American politicians argue that China has set the value of its currency about 40 percent below where it would be if it traded freely. Economists bicker about what the renminbi's value would be if it were freely traded, with some insisting it is fairly valued but most saying the Chinese currency is undervalued by between 20 and 40 percent. Undervaluation gives a huge tailwind to Chinese exports, effectively setting prices 20–40 percent below their normal market value. So when Li & Fung needs to ship Levi's blue jeans to the United States, it can get them made for a practically unbeatable price in China. And when American stores like Wal-Mart order made-in-China DVD players or toolboxes or tires, they too get rock-bottom prices, keep the profits for their investors, or pass on some of the savings to their American customers. Factories elsewhere in the world, including the United States, find it nearly impossible to compete with Chinese factory prices.

A revaluation of the Chinese currency of, say, 25 percent—or an across-the-board import duty of that magnitude—would instantly give factories elsewhere a better chance of doing battle against the Chinese juggernaut. The United States has been pressuring China for several years to let its currency rise to market levels, but China has resisted, fearing that it would create the instability that leaders fear.

Most Chinese companies are barely profitable anyway, and if Chinese factories lost their competitive advantage, they could be forced to lay off literally millions of workers in a land without a social safety net.

It isn't in the interest of the United States to have an unstable Chinese economy on the loose, but there are two more important long-term reasons why American politicians should think twice before pushing for a giant jump in the value of the Chinese currency. First, the benefits of the cheap Chinese currency go largely to two groups—American companies exporting from China and American consumers. Consumers pay less than they otherwise would at Wal-Mart for Chinese-made goods. And as was discussed in an earlier chapter, American companies contracting with factories in China to make their goods are usually the ones reaping the higher-than-average profits. There are more factory jobs than there would otherwise be for impoverished Chinese workers. Most of the lowest-paid factory work moved outside U.S. borders years ago, leaving few U.S. jobs threatened even if Chinese costs were effectively made 25 percent higher overnight. After all, even if average Chinese *daily* wages shot up from $1 or $2 per day to $3 or $4 per day, they would remain far lower than *hourly* rates at U.S. factories, and China would still have lower costs despite a new exchange rate. So if China revalued its currency, Americans would lose the benefits of lower prices without saving many jobs.

Second, if the renminbi's value rose, Chinese goods would be far less competitive when compared with those of other low-wage nations. Such a shift could force Chinese factory owners to start moving up the food chain in order to stay in business, leaving the cheap goods to be made in India or Vietnam. To justify higher costs, the Chinese factory juggernaut would begin building more complex, expensive goods—the very kind more likely to compete directly with factory goods still made in the United States. So while China's current exchange rate policy hurts other low-wage countries, the simple-sounding solutions American politicians propose could wind up triggering more competition for U.S. factories in the long term.

O

WITH THE BRISK GROWTH the global economy has enjoyed since 2002, these should be the best of times. As in past expansions, the U.S. unemployment rate was expected to fall—and it did. American workers have become more productive each year, which normally leads to widespread raises. But the swelling economy has not led to fat paychecks this time; instead, median hourly wages after inflation declined 2 percent from 2004 to mid-2006.[5] For Americans, the missing link in a suddenly internationalized economy is improved pay. Much factory work has already moved overseas or been automated, and America's blue-collar workers are earning less than they did in 1973.[6] The migration of white-collar jobs has begun. Those who have lost jobs frequently must accept pay cuts when they find new work. Most of those who have kept their jobs aren't getting raises that run ahead of inflation, much less ahead of productivity increases.[7] The reality is that many workforce changes have already begun and are likely to accelerate in coming years as more and more companies move jobs offshore and otherwise adjust to the rise of India and China.

Unfortunately, most households are unprepared for the turmoil: during the 1990s, the American savings rate began its plunge from over 8 percent to negative 1 percent in 2006.[8] Americans didn't register much of the pain of smaller savings, first because stock prices soared in the 1990s, then because house prices began to zoom upward about the time the stock bubble burst. Housing prices have halted their powerful run-up, so Americans may soon feel the full weight of their unprecedented, credit-fueled spending binge.

Those looking closely see that American standards of living are already being pinched for all but the richest Americans. Middle-class expenses are way up, largely because of increased health care and college costs. Unless Americans make big changes, keeping up with the Joneses may mean going backward and downsizing the American standard of living. Some indicators show that Americans have in the past decade already begun the slide, but many haven't yet begun to feel it.

○

WHEN ALL THE PIECES of the global economy work together smoothly, all the players involved benefit. In this decade, a clear pattern emerged: China became factory to the world, the United States became buyer to the world, and India began to become back office to the world.

But there are risks for both East and West as the strands of the global economy intertwine. As the world economy interconnects, the United States, China, and India become more vulnerable to local disruptions in each other's economies. For instance, if the U.S. housing bubble bursts as quickly as the American stock rally ended in 2001, home prices in the country could plunge. Many Americans who had been feeling flush would suddenly feel poor, and many would be saddled with payments for home loans worth more than their houses. If that happened, a broad economic slowdown would follow, and many Americans would be forced to tighten their belts drastically, spending less on everything—including made-in-China goods stacked on store shelves. A U.S. recession could force Chinese factories to shut down or lay off workers, most for the first time ever. Indeed, worries about a U.S. slowdown push stories about the U.S. housing market to the front page of newspapers half a world away in China. At the same time, India's army of computer programmers and call-center employees could also feel the ripple of a downturn in the U.S. economy. Indians wouldn't be answering so many 800-number calls from shoppers buying plane tickets or other goods. On the other hand, because service jobs can move across the globe quickly, American companies fighting to stay afloat might accelerate their movement of white-collar jobs overseas in a downturn that desperately crimps their profits.

The potential for trouble goes both ways. Indeed, the scale of U.S.-China trade dependence is worrying even some stalwart free traders. "In the globalized world of today, there is no risk if America, Europe, and Japan stop producing T-shirts or television sets," said Jean-Pierre Lehmann, professor of international political economy at IMD, the international business school in Lausanne, Switzerland. "My concern is that the U.S., in particular, is far too overdependent on China not just for goods but also for finance," with the massive Chinese purchases of U.S. debt. "So there is nothing wrong, on the contrary, with

the U.S. sourcing its consumables outside the U.S., but it is dangerous that so much of it should be coming from the same source, and it
is certainly dangerous that the U.S. should be so dependent on Chinese finance."[9]

A number of scenarios could trigger a Chinese-American economic
meltdown. A political spat could erupt between the United States and
China that would cause China to dump those huge holdings of U.S.
bonds, creating a financial tidal wave that could quickly swamp
America's economy. Massive bond sales by China would be the economic equivalent of firing a long-range missile at American shores.
Such a chain of events could be triggered by an Asian-financial-crisis-
like calamity for China, political revolt there, or any abrupt change in
Chinese attitudes toward the United States. Imagine an incident like
the 2001 spy plane crisis, in which an American spy plane collided
with a Chinese fighter jet, which then crashed in the South China
Sea, producing raging, nationalistic Chinese protests against the
United States and a furious response from the Chinese government.
Because the incident took place in 2001, before the United States and
China were so interlinked, China had little economic power over the
United States, but a similar situation in the present circumstances
could lead to financial catastrophe for the United States with light-
ning speed if China chose. For the United States, it is the economic
equivalent of having your coastline encircled by a powerful navy.

It is ironic that China's communists have such a huge influence
over the U.S. economy—one that is now working in America's favor
but that could be used to attack the United States economically. The
Cold War may be over in political terms, but it could now be resur-
rected with financial weapons if China chose to exercise its economic power or if the United States insisted on protectionism.
Incidentally, Japan wields nearly the same economic power over the
United States, because Japan, too, has enormous holdings of U.S. dollars. But Japan is a longtime American ally with decades of political
and economic stability under its belt, and more experience maneu-
vering a powerful economy in global financial markets, so such an
attack from Japan is far less likely.

The good news is that this growing international economic interdependence is a little like nuclear deterrence: nations with such far-reaching trade and financial ties have an interest in preserving steady economic relations rather than triggering a round of financial shocks that could quickly spiral around the globe. China doesn't want to lose its best customer: the United States. If Chinese factories selling to Wal-Mart and other American companies shuttered as a result of a blowup in trade tensions, millions of Chinese workers could find themselves unemployed—and angry at their government. Of course, an army of newly unemployed Chinese workers could lead to national instability—the last thing the Communist Party wants. Likewise, if offshoring stalls in India and the economy tumbles, voters will likely hoist their leaders out of office in the next elections. So both the Indian and the Chinese governments are trying to keep their economies growing and globalizing fast, while the United States and Europe are finding themselves alarmingly and inextricably linked to the job markets of the international economy's fast-growing Asian giants. For now, we have a global economic détente.

○

How should the West respond to the economic metamorphoses brought about by the rise of India and China? Those who fear they will be hurt by the changes at hand usually call for protectionism. Those who expect to benefit tend to insist that the free market instead be given free rein. Neither option works very well. In the United States as well as in Europe and other developed economies, every job moved offshore leaves a tiny hole in the fabric of middle-class life; every layoff triggers trauma for the family of one who lost a job, a difficult search for a new job, and often the dawning realization that the unemployed worker was on the wrong side of the changes underway in the global economy. There are gains to the world economy, and even to the American economy, but those are not so immediate as the pain of a lost job. For those who have been laid off or are worried they will be, it is tempting to fight to stop—or at least delay—the changes that produce such suffering. Already, calls for protectionism are growing louder in the United States. In 2006, senators threatened to slap a 27.5 percent duty on all imports

from China in retaliation for its undervalued currency. Other politicians, aiming at India, have called for limits on white-collar work
moving overseas.

These efforts, however satisfying in the short term, tend to backfire in the long run, just like advocating a change in exchange rates.
Technology makes it more difficult to engage in protectionism
anyway: it is easier to turn back ships pulling into American ports
with goods made in overseas factories than it is to regulate—or even
measure—what kind of overseas service work crosses American
shores via computer connections or phone calls. In addition, protectionism is tough to pull off now that the world's supply chains have
been knitted together. Much of what is shipped back and forth across
borders is simply pieces of products heading to the next step in the
disassembly line, rather than finished products on their way to
customers.

Of course slowing down trade requires only collective will, not regulations. What if buyers decided to resist the siren song of low prices
emanating from the nearest Wal-Mart and buy instead from mom-and-
pop stores stocked with higher-priced, locally made goods? Globalization would decelerate. Offshoring could be slowed, too, if vast numbers
of buyers agreed to pay more for services whose workers are based in
their home countries. Such a scenario, however, seems unlikely. In the
1970s, car buyers didn't hesitate to choose Toyotas and Hondas when
they proved cheaper or more reliable than Fords and Fiats. Shoppers
didn't object in the 1980s and 1990s when factories making their toys
and tennis shoes moved to Mexico or China. Today it is nearly impossible for consumers to know which piece of a product was made in
which country. And realistically, customers are unlikely to care—or
know—whether their computer program was written in India or the
United States. For customers, it doesn't make much difference if their
tax preparer, telephone operator, or loan processor wears a sari and
works in Delhi or wears a baseball cap and works in Baltimore. A "buy
America" movement seems as unlikely to catch on now as it proved in
the past, and without it, the economy is likely to grow ever more
global, with jobs flowing toward low-wage countries.

It is tempting to turn to protectionism. But however well-meaning, the failure of efforts to keep jobs in developed countries is already on display. The poster child of government attempts to protect jobs is continental Europe, where companies are reluctant to hire new workers because they must pay costly employee benefits and because it can be difficult to fire workers who are later unneeded. Those restrictions are designed to help workers, but have instead in the long term led to unemployment rates in most of Europe that are twice as high as those in the United States. Western Europe's inflexible labor laws are a big reason so many Europeans are unemployed.

Engaging in protectionism in response to the rising fortunes of India and China—however personally or politically appealing—would leave most of the world's people from rich countries and poor countries alike worse off in the long run, economists concur. Not only does protectionism tend to backfire—to eventually cost jobs rather than to save them—but the global economy has already grown so interconnected that bashing China and making a scapegoat out of India could wind up hurting America's economy. Economists calculate that international trade adds about $1 trillion a year in benefits to the U.S. economy.[10] Even the offshoring of white-collar jobs, despite the hardship it brings for laid-off workers, is a net gain for developed nations like the United States and Japan, as well as for the country where the jobs land. Every dollar of spending that U.S. companies transfer to India creates $1.46 in new wealth, according to McKinsey & Company. Destination countries like India, China, or the Philippines keep 33 cents of that gain, while the United States keeps $1.13 for every dollar spent on offshoring. The country moving jobs keeps 78 percent of the value created globally by the more efficient operation of companies, in the form of lower prices for customers or higher corporate profits, according to McKinsey.

○

JUST WHEN MODERN TECHNOLOGY has dramatically speeded up the connections between East and West, between developing countries and the rich countries of the world, two nations with more than a billion people each have suddenly embraced capitalism and rejoined the world economy. After half a century's absence, India and China are now competing in commerce with the United States and the rest of the developed world. Hundreds of millions of poor people have been lifted from desperate poverty as a result, and the West should not try to stop the rise of India and China.

But the powerful, swift changes in the global economy will also trigger strong repercussions in the West, where many people stand to lose their jobs. For them and their families, the threat is grave. While protectionism would backfire, relying solely on free market forces would be naïve. Too many Americans would find their standards of living falling. Too many would be left behind. The United States must strive to create jobs and to weave a stronger safety net ahead of the inevitable job losses. Without a concerted effort now, the United States risks seeing American children become worse off than their parents.

○

THE GOOD NEWS IS that we know the way forward. Robert Rubin spearheaded the founding in 2006 of the Hamilton Project, a mini–think tank within the Brookings Institution.[11] The same year, alarmed by the new challenges to the United States, members of the nonpartisan Council on Competitiveness[12]—mostly American academic and business leaders—pushed for legislation that would encourage innovation: they called on the United States to "innovate or abdicate" its global leadership role. Of particular interest is that these separate efforts, one driven by Mr. Rubin's coterie of prominent Democrats, the other made up of some of the nation's most respected academic leaders along with mostly Republican business leaders, have come up with remarkably similar policy recommendations. Outside of those efforts, economists who have looked most closely at the issue agree with them. "The best response from the high-wage developed world is to uncover new sources of job creation rather than protect the old ones," says Morgan Stanley's globetrotting Stephen Roach. "That's precisely what worked when farmers were displaced by the Industrial Revolution, when sweatshop workers lost their jobs to automated assembly lines, and when the U.S. Rust Bowl was hollowed out in the early 1980s."

Back in Mr. Rubin's quiet New York office, his serious tone of analysis takes on an edge of frustration. From where he sits, its seems that as the United States focuses on fighting the war on terror and a war in Iraq and Afghanistan, it isn't paying enough attention to the gathering storm right outside his windows: America isn't fighting the economic war that has already reached its shores. Mr. Rubin isn't really worried about the rise of India and China. He's worried about America. "What we've really got to do is get serious," Mr. Rubin says. "We have to address the various challenges we have and create the best possible environment in this country."

He reels off a rather gloomy list of what America must do to compete—matters that the nation has put on the back burner in recent years. "We've got to have a public education system that's first-rate. We've got to get our basic research back. We've got to get our fiscal house back in order" by reining in the budget deficit. He adds that the United States must recognize that "in the long run, good environmental policy is good economic policy." Then he pauses, and his almost perpetually worried look gives way as he thinks about how making those changes could change America. "We've got to put in place the ability to be the best we can be," Mr. Rubin says. A small smile emerges: "The best we can be might actually be pretty good."

○

MAKE NO MISTAKE: the United States doesn't have a billion people, but it has enormous advantages and resources when it comes to competing in the world economy, even one in the midst of an historic shakeup. It is the world's largest economy by far, with one of the best-trained workforces. Its citizens are better educated and make more money than those of most other nations, and its government is powerful. U.S. companies own the majority of the world's dominant, cutting-edge technology. The U.S. labor market is one of the most flexible in the world, and that will help with the necessary adjustments. There is something harder to measure but equally important: Americans have a can-do spirit that is not found as often in other, more risk-averse societies. Most Americans—even new immigrants drawn to the United States—share an unshakable belief in the American Dream. Like Sybase's Mr. Chen, Americans believe in the idea that with hard work and the fair chance they expect in the U.S.A., they'll get ahead. The American system is renowned for its ability to foster the kind of creativity and flexibility that has helped it rise above past challenges. Those are the traits that helped America send a man to the moon after President Kennedy called on the nation to concentrate its efforts.

Today's challenge is to ready the nation for the coming wave of stiff competition from India and China. The good news is that what the United States must do is clear: it must strengthen its educational and economic foundations and foster the innovation that will keep the United States ahead in the technology that underpins so many parts of the nation's culture and the global economy. Now is the time for the United States to recognize the threat to American standards of living and to resolve to raise its game and compete on the new global terms. Forget protectionism. Forget letting the free market ride. To meet the challenges, the United States must choose a third way: the nation must focus on creating jobs, even as it increases support to those losing jobs.

In readying for a storm of competition, America must return to basics. The most critical building block is education. Federal, state, and local governments—and the individuals who elect them—will be catastrophically irresponsible unless they insist on dramatically improved education, starting with elementary school. Despite years of hand-wringing and despite higher spending than that of other industrialized nations, America's schools threaten to leave the nation less competitive in global labor markets. A barrage of test scores shows American students are already far behind the world's academic leaders. U.S. universities are still considered the best in the world, but shockingly, American fifteen-year-olds are tied for twenty-first place in average academic performance globally.[13] American eighth graders ranked fifteenth in math—just beating out Lithuania's kids—and ninth in the world in science in 2003.[14] When those American children grow up and start working, they will not have the skills to compete with better-educated foreign counterparts, much less to earn wages ten times higher. Reading, language skills, and geography are other basic skills in which American students are laggards.

Business leaders—the ones busy hiring Indian and Chinese college graduates—warn that judging by America's current education efforts, the nation is already falling behind. "The competitiveness of the U.S. workforce depends on a strong educational foundation, particularly in the math and science skills required to succeed in the information technology industry," says Craig R. Barrett, chairman of Intel Corporation. "We need to raise our sights and not tolerate the mediocrity we already have."[15] The government must fix America's K–12 education system, and parents must demand that their children prepare more rigorously for the tough competition they'll face. "Ten years ago, half the world's population was not playing, and now they are," Mr. Barrett says.

Mr. Chen badgers his own children to learn Mandarin and to study harder. Once a year, he buys Chinese textbooks in Hong Kong and brings them home to California to show his kids that Chinese students are studying more-advanced material than they are in each and every grade. "We are not equipped as an economy to go to the next knowledge base," says Mr. Chen, the American immigrant. "I don't see us training ourselves. I don't see us training our K–12th grades," he complains. "Yes, we have the best university system in the world, but we're not feeding that system. We're not investing in creativity."

Meanwhile, at the very time a university education has become critical for the nation's competitiveness, America's colleges and universities have since the early 1990s become less affordable.[16] If trends continue, the proportion of American workers with high school diplomas as well as the proportion with college degrees is expected to drop over the next fifteen years, and as a result, incomes will, too.[17]

The United States also needs to shore up its financial foundations. Individuals as well as the government are spending beyond their means, leaving less of a cushion against the likely storm of global competition ahead. America's twin deficits—the budget deficit and the current-account deficit—are at record highs. The massive budget deficit means the government can't as easily find money to spend for better education and for beefing up infrastructure when it needs to do so. The current-account deficit means the United States increasingly depends on foreigners—particularly China and Japan, and recently

Middle Eastern nations flush with profits from selling high-priced oil—to lend America money.[18] If the United States were to lose the trust of the global financial markets—if the dollar lost its economic credibility in the same way the United States has bruised its diplomatic standing in recent years—the financial effects could be dire as nations sold their dollar holdings.

Meanwhile, Americans are continuing their spending spree; collectively, Americans are spending more than they earn. Americans became net borrowers, not net savers, in 2005, when the national savings rate reached minus 0.4 percent, according to the Commerce Department. In 2006, the savings rate dropped to minus 1 percent. These levels were last seen during the Great Depression. If Indians and Chinese can earn $5,000 a year and salt away $1,500, Americans earning $40,000 a year should be able to save at least that much each year—but Americans don't.

Sometimes, it is easier to put things in perspective from the other side of the world. "It is not the best feeling in the world to know that I'm taking away someone's job," said Sheelan Chawathe, who answers the phone for Delta Air Lines in Mumbai. He offered some advice: "Stop trading in your car every year and a half, and cut down going to Applebee's seven days a week to once a week. If you cut back, you can keep a pretty high standard of living."[19] After all, the average Western standard of living remains a dream for most of the Indian and Chinese workers who are "taking away someone's job." A McDonald's Value Meal costs just $2 in most of Asia, but is so far out of reach that it is considered an upper-middle-class treat.

Stronger educational and financial fundamentals are essential, but the nation's physical foundation—its infrastructure—also needs work. The flood walls that failed New Orleans during Hurricane Katrina are only the most dramatic example. "If you went to Kennedy Airport and Shanghai airport, which would you say is the more advanced country?" asked Mr. Rubin,[20] decrying the shabby state of New York's international airport. Similarly, China's roads are in better shape than many found in the United States, starting with the potholed, neglected highways near the Detroit auto factories that put America on wheels in the first place. Like China, America built highways across the nation as its economy boomed, but many of those were built in the 1950s and are now aging and overdue for upgrades.

Not all of the U.S. infrastructure shortcomings can be explained by the passage of time. The United States lags far behind Asian leaders in high-speed, broadband Internet connectivity today, even though the Internet was invented in America. Japan, Korea, most of Europe, and even China and India have far more reliable and advanced cell phone networks. On trains zipping past Indian fields, passengers surf the Internet on their laptop computers. On subway cars deep underground in China, riders chat on cell phones. Not in America. This inadequate infrastructure is already triggering job losses in the United States. Mr. Barrett's Intel and other companies have hired Chinese researchers to work on the next generation of cell phone and mobile Internet technology because Chinese workers are already using cutting edge services and technology unfamiliar to Americans.

Upgrading shabby infrastructure would have another benefit besides making it attractive to keep high-tech jobs in the United States: it would create low-tech jobs of the sort that cannot be moved offshore. Those jobs—in construction, pipe fitting, road laying—form a natural safety net for some whose factory work moved overseas in coming years.

Newer infrastructure, stronger economic foundations, and a better educational system are musts for keeping the United States at the top of its game. But there is one more important ingredient: innovation, the kind that led to the creation of the Internet. The nation's long-term standing in the world depends on whether the United States can encourage the inventions and innovation necessary to create the jobs of the future. To push progress, the United States should increase funding for basic research, the kind of noncommercial, scientific research that can lead to huge gains like the Internet, spawned by efforts to improve communication at the Department of Defense, or, a century before, the first telegraph line.[21]

The United States has instead been going the other way, reducing its spending on basic research as well as applied research and development, according to the National Science Foundation.[22] Companies have stepped in to fill the void, increasing their funding of research and development, but the vast majority of their spending increases have gone to product development, not to basic research.[23] The Council on Competitiveness noted that federal funding for the life sciences has increased fourfold since the 1980s, with remarkable breakthroughs, including scientific triumphs like the sequencing of the human genome. The new discoveries created jobs. But research spending on the physical sciences, engineering, and math was stagnant during that time. The Council on Competitiveness recommended that government R&D spending be increased across the board so that it totals 1 percent of U.S. GDP. In addition, the council suggested that 3 percent of all federal agencies' R&D budgets be allocated to "innovation acceleration" grants meant to encourage exploratory, high-risk research.[24]

The federal government has a critical role to play, but state and local governments must also take up the cause of creating jobs. Cities must encourage innovation by trying to attract and keep jobs in emerging fields like nanotechnology or biotechnology that will keep America ahead of other nations by creating new, higher-skilled jobs fast enough to replace those lost to offshoring. The Council on Competitiveness suggests the United States embark on a national campaign to create "regional innovation hot spots" in the same way China builds industrial parks to attract a concentration of new factories. They can't all focus on the same field, of course; cities would have to decide which specializations best suit the attributes of the existing workforce and companies, and make sure there is adequate nearby training to encourage workers to keep skills up to date. The American hot spots would try to foster a "Silicon Valley effect" that encourages a climate of innovation and entrepreneurship. The hot spots might be located near universities, laboratories, or nonprofit organizations and would combine public and private support for development, both in regional economic plans and in funding for start-up companies.

○

WHETHER OR NOT the federal and local governments effectively step up to face the challenges brought on by the rise of India and

China, much of the responsibility—and the consequences—will fall to individual families.

The stakes are high: without dramatic changes, standards of living could fall as more white-collar as well as blue-collar jobs move overseas to hungrier, harder-working, lower-paid Indians and Chinese. Americans should expect change and embrace it, rather than expect to work in the same job for an entire career like the previous generation. Americans must be ready for disruption and willing to undergo retraining to upgrade their skills and to be ready to change careers to jump on new job opportunities when they arrive. A laboratory scientist might fear that her drug testing work would move to India. Ideally, she could proactively retrain to become a biotechnologist, for instance. Those who successfully adapt and meet the challenges will be more likely to have stable or growing paychecks.

But lots of people will not have the ability to switch quickly to jobs that cater to local customers—the kind that cannot easily be moved overseas. Inevitably, many Americans will become less competitive in the expanded global labor market. Their paychecks will shrink as work migrates to places where it can be done for lower pay. Those Americans will need a safety net to catch them—a personal safety net of higher savings and a government-provided safety net, too.

"Displaced workers deserve retraining," said Morgan Stanley's Mr. Roach, for what he calls "the inevitable global labor arbitrage." While the free market should be allowed to work, both the government and corporations must install a safety net for those whose livelihoods are disrupted by the enormous changes afoot. Companies busy saving big bucks by offshoring jobs should set aside a small portion of their gains to provide for the American workers they are firing. The federal government should help, too. The Brookings Institution said that an insurance policy that would cost twenty-five dollars per worker would help those who were displaced to retrain or get a new job.[25] The Council on Competitiveness recommends the creation of "lifelong learning accounts" patterned after retirement accounts. They would allow tax-exempt contributions by workers and tax credits for contributions from their employers, and could be spent on tuition at training programs operated by public or private colleges and community colleges, other private training centers, and labor unions. The increased job churn will have an emotional component the nation must collectively come to terms with. Those losing jobs now tend to take it personally, to feel bad about themselves if they must accept smaller paychecks in the future or go back to retrain for another career, and the experience of losing a previously stable job is only going to become more widespread in America over the coming years. Creating company and government-funded safety nets is not only fairer than leaving workers blowing in the wind of globalization. Wage insurance and job retraining programs would also make workers more willing to accept the changes at hand,[26] changes that will benefit Americans, Indians, and Chinese collectively.

○

WHAT'S NEXT FOR AMERICANS?

Predicting which jobs will find favor in the future is difficult—the most stable job in the West may be that of a fortune-teller. Mostly as a result of offshoring, America has lost more than 1.1 million once-coveted information technology jobs in the past five years. On the other hand, since 2001, about 1.7 million new health care industry jobs have been created in the United States along with more than 900,000 new housing industry jobs—those of real estate agents, homebuilders, and mortgage brokers.[27] Anyone can try to guess where the jobs of tomorrow will be found. Israel's former prime minister Shimon Peres says America's hot careers will be in nanotechnology, which will create openings for jobs we haven't even imagined yet. Another may be in green engineering because of China's need to clean up its water and air and its willingness to spend billions to do so. That could jump-start the long-neglected field of environmental cleanup, dramatically increasing the demand for Western scientists and technicians who can develop new green technologies.

The economist Alan Blinder says that whether blue-collar or white-collar, Americans should concentrate on careers that cannot be moved offshore—on jobs that require one to be in the same city as one's work. Many believe that America's growing income inequality will create a raft of service jobs to serve the growing ranks of the rich in America—high-end hairdressers, personal trainers, closet designers, and florists, for instance, or expensive doctors happy to make house calls—none of which are likely to be moved offshore.

Nandan Nilekani, the Infosys CEO who has persuaded American companies to move tens of thousands of jobs to India, agrees with Mr. Blinder. "People should look at careers which cannot be delivered over a wire. If someone is a cardiac surgeon, they're not going to be displaced. But if they are a radiologist, somebody from Bangalore is liable to check X-rays over a wire."

But he predicts the American workforce will meet the challenge with customary American ingenuity. "People will have to really focus on education—that has to happen," Mr. Nilekani said. "If there is an expectation that there will be a lot of high-paying jobs without an investment in education," that's wrong. "The education investment is a must; it is nonnegotiable," he said. But America will find its way in the newly internationalized economy. "The capacity of the U.S. to constantly reinvent itself is really extraordinary."[28]

Most exciting of all are the unexpected possibilities not yet envisioned—the prospect of an invention on the scale of the Internet, which so revolutionized the way the world works, or even the invention of the iPod, which merely transformed the way the world listens to music. There is one thing impossible for any company to move overseas, and difficult for other nations to duplicate: America's essentially scrappy culture of thinking of, funding, and bringing to market new ideas and ventures—its people's inventive, can-do mind-set. Despite the coming turmoil, Americans should not assume the worst, but ready themselves to embrace the new opportunities that will come along, even though experts cannot say what they will be. Americans are flexible and creative, are risk-takers, are the world's optimists, and are at their best as underdogs. "Americans like to compete," said Intel's Mr. Barrett. "It is a fundamental strength and national characteristic that we have." The United States is the world's largest, strongest, most resilient economy by a good measure.

Americans must embrace that and walk tall into the ways of a new world shaped by the rise of India and China.

Let the rise of India and China be a catalyst to reestablish America's competitiveness. Let it be this generation's space race. If inward-facing India and communist China can transform themselves and face the world, so can the United States of America.

AFTERWORD

In January 2008, Manmohan Singh made his first visit to China as India's prime minister. As his plane descended over Beijing, Mr. Singh could see something that wasn't there when his predecessor, Atal Bihari Vajpayee, visited just five years earlier: the world's largest airport terminal, a futuristic masterpiece designed by Norman Foster and meant to evoke the form of a dragon.

After exiting the plane, Mr. Singh, wearing his trademark blue turban, accompanied proud Chinese officials to an exhibit of the other avant-garde buildings and landmark stadiums the government is constructing in preparation for the 2008 Summer Olympic Games. In addition to the tens of billions China has spent on Olympics-related projects, Mr. Singh knew that in 2007 alone, China managed to attract $67 billion in foreign direct investment—about five times what India did. "We in India admire the remarkable economic progress that China has made," Mr. Singh, an economist by training, told a gathering of Chinese academics two days later as he concluded his visit. "India is changing and I would like to acknowledge that the success of China has been a stimulus to change."

Despite India's strong growth—about 9 percent for the past three years—Mr. Singh's country is still playing catch-up to China. While Bombay's international airport has had a face-lift, the airport in India's capital city of New Dehli remains decrepit. "Both India and China are in the midst of rapid transformation," Mr. Singh told his

Beijing hosts. "When countries the size of China and India, together accounting for 2.5 billion people, begin to unshackle their creative energies, it impacts on the whole world. The world knows it and is watching with interest."

The changes Mr. Singh described continue to be felt across the globe. Stock markets in Bombay, Shanghai, and Shenzhen were hit hard in early 2008 after the American economy—and banks around the world—stumbled. The burgeoning subprime crisis made it harder to get a loan both in the U.S. and in China. But then a funny thing happened: China invested $5 billion in Morgan Stanley, just after the American investment bank reported bigger-than-expected losses. And remember the struggling trona miners of Green River, Wyoming, described in chapter 8? Tata Chemicals, part of Ratan Tata's Indian conglomerate, announced it would spend $1 billion to buy a trona mining company there. Chinese and Indian investments have helped some American companies and their employees, even as others have seen their jobs move halfway around the world to Asia.

Some of those jobs have moved to a new neighborhood outside Delhi called Gurgaon. It is a spot in India that has changed more than perhaps any other in the past few years. It looks like an entire swath of Silicon Valley has been plunked down in a new, warmer setting. New office buildings have created a suburban skyline, but traditional Indian touches remain. Bicycle rickshaw drivers pedal for passengers outside the gated apartment buildings that have sprung up in the neighborhood, and three white cows can occasionally be found striding nose-to-tail along the wide, new highway linking Gurgaon to Delhi.

Meanwhile in China, basketball is the latest American export. Yao Ming, the Houston Rockets center born in China, has inspired would-be NBA players there. Basketball courts are cropping up all over Beijing—and Nike ads are plastered near the hoops. When Americans tune in to the Beijing Olympics, they won't find the nation of bicycle riders they might expect. Instead, they are likely to marvel as much at China's modernism as its filthy air.

The approach of India and China is as inexorable as ever—they are intertwining with the West quietly and quickly. The rest of the world cannot avoid the changes they will bring. The only thing to do is face them, and adjust.

Robyn Meredith
Hong Kong
March 2008

ACKNOWLEDGMENTS

In hundreds of formal interviews and casual conversations over several years, many people have shared their ideas with me, and they have added to this book. I thank Narayana Murthy, Nandan Nilekani, Ram (Kris) Ramachandran, and Ratan Tata, along with Shekhar Gupta of the Indian Express and T. N. Ninan of the Business Standard, for their insights on India; thanks to David Abney for telling me about supply chains and to Diana Farrell for discussing her groundbreaking research on offshoring.

In China I have also had many gurus over the years, and I thank Tom Doctoroff, Jimmy Lai, Jim Thompson, Carl Walter, Andy Xie, and David Zweig. I thank also those who must remain unnamed but who have shared their time and experiences and feelings with me.

I am grateful to those who read early drafts, including Jean-Pierre Lehmann of IMD and the Evian Group and Ruth Shapiro, the visionary founder of the Asia Business Council, both of whom generously shared their wisdom about India and China. I also thank Michael Denneny, Marcia Hensley, P. V. Kannan, Aaron Lammer, Kristi Lu Stout, and Leonard (Bud) Pratt for reading chapters.

My gratitude goes to two people who tirelessly helped me research this book, Julian de Jonquieres and Ng Tze Wei, both of whom have since migrated to Beijing and are now concentrating on their own journalism.

I thank the Forbes brothers—Bob, Kip, Steve, and Tim—who have graciously supported my work for them and cheered me on as I wrote this book. I have been lucky enough to work with Tim Ferguson, Rich

Karlgaard, Dennis Kneale, Stew Pinkerton, and Larry Reibstein, and each has taught me about writing. Thanks also to Monie Begley, Jim Berrien, Christopher Buckley, Kendall Crolius, and Anne Mintz, and to Forbes editor Bill Baldwin for granting me a leave to write this book.

I am grateful for the insights my other journalistic colleagues have shared with me, particularly Reg Chua, Mark Clifford, Hugo Restall, and Cecilie Rohwedder. Photojournalists Rajat Ghosh and Grischa Rueschendorf showed us India and China through their camera lenses. Gene Mustain and Doreen Weisenhaus not only offered encouragement all along but also led me to the world's best literary agent, Alice Martell of the Martell Agency. Thanks to Bob Levey, who gave a kid reporter a break at the *Washington Post*, and to the *Post*'s Warren Brown for his advice along the way. I thank my journalistic rabbi, Charles Eisendrath of the University of Michigan's Knight-Wallace Fellows program. I salute the late Johnny Apple, who encouraged me to write this book and whose legacy lives on in the journalistic DNA of so many scribblers working around the world.

I am grateful to other friends for their ongoing support. Members of my Hong Kong book club offered both encouragement for and a welcome respite from writing, particularly Kyoko Altman, who will soon finish her own book, and Doveen Schecter, who created Dove of the East while I created *The Elephant and the Dragon*. I thank Diana Fortescue, Grant Kelley, Ann Park, and Anne Sawyer.

I congratulate my mother, Marcia Hensley, on her own book, *Staking Her Claim: Women Homesteading the West*, published by the High Plains Press.

Most of all, this book is for Christopher Bradsher, with the hope that his world will be one with billions of people linked closer together in peace and prosperity.

NOTES

Introduction: Tectonic Economics

1 The U.S. sent $13 billion in aid to Europe between 1947 and 1953, according to the U.S. State Department. Inflation-adjusted, that is about $100 billion, whereas foreign companies directly invested more than $700 billion in China between 1978 and 2007.

2 Hu Jintao, president of China, in "Why China Loves Globalization," *Globalist*, June 7, 2005.

3 There are many definitions of poverty. This is the Asian Development Bank's, which tracks the share of the population living below U.S.$1 a day in purchasing-power parity terms. www.adb.org/statistics.

4 India gets the same amount of foreign direct investment in a month as China gets in a week.

5 As pointed out by Ruth Shapiro, founder of the Asia Business Council.

6 Globalization has not benefited all nations: poverty has increased in much of the developing world over the past two decades, but China, India, and a number of other Asian countries are exceptions, Joseph Stiglitz notes in *Making Globalization Work* (New York: Norton, 2006).

7 India adds 2.7 million university graduates per year, according to "India and China: New Tigers of Asia, Part II," Morgan Stanley, June 2006. China had 4.95 million in 2007, according to the Ministry of Labor and Social Security. About 1.3 million Americans graduate each year, according to the National Science Foundation, Dec. 2005.

Chapter 1: Where Mao Meets the Middle Class

1 Hong Kong Trade Development Council and Guangdong Toy Association.

2 United Nations Comtrade database, at http://unstats.un.org/unsd/comtrade/.

3 Ibid. and People's Daily Online.

4 Organization for Economic Cooperation and Development, at http://www.oecd.org/document/8/0,2340,en_2649_201185_35833096_1_1_1_1,00.html.

5   Fang Zhenghui, ed., *Stories of China's Reform and Opening-Up* (Shenzhen: Story of China Publishing, Aug. 2004), p. 23. In 1978, China exported just $970 million in goods to the entire world. By 2003, after the multitude of factories moved in, exports had risen to $438 billion, shifting international trade patterns and remaking whole industries.

6   Fang, ed., *Stories of China's Reform and Opening-Up*.

7   On Xiaogang rural reform, see http://www.fengyang.gov.cn/en/index.php.

8   In fact, a much larger, successful project was carried out in Sichuan Province three years earlier, in 1975, but is seldom publicized in China because its architect was the reformer Zhao Ziyang, who remains a controversial figure in China. He was then the first party secretary of Sichuan County and in 1980 became premier of China and general secretary of the Communist Party, before being stripped of his leadership positions and put under house arrest until his death, in Jan. 2005, after opposing the martial law imposed to put down student demonstrations in Tiananmen Square in 1989.

9   United Nations Food and Agriculture Organization, http://faostat.fao.org, and U.S. Department of Agriculture, http://www.nass.usda.gov/census/census02/volume1/us/st99_2_008_008.pdf.

10 *Yi zi er shi* means "exchanging children to eat."

11 A number of Chinese and Western scholars have documented starvation and cannibalism during Mao's Great Leap Forward, but these accounts of what happened in China's countryside are taken from Jasper Becker, *Hungry Ghosts: Mao's Secret Famine* (New York: Free Press, 1996).

12 Fang, ed., *Stories of China's Reform and Opening-Up*.

13 Joachim von Braun, Ashok Gulati, and Shenggen Fan, "Agricultural and Economic Development Strategies and the Transformation of China and India," International Food Policy Research Institute, 2004–2005 Annual Report Essay, http://www.ifpri.org/pubs/books/ar2004/ar2004_essay01.asp. This paper details Indian and Chinese agriculture reform policies and gives detailed information on rural poverty reduction in both countries.

14 On Chinese rural reforms, see David Zweig, *Internationalizing China: Domestic Interests and Global Linkages* (Ithaca: Cornell Univ. Press, 2002), and *Freeing China's Farmers: Rural Restructuring in the Reform Era* (Armonk, N.Y.: M. E. Sharpe, 1997).

15 Fang, ed., *Stories of China's Reform and Opening-Up*.

16 Lee Kuan Yew, *From Third World to First: The Singapore Story, 1965–2000* (New York: HarperCollins, 2000). Lee Kuan Yew recalled the Deng visit at the Forbes CEO Forum in Singapore on Sept. 5, 2006.

17 Lee Kuan Yew, in a speech, June 23, 2004, at Nanyang Technological Univ., Singapore, http://www.ntu.edu.sg/corpcomms2/releases/Speech%20by%20SM%20Lee%20Kuan%20Yew%20at%20CCLC%20Conference.pdf.

18 Edwin Chan, chairman, ChanCo International Group Ltd., Hong Kong, July 25, 2002.

19 Jan Wong, "Beijing Massacre Spurs New Clashes," *Toronto Globe and Mail*, June 5, 1989.

20 Fang, ed., *Stories of China's Reform and Opening-Up*, pp. 35–37.

21 Adrian Gonzalez, director of the ARC Advisory Group, a consulting firm based in Dedham, Mass. arcweb.com.

22 On Chinese highways, see Xinhua News Agency, China's official news distributor, Sept. 29, 2005.

23 "Beijing Loosens Grip on Economic Zones," *South China Morning Post*, April 5, 2006.

24 Fang, ed., *Stories of China's Reform and Opening-Up*, p. 19.

25 Kenneth Lieberthal, interview in Ann Arbor, Mich., Jan. 21, 2006. Mr. Lieberthal is director for China at the Univ. of Michigan Business School's William Davidson Institute.

26 John Gittings, *The Changing Face of China: From Mao to Market* (Oxford: Oxford Univ. Press, 2005), p. 3.

27 According to the *Financial Times*, this estimate appeared in a World Bank report on pollution that was censored by the Chinese government, http://www.ft.com/cms/s/0/69333ff8-28bb-11dc-af78-00b5df10621.html. The remaining 151-page World Bank report can be found at http://siteresources.worldbank.org/INTEAPREGTOPENVIRONMENT/Resources/China_Cost_of_Pollution.pdf.

28 *Xinhua News* and U.S. Department of Labor, Mine Safety and Health Administration, http://www.msha.gov/FATALS/FABC2006.asp.

29 William Fung, group managing director, Li & Fung, interview in Hong Kong, Nov. 4, 2005.

30 Jasper Becker, *The Chinese* (London: John Murray, 2000), pp. 236, 373.

31 Zhang Weiqing, minister in charge of China's National Population and Family Planning Commission, told *Xinhua News*, March 22, 2006.

32 *The Tank Man*, by Antony Thomas, http://www.pbs.org/wgbh/pages/frontline/tankman/view.

33 Nationwide, Chinese incomes averaged $1,165, according to CLSA Asia-Pacific Markets, with wide disparities between cities and the countryside. China's National Bureau of Statistics said that for 2007, per capita urban disposable income rose 17 percent from the year before, to $1,915, while rural incomes grew 15 percent, to $575.

34 Jonathan Anderson, "China and Food," UBS Asian Focus, March 1, 2006.

35 Stephen Roach, interview in Boao, China, April 26, 2004.

36 Fang, ed., *Stories of China's Reform and Opening-Up* and http://english.peopledaily.com.cn/200504/13/eng20050413_180808.html.

37 Andy Xie, Morgan Stanley managing director, "2006 NPC: Leaning towards the Countryside" March 6, 2006.

38 See http://news.xinhuanet.com/english/2007-10/22/content_6925292.htm.

39 Skyscrapers: Emporis is a real estate research firm that monitors construction activity for thousands of cities worldwide through a network of more than 700 editors. Interviews via emails, Oct. 10, 2005.

40 Tony Ma, interview in Hong Kong, March 22, 2006.

41 China's National Bureau of Statistics.

42 Virginia Mannering, Bureau of Economic Statistics, U.S. Department of Commerce, email interview, Oct. 19, 2005. Jonathan Anderson, chief Asian economist at UBS in Hong Kong, argues persuasively in "China's True Growth: No
Myth or Miracle," *Far Eastern Economic Review*, Sept. 2006, that China's fast
growth is explained by its extraordinarily high savings rate, and that India's
economy is likely to follow a rapid, yet slightly more restrained, growth path
because India now has a high and growing savings rate.

43 Lee Kuan Yew, Singapore's minister mentor, comments to the Forbes CEO
Conference, Singapore, Sept. 5, 2006.

CHAPTER 2:
FROM THE SPINNING WHEEL TO THE FIBER-OPTIC WIRE

1   Gurcharan Das, *India Unbound* (New York: Anchor Books, 2002), pp. 214–15.

2   Ibid., pp. 219–21.

3   Larry Collins and Dominique LaPierre, *Freedom at Midnight* (New York:
Simon & Schuster, 1975), p. 64.

4   Jean-Pierre Lehmann, professor, IMD, Lausanne, Switzerland, interview, May
26, 2006.

5   Das, *India Unbound*, p. 175.

6   Katherine Frank, *Indira: The Life of Indira Nehru Gandhi* (London: Harper-
Collins, 2001). Feroze Gandhi was a Parsi from Gujurat with the relatively
common name Gandhi.

7   Das, *India Unbound*, pp. 170, 174, 208–9, 319, and J. Bradford DeLong, "Prelim-
inary Thoughts on India's Economic Growth," Berkeley, Calif., May 5, 2001.

8   Infosys material: interviews with Narayana Murthy in Sydney, Australia, Sept.
1, 2005, and with Nandan Nilekani in Beijing, May 16, 2005, and Bangalore,
Oct. 24, 2006.

9   Murthy graduated from the Univ. of Mysore and later earned his master's
degree at the Indian Institute of Technology in Kanpur.

10 As often happens in Asia, the wives controlled the family purse strings.

11 In 1992, the rupee became convertible on the trade account, but as of 2006 was
not yet convertible on the capital account.

12 Foreign companies in so-called nonpriority sectors of the economy were
required to dilute their stakes in their companies to less than 40 percent.

13 Infosys revenue reached $2 billion in March 2006 and is expected to hit $3 billion in March 2007. The company had 69,432 employees as of Jan. 2007 but is
adding workers at the remarkable pace of more than 25,000 a year.

14 Bill Gates planted a magnolia in 2002, the same year Zhu Rongji planted a scar-
let flame tree and Tony Blair a cannonball tree. Lee Kuan Yew planted a rosy
trumpet tree in 2005.

15 Ratan Tata, telephone interview, Aug. 3, 2005.

16 Tata Sons controls the Tata Group of companies, and many of the underlying
companies are publicly traded.

17 India's Center for Management Research: http://icmr.icfai.org/casestudies/

catalogue/Business percent20Reports/BREP017.htm; Godrej & Boyce website: http://www.godrej.com/GodrejNew/GodrejHome/News/Coldjolt.htm.

18 Nara Chandrababu Naidu, then the leader of the opposition, interview in Hyderabad, Andhra Pradesh, Oct. 25, 2006.

19 Anne O. Krueger, first deputy managing director of the IMF, speech to the Asia Society, Hong Kong, Dec. 14, 2005.

20 Vijay Kelkar, "India's Economic Future: Moving beyond State Capitalism," Oct. 26, 2005. Dr. Kelkar served as India's finance secretary in 1998–99 and as executive director of the IMF from 1999 to 2002.

21 Kamal Nath, interview in Hong Kong, Dec. 12, 2005.

22 *Destination India* (New Delhi: World Travel and Tourism Summit, April 8, 2005).

23 "India and China: New Tigers of Asia, Part II," Morgan Stanley, June 2006.

24 These particular scenes were observed on Oct. 23, 2006, at the Bangalore airport, but are typical of what I have seen there on a number of visits over the past few years.

25 Kamal Nath, interview in Hong Kong, Dec. 12. 2005.

26 *Destination India.*

27 V. T. Bharadwaj, Gautam M. Swaroop, and Ireena Vittal, "Winning the Indian Consumer," *McKinsey Quarterly*, 2005 special edition: "Fulfilling India's Promise." See this press release issued by the Telecom Regulatory Authority of India: http://www.trai.gov.in/trai/upload/PressReleases/533/pr22jan08no11.pdf.

28 Nandan Nilekani, interview in Beijing, May 16, 2005.

29 Das, *India Unbound*, p. xix.

30 See http://www.worldsteel.org/?action=stats&type=steel&period=latest&month =11&year=2007 for 2007 production: #1 China . . . #6 India.

31 Tata Steel announced Jan. 31, 2007, that it would buy Corus, the successor to British Steel. The combined company ranks as the world's fifth-largest steel company.

Chapter 3: Made by America in China

1 Pieter de Haan, interview in Shanghai, June 17, 2005.

2 Scholars believe that the Silk Road was first used as early as the first century B.C. It was flourishing by the seventh century, serving as an overland route that linked China with the Mediterranean by way of Iran and Central Asia. Most goods were carried in camel caravans that averaged twenty miles a day. In the seventeenth century, the Silk Road trade gave way to the Spice Route maritime trading, which linked India, China, Japan, and places in between to Europe. It was first led by the Portuguese, then the Dutch East India Company, and finally the British East India Company. Various accounts of the trade are found in Ainslie T. Embree and Carol Gluck, eds., *Asia in Western and World History: A Guide for Teaching* (Armonk, N.Y.: M. E. Sharpe, 1997), pp. 70, 320–21, 818.

3 Andy Xie, Morgan Stanley managing director, interview, May 30, 2006.

4 Tom Doctoroff, *Billions: Selling to the New Chinese Consumer* (New York:

Palgrave/Macmillan, 2004), p. 7, and Arthur Kroeber, managing director, Drag-
onomics Research and Advisory, Beijing.

5 In November 2007, China had 539 million mobile-phone subscribers, an increase
   of 78 million during the first eleven months of the year, according to a statement
   from the Ministry of Information Industry. See http://orange.advfn.com/news
   _China-Nov-mobile-phone-users-over-539-mln-Xinhua_23926722.html.

6 Chinese Ministry of Health reports.

7 David Jin, CEO, Greater China for Philips Medical Systems, interview in
   Shanghai, June 17, 2005.

8 Companies from Hong Kong, Singapore, and Taiwan and others owned by the
   Chinese diaspora were generally the first to rush to build factories in China.
   They were followed by American, European, Japanese, and Korean multinationals. Many of the Hong Kong and Taiwanese factories are now suppliers to
   the larger foreign companies.

9 Joe Studwell, *The China Dream* (London: Profile Books, 2003).

10 Ibid., p. 173.

11 Morgan Stanley, Jan. 2007.

12 Studwell, *China Dream*, p. 157.

13 Jimmy Hexter and Ananth S. Narayanan, "The Challenges in Chinese Procure-
    ment," *McKinsey Quarterly*, 2006 special edition: "Serving the New Chinese
    Consumer."

14 Shaun Breslin, "Power and Production: Rethinking China's Global Economic
    Role," *Review of International Studies* 31 (2005): 735–53.

15 Andy Rothman, "Reinventing China," CLSA Asia-Pacific Markets, Sept. 2006,
    p. 12.

16 The 27-country E.U. trade deficit with China reached a record 132 billion euros
    in just the first ten months of 2007, according to Eurostat.

17 Andrew Batson, "China's Fast Growth Spurs Effort to Spread Wealth," The
    Wall Street Journal Asia, Jan. 24, 2007.

18 Rothman, "Reinventing China," p. 4.

19 "India and China: New Tigers of Asia, Part II."

20 This figure was more than five times larger than what the China Banking Reg-
    ulatory Commission reported as of March 31, 2006, and was about the same
    size as China's huge foreign currency reserves. Beijing reacted furiously: the
    People's Bank of China called the accounting firm's report "ridiculous" and
    "distorted." Within days, Ernst & Young retracted the report and apologized to
    China. Economists at other Western financial firms say privately that the Ernst
    & Young report was likely accurate.

21 The S&L crisis cost the U.S. government approximately $150 billion plus inter-
    est. See Robyn Meredith, "Ultimate Tab for the S&L Crisis Pegged at $150B,
    Plus Interest," *American Banker*, Aug. 8, 1994.

22 "Banking on Reform," *China Business Review*, May–June 2006.

23 Mark O'Neill, "Central Bank Chief Seeks Break-up of Agricultural Bank,"
    South China Morning Post, May 22, 2006.

24 Merrill Lynch counts 320,000 Chinese and 83,000 Indians with financial hold-

ings of more than $1 million U.S. dollars, excluding the value of their primary residence. Interview, Aug. 9, 2006.

25 James McGregor, author of *One Billion Customers* (New York: Free Press, 2006), speech to Asia Society, Hong Kong, Oct. 14, 2005.

26 Carsten A. Holz, "China's Economic Growth, 1978–2025: What We Know Today about China's Economic Growth Tomorrow," Working Paper No. 8, Center on China's Transnational Relations, July 3, 2005.

27 National Bureau of Statistics Director Qiu Xiaohua, speaking at Peking Univ., June 12, 2006.

28 China's National Bureau of Statistics, quoted in *China Daily*, March 16, 2006.

29 J.Walter Thompson, Shanghai.

30 Gordon R. Orr, "What Executives Are Asking about China," *McKinsey Quarterly*, 2004 special edition: "China Today."

31 Mary Elizabeth Gallagher, interview June 16, 2006. Gallagher is assistant professor of political science at the Univ. of Michigan, Ann Arbor, and author of *Contagious Capitalism* (Princeton: Princeton Univ. Press, 2005).

32 "India and China: New Tigers of Asia, Part II."

33 Andy Xie, Morgan Stanley economist, interview on Aug. 7, 2006. There are many measures of a nation's savings rate. This one is savings as a percentage of a household's disposable income.

34 Diana Farrell and Andrew J. Grant, "China's Looming Talent Shortage," *McKinsey Quarterly*, Oct. 2005.

35 China had 4.95 million graduates in 2007, according to the Ministry of Labor and Social Security, and 800,000 of the 2006 graduates were in the science and technology fields, according to a July 28, 2006, report from China's National Development and Reform Commission.

36 "2003 College Graduates in the U.S. Workforce: A Profile," National Science Foundation, Dec. 2005.

37 Farrell and Grant, "China's Looming Talent Shortage."

38 Hu Jintao, "Why China Loves Globalization," *Globalist*, June 7, 2005.

39 Hexter and Narayanan, "Challenges in Chinese Procurement."

CHAPTER 4: THE INTERNET'S SPICE ROUTE

1 Diana Farrell, "U.S. Offshoring: Small Steps to Make It a Win-Win," *Berkeley Electronic Press*, March 2006.

2 Craig Barrett, interview in Richmond, Va., Oct. 2, 2003.

3 India's National Association of Software and Service Companies, http://www.nasscom.in/.

4 Microsoft announced on Dec. 8, 2005, that it would invest $1.7 billion and hire 3,000 workers in India over the next four years. Earlier that week, Intel announced it would invest $1.05 billion over five years. In Oct. 2005, Cisco Systems said it planned to invest $1.1 billion in India.

5 "Commerce Dept. to Bring 238 on Mission to India," press release, Nov. 20, 2006.

6   McKinsey Global Institute, McKinsey & Company's economic think tank, interview, June 9, 2006.

7   Called H1-B visas.

8   Farrell, "U.S. Offshoring," and http://www.nasscom.in/upload/41527/Annual%20Report-06-07.pdf.

9   P. V. Kannan, CEO of 24/7 Customer, a California-based offshoring firm, interview, June 9, 2006.

10   "India and China: New Tigers of Asia, Part II," Morgan Stanley, June 2006.

11   Chandrababu Naidu, leader of the opposition in Andhra Pradesh, interview, Oct. 25, 2006. His state graduates 100,000 engineers a year, while the U.S. produces 70,000 engineering graduates.

12   John C. McCarthy et al., "3.3 Million U.S. Services Jobs to Go Offshore," *Forrester Research*, Nov. 11, 2002. The estimate includes jobs moved from the U.S. to any country, not just to India.

13   Alan Blinder, "Fear of Offshoring," Center for Economic Policy Studies Working Paper No. 119, Princeton Univ., Dec. 16, 2005.

14   Farrell, "U.S. Offshoring,"

15   Ibid.

16   Blinder, "Fear of Offshoring."

17   Marcus Courtney, email interview, July 27, 2003.

18   Sunil Mehta, interview in New Delhi, India, July 15, 2003.

19   Ruth Shapiro, founder and executive director, Asia Business Council, interview, Oct. 20, 2005.

20   From a visit to Lupin Ltd.'s offices in Mumbai and outside Pune, Oct. 19, 2004.

21   Shashank Luthra, Ramesh Mangaleswaran, and Asutosh Padhi, "When to Make India a Manufacturing Base," *McKinsey Quarterly*, 2005 special edition: "Fulfilling India's Promise."

22   For 1991 Indian car and motorcycle sales, see http://www.indiainfoline.com/sect/atca/ch06.html. Data for 2007 car sales is from the Society of Indian Motor Manufacturers.

23   "DB Automotive Daily," Deutsche Bank Equity Research, Aug. 28, 2006. Deutsche Bank expects auto production capacity to rise to 3.3 million in India by March 2010, but some of the units made in India will be exported rather than sold in India.

24   World Bank's Education Statistics Database, 2000–2001. China's illiteracy rate was 9 percent in 2000.

25   Luthra, Mangaleswaran, and Padhi, "When to Make India a Manufacturing Base."

26   Interviews with Philips executives in Mumbai, July 23, 2005; in New Delhi, July 25, 2005; in Mohali, India, July 26, 2005; and in Bangalore, July 27, 2005.

27   "The Next 4 Billion: Market Size and Business Strategy at the Base of the Pyramid," by IFC, the private sector arm of the World Bank Group, and World Resources Institute, March 19, 2007.

28   Ram Ramachandran, interview in Mumbai, July 23, 2005.

29 Royal Philips Electronics, N.V., interviews with executives in India in July 2005, and additional interviews in Feb. 2006.

30 Ratan Tata, interview, Aug. 3, 2005.

CHAPTER 5: THE DISASSEMBLY LINE

1 On Henry Ford's assembly line, see Peter Collier and David Horowitz, *The Fords: An American Epic* (London: William Collins, 1987), p. 90.

2 David Abney, chief operating officer, UPS, interview in Shanghai, Feb. 20, 2006.

3 "The Challenge of Complexity in Global Manufacturing—Critical Trends in Supply Chain Management," a 2003 study by Deloitte Touche Tohmatsu.

4 Thomas Hout, interview, Feb. 22, 2006.

5 Progressive Policy Institute, "T-shirt Prices Are Falling," Feb. 15, 2006.

6 The Eyeball Factory is Tak Mei Toys Eye-Ball Factory Ltd.

7 Visit to UPS Shanghai shipping warehouses, Feb. 20, 2006.

8 Vijay Kelkar, "India's Economic Future: Moving beyond State Capitalism," Oct. 26, 2005.

9 "Global Economic Prospects," World Bank, Dec. 13, 2006.

10 Victor and William Fung, interviews in Nov. and Dec. 2005; William Fung, interview, Nov. 4, 2005.

11 Robin Hutcheon, *A Burst of Crackers: The Li & Fung Story* (n.p.: Li & Fung, 1991).

12 Visit to the yarn factory in Shuozhou, Nov. 10, 2005.

13 Visit to the Everbright factory in Dongguan, China, Nov. 8, 2005.

CHAPTER 6: INDIA'S CULTURAL REVOLUTION

1 Stawan Kadepurkar, interview at Infosys headquarters in Bangalore, Dec. 9, 2003, and follow-up telephone and email interviews March 18, 2004, and July 14, 2006.

2 Nandan Nilekani, interview in Beijing, May 16, 2005.

3 Vishwas Jain, interview at Infosys headquarters, Bangalore, Dec. 9, 2003.

4 Infosys headquarters, Bangalore, Dec. 9, 2003.

5 Infosys headquarters, Bangalore, Oct. 24, 2006.

6 Nandan Nilekani, interview at Infosys headquarters, Bangalore, Dec. 9, 2003.

7 Progeon workers earn $200–$300 a month, far less than the $2,000–$3,000 a month a comparable worker would earn in the U.S., according to "Case Study: Inside the Progeon-Greenpoint Mortgage Transaction," Knowledge@Wharton, Sept. 25, 2002.

8 Alpana Sinha and Akshaya Bhargava, interviews at Infosys headquarters, Bangalore, Dec. 9, 2003.

9 Nandan Nilekani, interview in Bangalore, Oct. 24, 2006.

10 Returned Non-Resident Indians Association, India.

11 P. V. Kannan, CEO of 24/7 Customer, Bangalore-based Indian offshoring firm, interview, July 24, 2006.

12 U.S. dollar millionaires, excluding the value of their primary residence, according to Merrill Lynch, interview, Aug. 9, 2006.

13 V. T. Bharadwaj, Gautam M. Swaroop, and Ireena Vittal, "Winning the Indian Consumer," *McKinsey Quarterly*, 2005 special edition: "Fulfilling India's Promise."

14 India's NASSCOM, the National Association of Software and Service Companies.

15 In Tamil Nadu and Karnataka, in the South, for instance, coffee is the favorite, not tea.

16 P. V. Kannan, interview, July 24, 2006.

17 R. N. Koushik, Infosys associate vice president, interview in Bangalore, Oct. 24, 2006.

18 "It Takes Guts to Send Your Groom Packing," *Times of India*, May 13, 2003.

19 India's NASSCOM.

20 Visit to Idulbera, near Jamshedpur, India, Oct. 21, 2004.

21 The immunization rate varies, according to UNICEF. In 2005, some 75 percent of all year-old children had had tuberculosis vaccinations; 81 percent, DPT1 for diphtheria, pertussis, and tetanus; 59 percent, DPT3; 58 percent, polio vaccinations; and 58 percent, measles vaccinations; see http://www.unicef.org/infobycountry/india_statistics.html#24.

22 Tour of Dharavi on July 24, 2005, with Celine D'Cruz, associate director and founding member of SPARC, the Society for Promotion of Area Resource Centers, a Mumbai nonprofit that advocates for secure housing and infrastructure for the urban poor. Estimates of Dharavi's population vary: a 1991 survey by the National Slum Dwellers Federation found 85,000 structures and 120,000 families, with an average of three children, giving Dharavi a population of 600,000. Others estimate its population at 1 million, but there are few reliable population surveys.

23 An astonishing two million people in Bombay lack access to latrines, according to Suketu Mehta, *Maximum City: Bombay Lost and Found* (New York: Vintage Books, 2004), p. 53.

24 Saritha Rai, "India, Looking Up," *International Herald Tribune*, May 28, 2005.

25 Bibek Debroy, secretary general of PHD Chamber of Commerce & Industry, "China vs. India: Myths and Realities," J. P. Morgan's Hands-On China series, June 2006.

26 United Nations Population Fund, "Silent Spring" report, Oct. 11, 2005. The natural birthrate averages 950 girls for every 1,000 boys.

27 India's National Crime Records Bureau recorded 6,787 dowry murders in 2005, but unofficial estimates say the total is closer to 25,000 deaths a year; see http://ncrb.nic.in/crime2005/cii-2005/CHAP5.pdf.

28 Naila Kabeer, "Social Exclusion and the MDGs: The Challenge of Durable Inequalities in the Asian Context," Institute of Development Studies, Univ. of Sussex, Brighton, March 2006, www.asia2015conference.org.

29 Mehta, *Maximum City*, p. 133.

30 Marlise Simons, "In a Belgian City, a Diamond Twilight," *International Her-*

ald Tribune, Jan. 2, 2006, and Amy Waldman, "A New Urban Lifestyle Lures India's Rural Poor," *New York Times*, Dec. 8, 2005.

31 Yuwa Hedrick-Wong, "The Corporate Superpower of the 21st Century: China versus India or China and India?" *Insights*, June 2006. The author is economic adviser of MasterCard Worldwide.

32 Oxfam report, Dec. 2002, http://www.oxfam.org.uk/what_we_do/issues/trade/downloads/bp34_cap.pdf.

33 Ratan Tata, interview, Aug. 6, 2006, and information from Tata Chemicals, whose Tata Kisan Sansars operate in the states of Uttar Pradesh, Haryana, and Punjab.

34 Amelia Gentleman, "Destitute and Dying on India's Farms," *International Herald Tribune*, April 19, 2006.

35 Ron Moreau and Sudip Mazumdar, "Bigger, Faster, Better," *Newsweek International*, July 17, 2006.

36 United Nations Population Division, medium variant.

37 William T. Wilson, "The Dawn of the Indian Century," 2005 report. Dr. Wilson is managing director and chief economist of Keystone-India.

38 Sanjay Mathur, "The Base of the Indian Pyramid," March 2, 2006. Mr. Mathur is senior economist for South/Southeast Asia, UBS.

39 Wilson, "Dawn of the Indian Century."

40 Mathur, "Base of the Indian Pyramid."

41 Wilson, "Dawn of the Indian Century."

42 Kelkar, "India's Economic Future."

43 Nandan Nilekani, interview in Bangalore, Dec. 12, 2003.

44 Bharadwaj et al., "Winning the Indian Consumer."

45 Mehta, *Maximum City*.

CHAPTER 7: REVOLUTION BY DINNER PARTY

1 Visit to Kodak factory, Shanghai, Sept. 24, 2004.

2 Diana Farrell, Ulrich A. Gersch, and Elizabeth Stephenson, "The Value of China's Emerging Middle Class," *McKinsey Quarterly*, 2006 special edition: "Serving the New Chinese Consumer."

3 Miles Mao, interview in Shanghai, Sept. 24, 2004.

4 Jonathan R. Woetzel, "Checking China's Vital Signs: The Social Challenge," *McKinsey Quarterly*, 2006 special edition: "Serving the New Chinese Consumer."

5 There are many measures of savings rates. This is the percentage of a household's disposable income that is saved. From Andy Xie, Morgan Stanley managing director, interview, Aug. 7, 2006.

6 See note 24 to chapter 3 on p. 224.

7 Ying Yeh, interview in Hong Kong, Sept. 18, 2004.

8 Farrell et al., "Value of China's Emerging Middle Class."

9 Doctoroff is also the author of *Billions: Selling to the New Chinese Consumer* (New York: Palgrave/Macmillan, 2004).

10   Christina Hudson, marketing director, Greater China, DTC Asia Pacific Ltd.,
      interviews in Hong Kong, Feb. 14, 2005 and Nov. 11, 2004.

11   J. Walter Thompson advertising agency, Shanghai, Aug. 11, 2006.

12   Hung Huang, interview at her home in Beijing, Nov. 9, 2004.

13   Claire Jackson, interview in Shanghai, Sept. 2, 2004.

14   "Me! Me! Me!" *CLSA Asia-Pacific Markets,* summer 2005.

15   Shanghai, Oct. 15, 2005. No doubt there has been far more construction in the
      area since then.

16   Li Zhensheng, *Red-Color News Soldier: A Chinese Photographer's Odyssey
      through the Cultural Revolution* (London: Phaidon Press, 2003).

17   William T. Wilson, "The Dawn of the India Century," 2005 report.

18   Woetzel, "Checking China's Vital Signs."

19   See http://www.chinadaily.com.cn/china/2007-01/25/content_792311.htm.

20   Jonathan Anderson, "What's All This Labor Shortage Talk?," Sept. 12, 2004.
      Mr. Anderson is a chief Asian economist for UBS in Hong Kong.

21   Kenichi Ohmae, speech in Hong Kong to the Asia Society, Aug. 29, 2003.

22   Visit to Shanghai Pudong Software Park and Codex's office there, Sept. 15, 2003.

23   Philip Snow, *The Fall of Hong Kong: Britain, China, and the Japanese Occupa-
      tion* (New Haven: Yale Univ. Press, 2003), p. 317.

24   China's value-added tax is 17 percent. Consumption taxes vary by product: golf
      clubs and yachts carry a 10 percent tax; sport utility vehicles and luxury
      watches are taxed at 20 percent.

25   Robbie Yang, interview in HP's Beijing office, Nov. 28, 2003. Lenovo completed
      the IBM deal in May 2005.

26   China's annual GDP growth averaged 9.37 percent since 1978, according to
      Carsten A. Holz, associate professor, Hong Kong Univ. of Science and Technol-
      ogy, in "China's Economic Growth, 1978–2025: What We Know Today about
      China's Economic Growth Tomorrow," July 3, 2005.

27   Xinhua news agency, Feb. 14, 2007.

28   http://www.chinaaidsorphans.org, Aug. 2006 interview.

29   It is 30,000, according to "Information Development and Information Control
      in the PRC," Nov. 22, 2005, http://www.usembassy.it/pdf/other/RL33167.pdf.
      It is 40,000, according to the Carnegie Endowment's Globalization101.org, a
      student's guide to globalization, http://www.globalization101.org/index
      .php?file=news1&id=8.

30   See Amnesty International, http://thereport.amnesty.org/eng/Regions/Asia
      -Pacific/China.

31   "Asia's Billion Boomers," *CLSA Asia-Pacific Markets,* Sept. 2005.

32   Woetzel, "Checking China's Vital Signs."

33   John Pomfret, speech at the Asia Society in Hong Kong, Oct. 13, 2006. Mr.
      Pomfret, a *Washington Post* reporter, is the author of *Chinese Lessons: Five
      Classmates and the Story of the New China* (New York: Henry Holt, 2006).

34   Woetzel, "Checking China's Vital Signs."

35   Amartya Sen, "Wrongs and Rights in Development," *Prospect* magazine, Oct. 1995.

36   Gross national savings rate figures include government savings, which are par-

ticularly high in China. "India and China: New Tigers of Asia, Part II," Morgan
Stanley, June 2006, p. 16.

37 Interviews with Beijing Food Safety Office Aug. 3, 2006, and various articles in
China Daily.

CHAPTER 8: GEOPOLITICS MIXED WITH OIL AND WATER

1 Visit to the Metropolitan Museum of Art's Varengeville Room, and interview
with Danielle O. Kisluk-Grosheide, curator, European sculpture and decorative
arts, Metropolitan Museum of Art, N.Y., Oct. 28. 2005. Ivory-inlaid furniture
and decorative arts from Vizagapatam, India, were also widely imitated in
Europe after being brought from India. See also Jeffrey Munger and Alice
Cooney Frelinghuysen, "East and West: Chinese Export Porcelain,"
http://www.metmuseum.org/toah/hd/ewpor/hd_ewpor.htm.

2 Angus Maddison is professor emeritus at the Univ. of Groningen, in the
Netherlands, and an honorary fellow of Selwyn College at Cambridge Univ.
His historical GDP figures are given in 1990 international dollars adjusted with
Geary-Khamis purchasing power parity converters. For more information,
see his website: http://www.ggdc.net/Maddison/content.shtml. For figures on
China's fast-growing economy, see http://www.ggdc.net/Maddison/articles/
China_Maddison_Wu_22_Feb_07.pdf.

3 Angus Maddison, report to the House of Lords, Feb. 20, 2005. The calculations
used 1990 international U.S. dollars. See http://www.ggdc.net/Maddison/arti-
cles/world_development_and_outlook_1820-1930_evidence_submitted_to_the
%20house_of_lords.pdf. Of course, the U.S. will remain far richer per person for
many decades to come because of India's and China's far larger populations.

4 U.S. Geological Survey, Mineral Commodity Summaries, Jan. 2006; Testimony
of Marion Loomis of the Wyoming Mining Association before the Senate Sub-
committee on Public Lands and Forest, July 14, 2004; Sierra Club; Jeff Gearino,
"Royalty Break Clears Congress," *Casper Star-Tribune*, Sept. 30, 2006; Sublette
County Wyoming, http://sublette-se.org/; and Dennis S. Kostick, senior mineral commodity specialist, Soda Ash, Salt and Sodium Sulfate, U.S. Geological
Survey, interview, Oct. 16, 2006.

5 Commodity prices have more than doubled in real terms on the average in the
past seven years, and estimates suggest that between 1998 and 2003 almost all
of the increase in worldwide demand for copper, nickel, and steel and three-
quarters of the higher demand for aluminum were attributable to China,
according to the IMF.

6 Data for 2006 are from U.S. Department of Energy, Energy Information Administration, www.eia.doe.gov.

7 U.S. sales of passenger cars, pickups, minivans, and sport utility vehicles were
16.1 million in 2007; Chinese sales of passenger vehicles rose 21 percent, to
5.2 million vehicles, according to J.D. Power and Associates. In China, an
additional 3.3 million commercial vehicles, trucks, and buses were sold. In
Japan, auto sales fell to 2.95 million. Car sales in India reached 1.5 million in

2007, according to the Society of Indian Automobile Manufacturers, up from the 675,000 sold in the fiscal year ending March 2002.

8   Other notable reasons are increasing demand from the U.S., ongoing political instability and military skirmishes in the Middle East, temporary disruption of oil pipeline flows as a result of weather and other factors, and, in general, demand that is growing faster than new production sources are brought online, according to the U.S. Department of Energy's Energy Information Administration.

9   Ivo Bozon, Subbu Narayanswamy, and Jonathan R. Woetzel, "Meeting China's Energy Needs through Liberalization," *McKinsey Quarterly*, 2006 special edition: "Serving the New Chinese Consumer."

10 The editorial "The Latest Darfur Outrage," *Asian Wall Street Journal*, Sept 6, 2006, notes that China and Russia abstained on an Aug. 31, 2006, UN Security Council vote to send 20,000 troops to attempt to quell the violence in Darfur, giving Sudan the opportunity to reject the presence of the UN contingent.

11 Nicholas D. Kristof, "China and Sudan, Blood and Oil," *New York Times*, April 24, 2006.

12 Miguel Poklepovic, Chilean consul general in Hong Kong, speech at the Foreign Correspondents' Club, Hong Kong, July 6, 2006, and subsequent interview, Oct. 16, 2006.

13 Irwin Abrams, ed., *The Nobel Prize Annual 1991* (New York: IMG, 1992). Suu Kyi's biography is reprinted on Nobelprize.org.

14 Jill McGivering, "India Signs Burma Gas Agreement," BBC News, March 9, 2006.

15 David E. Sanger, "A Safer World?: Bush Gambles in a Bid to Rewrite Atomic Rules," *International Herald Tribune*, March 6, 2006.

16 "Mission of Peace," in Fang Zhenghui, ed., *Stories of China's Reform and Opening-Up* (Shenzhen: Story of China Publishing, Aug. 2004).

17 There were 4.238 million Chinese troops when Deng announced his plan in 1985. The number dropped to 3.235 million by 1987, according to China Military Online, sponsored by the Chinese People's Liberation Army, http://english.chinamil.com.cn/.

18 Roger Cliff, "Advances Underway in China's Defense Industries," testimony presented to the U.S.-China Economic and Security Review Commission on March 16, 2006. Mr. Cliff, of the RAND Corp., Santa Monica, Calif., testified that China buys much of its modern weapons from Russia and gets significant technical assistance from both Russia and Israel.

19 Estimates of Chinese military spending vary widely. China announced that its 2007 defense budget was $45 billion, see http://www.globalsecurity.org/military/world/china/budget.htm. Globalsecurity.org estimates China's 2004 military expenditures at $65 billion and the U.S.'s at $466 billion. Michael Swaine, senior associate at the Carnegie Endowment for International Peace, estimates that China spends $45 billion–$70 billion annually.

20 Quadrennial Defense Review Report, Feb. 6, 2006.

21 "China's Peaceful Development," a speech by Xie Xiaoyan, deputy commissioner of China's Ministry of Foreign Affairs in Hong Kong, given at the Foreign Correspondents' Club, Hong Kong, Sept. 28, 2006.

22 George Friedman, "U.S. Perceptions of a Chinese Threat," *Stratfor Geopolitical Intelligence Report*, May 31, 2006.

23 Cliff, "Advances Underway in China's Defense Industries."

24 "CVX-US Navy Carriers for the 21st Century," *Popular Mechanics*, Oct. 1998.

25 Workshop held on May 15, 2006, by the Hong Kong Univ. of Science and Technology's Center on China's Transnational Relations in Hong Kong under Chatham House rules.

26 The United States spends 90 percent of what the entire world spends on military space programs, according to Joan Johnson-Freese and Andrew S. Erickson of the U.S. Naval War College. In 2006, China proved it could temporarily disable communications satellites by harmlessly illuminating an American reconnaissance satellite with a laser, according to *Aviation Week*.

27 "Win-Win Approach for China's Peaceful Rise," speech by Singapore Minister Mentor Lee Kuan Yew at China's Boao Forum, April 23, 2005.

28 Willy Wo-Lap Lam, *Chinese Politics in the Hu Jintao Era: New Leaders, New Challenges* (Armonk, N.Y.: M. E. Sharpe, 2006).

29 Ibid.

30 On troop strength and budget, see globalsecurity.org. On military acquisition plans, see Renae Merle, "India's Defense Buildup Attracts U.S. Contractors," *Washington Post*, Sept. 1, 2006.

31 Lam, *Chinese Politics in the Hu Jintao Era*, pp. 169 and 187.

32 The top twenty most polluted cities, on the basis of the amount of particulates, according to 2004 data collected by the World Bank, are Cairo, Delhi, Calcutta, Tianjin, Chongqing, Lucknow, Kanpur, Jakarta, Shenyang, Zhengzhou, Jinan, Lanzhou, Beijing, Taiyuan, Chengdu, Ahmadabad, Anshan, Wuhan, Bangkok, and Nanchang. China has twelve cities on the top twenty, while India has five. See http://siteresources.worldbank.org/DATASTATISTICS/Resources/table3_13.pdf.

33 Worldwatch Institute.

34 Bloomberg, "Capital Endures a Terrible Month for Air Pollution," *South China Morning Post*, Feb. 15, 2006.

35 Zijun Li, "Filthy Air Choking China's Growth, Olympic Goals," Worldwatch Institute, Feb. 14, 2006.

36 Jonathan R. Woetzel, "Checking China's Vital Signs: The Social Challenge," *McKinsey Quarterly*, 2006 special edition: "Serving the New Chinese Consumer."

37 U.S. Department of Energy, Energy Information Administration, http://www.eia.doe.gov/pub/international/iealf/tablee1.xls and http://www.eia.doe.gov/pub/international/iealf/tableh1co2.xls. Of course, both India and China use far less energy on a per capita basis than do the U.S., Europe, or Japan.

38 Pacific Research Institute, "Special Report: China's Litany," Environmetal Index 2006, San Francisco.

39 Shai Oster and Mei Fong, "Village's Battle against Pollution Shows China's Enduring Struggle," *Wall Street Journal Asia*, July 19, 2006.

40 Xinhua report of May 30, 2006, quoted in *Wall Street Journal Asia*, June 1, 2006.

41   Kenneth Lieberthal, interview in Ann Arbor, Mich., Jan. 21, 2006.

42   Le-Min Liu (Bloomberg), "A Chinese Time Bomb Is Dripping," *International Herald Tribune*, Feb. 24, 2006.

43   World Bank's World Development Indicators, ranked by micrograms per cubic meter of particulates, 2002, http://devdata.worldbank.org/wdi2006/contents /Section3.htm. Unfortunately, Delhi's air quality has since worsened, and by 2004 it was back to the world's second-worst pollution levels.

44   Global Wind Energy Council, "Record Year for Wind Energy: Global Wind Power Market Increased by 40.5 percent in 2005," Feb. 17, 2006.

45   "Stronger Future for Nuclear Power," *Physics Today*, Feb. 2006, p. 19.

46   Sasol Ltd., a partially state-owned company in South Africa, is the pioneer in this technology. Patrick Barta, "South Africa turns coal into oil, and China looks to tap expertise," *Wall Street Journal Asia*, Aug. 17, 2006.

47   Kenneth G. Lieberthal, speech at the Asia Society, Hong Kong, May 29, 2006. Prof. Lieberthal is director for China at the Univ. of Michigan Business School's William Davidson Institute and from 1998 to 2000 worked at the White House as special assistant to the president for national security affairs and senior director for Asia at the National Security Council.

48   Terence Chea, "China's Growing Air Pollution Reaches American Skies," Associated Press, July 29, 2006.

49   Athar Hussain, Robert Cassen, and Tim Dyson, "Demographic Transition in Asia and Its Consequences," March 2006. Hussain is director, Asia Research Centre, London School of Economics; Cassen represents the Social Policy Department, Centre for Analysis of Social Exclusion, Suntory and Toyota International Centres for Economics and Related Disciplines, LSE; Dyson comes from the Development Studies Institute and Social Policy Department, LSE. See www.asia2015conference.org.

50   Zhang spoke on Oct. 24, 2005, at a Beijing conference on air quality. His speech was quoted in Andrew Batson, "China Warns Pollution Will Grow with Economy," *Wall Street Journal Asia*, Oct. 25, 2005.

51   Kenneth G. Lieberthal, interview in Ann Arbor, Mich., Jan. 21, 2006.

52   Russian Federation President Vladimir Putin forcefully accused the United States of these moves in a Feb. 10, 2007, speech in Munich, but many of America's friends have worried about the same development.

CHAPTER 9: A CATALYST FOR COMPETITIVENESS

1   Robert Rubin, director and chairman of the executive committee, Citigroup Inc., interview in his Citigroup office in Manhattan, Jan. 5, 2006. Mr. Rubin was treasury secretary under President Clinton from Jan. 1995 until July 1999.

2   John Chen, CEO of Sybase Inc., various interviews: in Hong Kong, Sept. 13, 2006; in Singapore, Sept. 3, 2006; and in Hong Kong, Sept. 19, 2003.

3   Steffie Woolhandler, Terry Campbell, and David U. Himmelstein, "Cost of Health Care Administration in the United States and Canada," *New England Journal of Medicine*, Aug. 21, 2003.

4   Tyco International's CEO L. Dennis Kozlowski, was sentenced in Sept. 2005 to up to twenty-five years in prison for looting the company he led. He was paid $267 million from 1999 to 2001, but the company paid for a $6,000 gold-threaded shower curtain, not to mention an $18 million Manhattan apartment.

5   Steven Greenhouse and David Leonhardt, "The Future Looks Leaner as U.S. Wages Stagnate," *International Herald Tribune*, Aug. 29, 2006. Until 2005, stagnating wages were partially offset by rising spending on benefits like health insurance. From 2000 to 2005, worker productivity rose 16.6 percent while total compensation rose 7.2 percent.

6   C. Fred Bergsten, Bates Gill, Nicholas R. Lardy, and Derek Mitchell, *China: The Balance Sheet* (New York: Public Affairs, 2006), p. 77.

7   For the U.S., Euro-zone, Japan, the U.K., and Canada combined, the real compensation share of national income has been falling since 2002—the very years of the strongest period of global growth in thirty-five years, as Stephen Roach, chief economist of Morgan Stanley, points out in "Global Growth Paradox," his Sept. 5, 2006, report. In the U.S., labor productivity grew 3.3 percent a year between 2002 and 2005, but real hourly compensation grew just 1.4 percent, Mr. Roach points out in the report.

8   U.S. Department of Commerce, Bureau of Economic Analysis, http://www.bea.gov.

9   Jean-Pierre Lehmann, interviews, Jan. 16 and Feb. 22, 2006.

10 Peter Orszag and Michael Deich, "Growth, Opportunity and Prosperity in a Globalizing Economy," Hamilton Project, Brookings Institution, July 2006.

11 http://www.hamiltonproject.org.

12 http://www.compete.org/.

13 OECD, 2003 Programme for International Student Assessment, "PISA 2003 Technical Report."

14 National Center for Education Statistics, 2003 data from the Trends in International Mathematics and Science Study (TIMSS).

15 Craig R. Barrett, testimony before the Senate Commerce Committee, March 15, 2006.

16 National Center for Public Policy and Higher Education, http://measuringup .highereducation.org/nationalpicture/snapshot.cfm?cmbCategory=GradeAff&c mbYear=2006.

17 National Center for Public Policy and Higher Education, "Income of U.S. Workforce Projected to Decline If Education Doesn't Improve," Nov. 2005 report.

18 William J. McDonough, vice chairman of Merrill Lynch and former president of the New York Federal Reserve Bank, pointed out in a speech in Hong Kong on March 7, 2006, that the U.S. current account deficit had reached 6.5 percent of GDP, and he was alarmed when it was 3 percent. "For every dollar we spend, almost 7 cents has to be loaned to us by some foreigner somewhere," McDonough explained. "In the world economy, we have become the consumer of last resort."

19 Sheelan Chawathe, interview, Dec. 11, 2003, at Wipro's Spectramind subsidiary, Bombay.

20 Robert Rubin, speech to the Hong Kong General Chamber of Commerce, in Hong Kong, Dec. 7, 2005.

21   Joseph Stiglitz, *Making Globalization Work* (New York: Norton, 2006).

22   National Science Foundation, Science and Engineering Indicators 2000, data from 1985–2000.

23   National Science Foundation, Science and Engineering Indicators 2000 CD-Rom, 1987–2000 data.

24   Council on Competitiveness, "Innovate America," 2005, http://www .compete.org.

25   Lael Brainard, Robert E. Litan, and Nicholas Warren, "Insuring America's Workers in the New Era of Offshoring," Brookings Institution Policy Brief No. 143, July 2005.

26   Denmark's "flexicurity" model, while expensive for taxpayers, seems to have worked well. See: http://www.oecdobserver.org/news/fullstory.php/aid/1402/ Mobile,_yet_secure.html.

27   Michael Mandel, with Joseph Weber, "What's Really Propping Up the Economy," *BusinessWeek*, Sept. 25, 2006.

28   Nandan Nilekani, interview, Dec. 9, 2003.

INDEX

Page numbers beginning with 219 refer to endnotes.

abortion, 32, 129, 153
Accenture, 81
acid rain, 179
adivasis (tribal groups), 129
Advanced Micro Devices, 105
AETNA, 120
Afghanistan, 204
Africa, 60, 104
    China's foreign policy in, 165,
        166, 174, 175
Agricultural Bank of China, 69
AIDS, 151–52
Airbus, 120
Air Deccan, 55–56
Air India, 43
airline industry, 40, 43, 55–56
air pollution, 31, 94, 179–80, 183
Allianz Cornhill Insurance, 120
aluminum, 162–63
Amazon.com, 120
Ambani, Mukesh, 131–32, 136
America Online, 84
Amnesty International, 152
Andhra Pradesh, 51–52, 84
Angola, 166
Anhui Province, China, 16–17, 19

Apollo (hospital chain), 94
Apple computer, 102, 120
Argentina, 166
Armani, 70
Asian Airlines, 98
Asian Development Bank, 128,
    185
assembly line, 99–100, 101, 102,
    105, 108
AT&T, 51
A. T. Kearney, 65
Audi, 70
Aung San Suu Kyi, 167
Australia, 104, 170
auto parts industry, 16, 91, 100,
    102–3, 130
Avon, 141

Bajaj company, 44
Bangalore, India, 46, 49, 81, 92, 93,
    94, 108, 117–18, 119, 121
    airport of, 53–54
    Ejipura slum of, 128
    Infosys headquarters in, 119–20
Bangladesh, 104, 107
banking industry, 40, 68–69, 151

Bank of America, 120
Barrett, Craig R., 77, 96, 206, 208, 212
Beijing, China, 30, 51, 147, 179, 182
    pollution in, 179–80
Beijing National Stadium, 157
Beijing University, 33
Belgium, 130
B. F. Goodrich, 36, 73
Bhargava, Akshaya, 120–21
Bhaskaran, Manu, 175, 185
biofuels, 181
biotechnology industry, 54, 209
    offshoring practice and, 88–89
bird flu, 108, 152
Blair, Tony, 49, 222
Blinder, Alan, 83, 85, 211–12
BMW, 70
Boeing, 120
Bombay, India, 88, 135
    Dharavi slum of, 126–28
    pollution in, 180
    train bombings of 2006 in, 177
Bombay stock market, 40
bo pu zu (intellectuals), 142
Boston Consulting Group, 101
"bottom of the pyramid," 93–94
Brazil, 114, 166–67
British East India Company, 42
British Steel, 57, 223
British Telecom, 84
Brookings Institution, 203, 210
Buffett, Warren, 51
"bureaucratic" capitalism, 31
Bureau of Economic Analysis, 66
Burma (Myanmar), 165, 167–68, 172
Bush, George W., 168, 176
"buy America" movement, 201

California, 184
Cambodia, 104

Canada, 64, 102
capitalism, 21, 31, 71, 95, 164, 168, 185, 202
    "bureaucratic," 31
    in China's economic transformation, 23, 24–27
    "democratic," 155
    "state," 31
Capitalist Roaders, 144–45
caste system, 129
cell phones, 61, 182
Center for Economic Studies, 83
Center on China's Transnational Relations, 22
Central Bank (China), 69
Central Bank (India), 40
Central Military Commission, Chinese, 169
Chan, Edwin, 23–24
Chang, David, 63
Chawathe, Sheelan, 207
Chen, John, 188–90, 204, 206
Chennai, India, 93
Chernobyl disaster of 1986, 184
Chidambaram, P., 39–40, 52
Chile, 166
China, People's Republic of, 9, 42, 83, 85, 95, 108, 132, 138–58
    Africa policy of, 165, 166, 174, 175
    agrarian reforms in, 16–17, 21–22
    authoritarian political system of, 31–32, 55, 145, 150–51, 154, 156–57
    ballistic missile developed by, 172
    banking system of, 68–69, 151, 224
    bureaucracy in, 150–51
    car sales in, 163, 231
    cell phone use in, 61

cheap labor in, 59–61, 74–75,
    104
Clinton's 1998 visit to, 174
collectivized farming in, 18–20
Communist Party and foreign
    businesses in, 61, 113–14
constitution of, 152–53
as consumer market, 142–44
corruption in, 69–70, 150–51,
    182, 185
currency controversy and,
    174–75, 195–96, 201
democracy in, 23, 24–27, 155,
    167
demographic time bomb and,
    153–54, 185–86
disassembly line and, see disas-
    sembly line
disposable income in,
    141–42
education system of, 72–73,
    219
effect of U.S. trade with,
    191–95
environmental issues and, 151,
    182–85
exports of, 220
famine in, 18–19, 33
fear of, 67, 190
five-year plans of, 27, 34, 61
food imports of, 166–67
foreign company employment
    in, 59–61, 63–65, 72–75,
    148–49
foreign currency reserves of,
    194
foreign investment in, 10, 12,
    30–31, 59–62, 64–68, 70,
    74–75, 92, 95, 219
foreign policy of, 164–68, 174
free speech in, 152
future superpower status of, 11
GDP of, 65, 68, 71, 145, 151

global economy and, 67–68
globalization and, 11, 12–14, 59
global power ambition of, 176
gold-collar workers of,
    141–42
government abuses in,
    151–53
"Go-West" system of, 34
growing energy needs of,
    162–64
health care in, 62–63
historic global economic role
    of, 159–60, 186
Hong Kong returned to, 49–50
hospital modernization in,
    62–63
housing development in, 29–30
India and rise of, 49–52
India contrasted with, 10–11
India's synergy with, 94–95
industrial revolution of, 176–77
industries of, see specific
    industries
infrastructure of, 27–30, 31,
    33–34, 51, 61, 68, 103, 106,
    175
intellectual property protection
    and, 63
Internet and, 208
Japanese occupation of, 177
job creation in, 72
large-scale projects in, 151
literacy rate of, 155–56
local disruptions in, 196–202
luxury-goods market and,
    70–71
marriage traditions of, 143
mass production in, 91
media in, 33, 152
middle class of, 58–59,
    141–43
migrant workers in, 73–74
migration to cities in, 146

China, People's Republic of
  (*continued*)
  military modernization of, 160,
    168–74, 176
  military spending in, 171, 232
  modernization of, 15–16,
    138–39
  multigarchs of, 185
  nationalism of, 149–50, 157,
    178, 199
  national language of, 11, 151
  natural resources and, 160,
    164–66
  nuclear power in, 28, 172, 184
  oil use in, 163–64
  Olympics of 2008 and,
    157–58
  one-child policy of, 32, 153
  political instability as fear in,
    151, 154
  pollution in, 31, 33, 178–81
  population of, 18, 133, 154
  potential workforce of,
    72–73
  poverty in, 146–47
  prosperity of, 70, 139–40,
    144–45
  rich-poor gap in, 71, 150
  rural poverty in, 146–47
  rural-urban conflict in, 33–34
  savings rate of, 140–41, 156,
    222
  Singapore model and, 22–23,
    25, 27, 29, 51, 155
  social unrest in, 26–27
  space race and, 173, 233
  special economic zones of,
    23–24, 27, 30, 55, 59
  state-owned enterprises in, 31,
    71–72, 151
  stratification of incomes in,
    141–42
  Taiwan dispute and, 149, 177–78

  taxes in, 230
  threatening problems of,
    150–51
  Tibet repression of, 175
  in tripolar world, 186–87
  U.S. companies in, 65–66
  U.S. protectionism and, 200–3
  U.S. trade dependency and,
    198–200
  Vajpayee's delegation to, 9–10,
    11, 16, 52
  wages and income in, 10, 24,
    31–32, 33, 60, 66–67, 71,
    72, 74, 115, 140–42, 146,
    196
  water quality of, 180–81
  West's trade deficits with,
    67–68
  working-age population of, 154,
    185
  Xiaogang peasants' pact and,
    16–17, 21
"China" (porcelain), 159
China Banking Regulatory Com-
  mission, 224
China Economic Quarterly, 156
China Institute of Industrial
  Relations, 74
China Interactive Media Group,
  138
China Mobile, 71
"China price," 192
China Telecom, 71
*Chinese Politics in the Hu Jintao
  Era* (Lam), 174
Chongqing, China, 178–79
Chrysler, 89
Cisco Systems, 77, 117, 120, 225
Citibank, 69, 148
Cliff, Roger, 170, 172
Clinton, Bill, 174
coal, 161–62, 179, 184
Coca-Cola, 48

Codex, 148

Cold War, 13, 25, 151, 160, 164, 165, 173, 185, 186

Commerce Department, U.S., 66, 207
  India business development mission of, 78

Commerce Ministry, Indian, 55, 135

Committee to Protect Journalists, 152

communism, 24, 31, 71, 164, 168, 186
  agrarian reforms of, 16–17
  banking system and, 68–69
  Eastern Europe collapse of, 25–26
  in India, 41
  Mao's version of, 18–19, 71
  market economy and, 138–39

Communist Party, Chinese, 11, 18, 20, 25, 26–27, 29, 31, 96, 145, 150, 154, 155, 157, 188, 200
  foreign investment companies and, 64–65

Congress Party, India, 38, 42–43, 49, 52, 134, 135

consumer electronics industry, 60

copper, 166

Corus, 57, 223

Council on Competitiveness, 203, 209, 210

Courtney, Marcus, 86

Crate & Barrel, 131

Cultural Revolution, 11, 19–20, 35, 72, 138, 143, 144–45, 147

Dalian, China, 147

dalits (untouchable caste), 129

Dana Corporation, 105

dan shen qui zu (single aristocrats), 142

Darfur genocide, 166

Das, Gurcharan, 56

De Beers Group, 143

Defense Department, U.S., 208

de Haan, Pieter, 58

Delhi, India, 183

Delhi School of Economics, 50

Dell Computer, 101, 105

Deloitte Touche Tohmatsu, 101

Delta Air Lines, 207

democracy, 26, 167, 177–78
  in China, 23, 24–27, 155, 167
  in India, 43–44, 49, 76, 134, 156

Democrats, U.S., 203

"demographic dividend," 132–33

Deng Xiaoping, 20, 39, 55, 157, 169
  agrarian reforms of, 21–22
  demilitarization policy of, 169–70
  industrial reforms of, 22–25
  Singapore visit of, 22–23
  Tiananmen Square uprising and, 26

Deutsche Bank, 84

Dharavi (Bombay slum), 126–28, 228

DHL International, 120

diamond industry, 130

disassembly line, 97–116
  cheap labor and, 101
  China and, 103–4
  developing countries and, 106–7
  example of, 100–101, 111–16
  globalization and, 101–2, 107–8, 111, 112
  global trade and, 106–7
  infrastructure and, 106
  job migration and, 104
  Li & Fung and, 108–11
  lowered costs and, 102–3

disassembly line (*continued*)
   new product creation and, 102
   services adapted to, 105–6
   specialization and, 101–2
   subassemblies and, 99
   supply chains and, 99–100, 103,
      111, 201
   trans-border shipments and,
      97–98, 107–8
   transportation and, 104–5
Doctoroff, Tom, 142–44
dollar, U.S., 40, 46, 194, 199, 207
Domino's, 123
Dongguan, China, 23, 114
dowry murders, 130, 228
Dutch East India Company, 59,
   159

Eastern Europe, 83
Edison, Thomas, 63
EDS, 78, 81, 82, 84
Eileen Fisher company, 98, 111,
   114–15
Ejipura (slum), 128
environment, 151, 160, 182–85,
   211
   see also pollution
Environmental Protection
   Agency, U.S., 184
Equatorial Guinea, 166
Ericsson, 64
Ernst & Young, 68, 70, 224
Europe, 12, 59, 95, 104, 110, 131,
   159, 164, 182, 193, 198, 208
   rise of India and China and,
      190–91
European Union, 67, 131
Everbright Knitting Factory,
   114–15

Falun Gong, 151
farm center network (Kisan
   Sansar), 131–32

Farrell, Diana, 85
Federal Reserve Board, 83
FedEx, 97
Fengyang County, 16–17, 35
Ferrari, 144
Finance Ministry, Indian, 135
Food and Drug Administration,
   U.S., 88
Footlocker, 98
Forbes, 49
Ford, Henry, 96, 99, 101, 102–3,
   106, 111
Ford Motor Company, 87, 102
Foreign Affairs Ministry, Chi-
   nese, 171
France, 46, 98, 111, 116, 175
France Telecom, 83
Fujian Province, 23
Fung, Victor, 109–11
Fung, William, 109–11
Fung family, 109–10
Fung Pak-liu, 109

Gandhi, Feroze, 44
Gandhi, Indira, 44–45
Gandhi, Mohandas K. (Mahatma),
   11, 12, 41–43, 46, 91, 94,
   125, 135, 167
   legacy of, 41–42, 49
Gandhi, Rajiv, 38–40, 52
   economic reforms of, 45–46
Gandhi, Sonia, 38, 52, 135
Gap, 120, 131
Gates, Bill, 46, 49, 222
General Electric (GE), 50, 54, 81,
   82, 84, 96, 148, 184
General Motors, 87, 104, 130
Germany, 67, 79, 112, 163,
   186
Gittings, John, 31
globalization, 11, 12–14, 52, 59,
   186, 201, 211
   China and, 11, 12–14, 59

corporate and consumer effects of, 191–95
disassembly lines and, 101–2, 107–8, 111, 112
India and, 11, 12–14, 52
global warming, 184–85
Gobi Desert, 179–80
Godrej & Boyce, 50
gold-collar workers, 141–42
Goldman, Sachs, 84
Google, 152
Gorbachev, Mikhail, 23, 25
Gordy, Berry, Jr., 106
"Go West" campaign, 34
Great Britain, 12, 19, 49, 57, 67, 121, 122
fear of job losses in, 76
GDP of, 145
Hong Kong returned to China by, 49–50
Indian independence and, 39, 41, 42, 177
offshoring practice and, 79
Great Depression, 207
Greater China, 142
Great Leap Forward, 17–18, 20
Great Wall of China, 36
greenhouse gases, 180, 184–85
GreenPoint Mortgage, 120
Green River, Wyoming, 162
Greenspan, Alan, 46
Guangdong Province, 15–16, 23, 28
Guangzhou, China, 109, 114, 147, 182
Guantanamo Bay, 168
Guess Jeans, 115
Gulf War of 1991, 45

Hai gui pai (sea turtles), 73
Hamilton Project, 203
Hangzhou, China, 95
Harvard Business Review, 88

Henan Province, 18–19, 151
Hewlett Packard (HP), 78, 149
Hindus, 129–30, 177
Holden, James P., 89
Honda, 201
Hong Kong, 23, 24, 28, 30, 32–33, 36, 68, 84, 97–98, 105, 107, 109, 110, 113, 115, 148, 172
China's treatment of, 155
returned to China, 49–50
Hong Kong University of Science and Technology, 22
Hout, Thomas, 101
HSBC, 69, 81, 84, 147
Hu Jintao, 166, 167, 174
Hunan Province, 115
Hung Huang, 138, 143
Hurricane Katrina, 127, 208
Hyderabad, India, 51–52, 102, 123
hydropower, 183

IBM, 48, 81, 84, 120, 148, 149
India investment of, 77–78, 79, 82
Idulbera, India, 125–26, 128
India, 9–16, 114, 117–37
agriculture in, 131–32
automobile production in, 226
bureaucratic patronage in, 44, 47, 89
car sales in, 163, 231–32
caste system of, 129
cheap labor in, 102
China and rise of, 49–52
China contrasted with, 10–11
China model and, 54–55
China's synergy with, 94–95
college graduates in, 84
colonialism and, 41–42, 76, 135
computer revolution in, 46–47
controlled stock market of, 48–49

India (*continued*)
  corruption in, 182
  currency devalued by, 39–40
  democracy in, 43–44, 49, 76,
      134, 156
  demographic future of, 132–24,
      154–55, 160
  economic development and
      reforms in, 45–46, 52–57
  economic nationalism of,
      41–42
  education system of, 128, 219
  English language in, 76, 106
  environmental regulation in,
      183–85
  financial crisis of 1991 in,
      38–40, 41, 51, 128
  foreign investment in, 10, 12,
      42, 47–48, 50, 90–93, 225
  freedom movement of, 42–43
  future superpower status of, 11
  GDP of, 37, 83, 134
  globalization and, 11, 12–14, 52
  growing energy needs of,
      162–64
  and historic place in world
      economy, 159–60
  illiteracy in, 90, 128–29, 156
  immunization rates in, 126,
      228
  impediments to economic
      development in, 135–37
  independence of, 39, 41, 42, 43
  industries of, *see specific
      industries*
  jobs program in, 134–35
  leftist parties in, 135
  "license raj" of, 44, 47, 89
  marriage traditions of, 123–24,
      129
  mass production in, 91
  middle class of, 119, 122, 125,
      136

  military modernization of, 160,
      169
  movement of jobs in, 76–77
  natural resources of, 160,
      164–66
  and need for leadership, 136–37
  offshoring and, 77–78
  oil use in, 163–64
  one-party rule in, 43
  Pakistan and, 176–77
  pariah states and, 165–67
  political stability of, 154–55
  pollution in, 179–80
  popular culture of, 122–23
  population of, 42, 132, 133
  postwar economy of, 42–43
  poverty in, 82, 88, 124, 125–28,
      134–35
  professional opportunities in,
      121–22
  prosperity of, 117–22
  religious strife in, 129–30, 177
  rising expectations in, 124–25
  savings rate of, 156, 222
  16th century trade and, 159
  slums of, 82, 126–28
  socialism in, 41–42, 44, 45
  Soviet Union's barter relation-
      ship with, 45
  special economic zones of, 135
  tribal groups in, 129
  in tripolar world, 186–87
  U.S. Commerce Department
      mission to, 78
  U.S. nuclear technology shared
      with, 168, 175–76
  village life in, 125–26
  wages and income in, 60,
      117–22, 136
  Western merchandise in, 123
  women's rights in, 123–24,
      128–29
  worker training in, 82–83

working-age population of, 133
    yuppies of, 120–21
Indian Airlines, 55–56
Indian Institutes of Technology,
    46
India Unbound (Das), 56
Indonesia, 172
Industrial Revolution, 13, 179,
    203
infanticide, 129, 153
inflation, 38, 40, 194, 197
Infosys Technologies, 46–49, 51,
    54, 56, 78, 86, 89, 117–18,
    124, 134, 136, 212, 222
    Bangalore headquarters of,
    119–20
    clients of, 120
    offshoring practice and, 81–83
infrastructure:
    Chinese, 27–30, 31, 33–34, 51,
    61, 68, 103, 106, 175
    Indian, 53, 89–90, 91, 106, 121,
    130–31, 133, 135, 161
    of U.S., 207–8
Inner Mongolia, 184
Institute of Policy Studies, 175,
    185
Intel Corporation, 54, 74, 77, 96,
    148, 206, 208, 212, 225
intellectuals (bo pu zu), 142
interest rates, 194
International Monetary Fund
    (IMF), 39–40, 156
Internet, 32, 54, 79, 80, 81, 101,
    117, 118, 124, 125, 146,
    152, 182, 208, 212
    offshoring and, 77–78
iPod, 102, 212
Iran, 168, 174, 175
    China and, 165–66
Iraq, 169
Iraq War, 164, 204
Iron Rice Bowl, 65

Israel, 211
Italy, 114

Jackson, Claire, 144
Jain, Vishwas, 119
Jamshedpur, India, 125–26
Japan, 12, 29, 70, 83, 95, 98, 104,
    110, 114, 132, 142, 147–49,
    163, 170, 171, 182, 186,
    190, 192, 193, 198, 206,
    208
    car sales in, 163
    China and, 177–78
    GDP of, 145
J. C. Penney, 100
Jeep, 65
Jet Airways, 55–56
Jharkhand State, 161
Jiang Hou Wen, 112–13, 114
Jilin Province, 28
John F. Kennedy Airport, 207
Johnson & Johnson, 36
Johnson Controls, 120
J. P. Morgan, 84
J. P. Morgan Chase Bank, 28
J. Sainsbury, 120
J. Walter Thompson agency, 142
J. W. Marriott, 144

Kadepurkar, Stawan, 117–19,
    122–23
Kalam, A. P. J. Abdul, 167
Kashmir, 130, 177
Kazakhstan, 120, 172, 174
Kelkar, Vijay, 53, 134
Kennedy, John F., 205
Kerry, John, 86, 188
KFC, 64
Kingfisher Airlines, 55–56
Kisan Sansar (farm center net-
    work), 131–32
Kleisterlee, Gerard, 63
Kodak, 139–41, 142, 146

Koizumi, Junichiro, 177
Korea, People's Democratic Republic of (North Korea), 169, 175
Korea, Republic of (South Korea), 29, 95, 98, 104, 168, 208
  GDP of, 145
Koslowski, L. Dennis, 235
Koushik, R. N., 124
Kraft Foods, 120
Krishna, Raj, 50
Kristof, Nicholas D., 166
Kroeber, Arthur, 156
Kyrgyzstan, 174

Labor Ministry, Chinese, 146
Lakme company, 43
Lam, Dennis, 73
Lam, Willy Wo-Lap, 174
Lancôme, 141
Latin America, 166, 175
"learning accounts," 210
Lee Kuan Yew, 22–23, 37, 49, 156, 222
Legend (Lenovo), 149
Lehmann, Jean-Pierre, 198
Lenovo Group (Legend), 149
Levi's, 195
LG company, 50
Li & Fung, 109–10, 195
"license raj," 44
Lieberthal, Kenneth, 31, 181, 184, 185
Limited, The, 115
Lithuania, 205
Li To-ming, 109
little capitalists (xiao zi), 142
Little Red Book, 20
London School of Economics, 185
Louis Vuitton, 70
Lufthansa, 140
Lupin (biotech company), 88

Ma, Tony, 35–36, 73
Macao, 109
McDonald's, 36, 123, 207
McDonough, William J., 235
McKinsey & Co., 66, 76, 84, 122, 136, 202
McKinsey Global Institute, 76, 85
Maddison, Angus, 160
Maersk Sealand, 84, 105
Malaysia, 83, 84
Mall of America, 144
Mao, Miles, 140–41, 142
Mao Zedong, 11, 12, 17, 19–20, 21, 25, 27, 32, 33, 35, 41, 57, 70, 71, 138, 143, 157
  communism of, 18–19, 71
  farm collectivization policy of, 18–20
Marshall Plan, 10
Marxism, 18
medical equipment market, 62
Mehta, Sunil, 87
Mercedes Benz, 70, 120, 144
Merrill Lynch, 141, 224–25
"Messengers of Faith" dolls, 15
Metropolitan Museum (New York), 159
Mexico, 13, 46, 85, 103, 201
Michigan, University of, 31, 93, 181
Microsoft, 48, 49, 73, 74, 82, 147, 225
  Global Technical Engineering Center of, 73
  offshoring practice and, 77–78
middle class, 82, 93, 193, 197
  Chinese, 58–59, 141–43
  and fear of job losses, 76–77
  globalization and, 13
  Indian, 119, 122, 125, 136
  offshoring and, 86
Middle East, 165, 169, 175, 206–7
Mindspace boomtown, 81–82

Mohali, India, 92
Mongolia, 174
Monsanto, 120
Morgan Stanley, 34, 53, 60, 84, 191, 203, 210
Motorola, 56, 64, 130
Motown Records, 106
Mumbai, India, 81–82, 88, 89
  religious rivalry in, 130
Murthy, Narayana, 46–49, 51, 56, 81, 82, 86, 117, 136
Muslims, 129–30, 164, 175, 177
Myanmar (Burma), 165, 167–68, 172
Mysore, India, 46

Naidu, N. Chandrababu, 51–52
Nanking, rape of, 149
nanotechnology, 209, 211
NASSCOM, 48
Nath, Kamal, 53–57
National Association of Software and Service Companies, 87
National Bureau of Statistics (China), 181
National Health Service, British, 84
nationalism:
  Chinese, 149–50, 157, 178, 199
  economic, 41–42
  Indian, 41–42
National Rural Employment Act (India, 2005), 134
National Science Foundation, 208
National Security Council, U.S., 181
natural gas, 161–62, 164–66, 168
natural resources, 160, 161–66
Navy, U.S., 171
NEC, 139
Nehru, Jawaharlal, 12, 41–45, 46, 49, 52, 55, 135
  legacy of, 41–45, 91

neoIT, 81
Nepal, 177
Netherlands, 59, 105
New Balance, 98
New Delhi, India, 47
New Orleans, La., 127, 207
New York Times, 166
New Zealand, 149
Nigeria, 166
Nike, 41, 101
Nilekani, Nandan, 46, 56, 117, 118, 120–21, 134, 135–36, 212
Ningbo, China, 105
Noamundi, India, 161
Nobel Peace Prize, 167
Nokia, 54, 64, 130
Nordstrom, 120
Nortel, 120
Norwich Union, 84
Novell, 41
Nuclear Nonproliferation Treaty, 168
nuclear power, 165–66, 172, 184

offshoring, 76–96, 200, 201, 202, 210, 211
  biotechnology industry and, 88–89
  "bottom of the pyramid" products and, 93–94
  Commerce Department mission and, 78
  competition for jobs and, 82
  concealed jobs and, 86–97
  economic growth and, 88–89
  emergence of, 80
  foreign investment and, 90–91
  in India, 77–78
  Infosys and, 81–83
  infrastructure and, 89–90
  Internet and modern technology and, 79–80

offshoring (*continued*)
Microsoft and, 77–78
Mindspace boomtown and, 81–82
number of jobs involved in, 84–85
spinoff jobs and, 88–89
tech bubble and, 81
as third industrial revolution, 85
three ways of, 78–79
U.S. middle class and, 86
wages and, 79, 83–84, 87, 125
Western job losses and, 83–86
women and, 123–24
Y2K scare and, 80
Ogilvy & Mather, 144
Ohmae, Kenichi, 147–48
oil, 13, 45, 160, 161–63, 175, 185, 207
China's military buildup and, 171–72
foreign policy and, 164–66
U.S. conservation of, 163–64
Oil of Olay, 141
Olympics of 2008, 157–58, 179
one-child policy, 32, 183
100–Yen stores, 192
Oracle, 48
Oregon, 184
Otis Elevators, 41
outsourcing, 78, 111, 118

Pakistan, 98, 129, 103, 165, 174
India and, 176–77
Palmisano, Samuel J., 77–78
Patni Computer Systems, 46
People's Bank of China, 69
People's Daily, 23
People's Liberation Army, Chinese, 169
PepsiCo, 120
Peres, Shimon, 211

permafrost peace, 173, 186
PetroChina, 71
petroleum, *see* oil
Philippines, 83, 202
Philips Electronics, 54, 58–59, 61, 74, 77, 105
India investment of, 77–78, 92–93
"Innovation Campus" of, 94–95
Malu factory of, 63–64
Mohali factory of, 92–93
Pierre Hotel, 51
Pinedale, Wyoming, 162
Pizza Hut, 123
Poland, 85
pollution, 31, 160, 178–81, 183–85, 233
across borders, 184–85
air, 31, 179–80, 183
in Beijing, 179–80
in Bombay, 180
in China, 31, 33, 178–81
in India, 179–80
water, 31, 180–81
Porsche, 120
PortalPlayer, 102
poverty, 106, 219
"bottom of the pyramid" products and, 93–94
in China, 146–47
in India, 82, 88, 124, 125–28, 134–35
offshoring business model and, 134
Prada, 70
Prahalad, C. K., 93
Princeton University, 83
Procter & Gamble, 44
Progressive Policy Institute, 101
protectionism, 199, 200–203, 205
Pudong Software Park, 148

Putin, Vladimir, 154, 234
Pu Yi, 166

Qian Jun, 148
Qiao Jian, 74
Quadrennial Defense Review
    Report, 171, 173
Qualcomm, 56
Qualiman Industrial Company,
    15
Quanta Computer, 105

Ramachandran, Ram, 94
RAND Corporation, 170, 172
Rao, Narayan, 40–41, 49
Rao, P. V. Narasimha, 38–39, 40,
    46–47, 49
Red Guards, 35
Rediff Matchmaker, 124
Reebok, 41, 120
Reliance Industries, 131, 136
renminbi, Chinese, 175, 195–96
Republicans, U.S., 203
Reserve Bank of India, 39–40, 46
retraining, 210–11
Ricoh, 139
Roach, Stephen, 34, 191, 203, 210
Robert Bosch company, 130
Rubin, Robert, 188, 189–90, 191,
    203–4, 207, 234
rupee, Indian, 40, 46
Russia, 164, 165, 166, 172, 174,
    175
Rust Bowl, 203

Sadar, Negi Singh, 125–26
SARS, 152
satellites, 173
Satyam Computer Services, 148
Saudi Arabia, 166
Seagate Technology, 104–5
"sea turtles" (hai gui pai), 74
Sen, Amartya, 126

September 11, 2001 terrorist
    attacks, 164, 169, 175
Shaadi.com, 124
Shanghai, China, 28, 29, 30, 34,
    51, 58–59, 62, 63, 70–71,
    73, 104, 147, 150, 182
  Pudong region of, 139
  Pudong Software Park of, 148
  Tomorrow Square of, 144
Shanghai Art Museum, 144
Shanghai Cooperation Organiza-
    tion, 174
Shanxi Shuofang Flax Textile
    Company, 112
Sharma, Nisha, 124, 128
Sharp, 139
Shenyang, China, 63
Shenzhen, China, 30, 51, 102,
    147
Shiseido, 141
Shuozhou, China, 111–14
Sichuan Province, 115, 220
Siemens, 81, 117, 139
Silk Road, 14, 66, 79, 160, 223
Singapore, 24, 25, 27, 49, 51, 84,
    95, 156
  Deng's visit to, 22–23
Singh, Manmohan, 39–40, 47, 52,
    54, 136–37, 160
single aristocrats (dan shen qui
    zu), 142
Sinha, Alpana, 120
Sinopec, 36, 165
soda ash, 162
Soe Win, 167
solar power, 183
Sony, 119, 148
South Africa, 184
South America, 60, 165
Southeast Asia, 60
Soviet Union, 18, 23, 27, 42, 154,
    165, 173, 174, 185
  Chernobyl disaster in, 184

Soviet Union (*continued*)
  collapse of, 25–26, 45, 185
  India's barter relationship with, 45
soybeans, 166–67
Spain, 64
special economic zones, 23–24, 27, 30, 54–55, 135
Spice Route, 14, 59, 160, 223
Spielberg, Steven, 157
Srinivasan, Chandramowli, 84
Starbucks Coffee, 36, 143–44
"state" capitalism, 31
State Environmental Protection Administration, Chinese, 181, 185
steel industry, 19, 43, 51, 57, 161, 162
Strait of Malacca, 171–72
Sudan, 165
  Darfur genocide in, 166
Sun Microsystems, 148
supply chain management, *see* disassembly line
supply chains, 99–100, 103, 111, 201
Supreme Court, Indian, 183
Suzhou, China, 105
Swadeshi Mills, 43
Sybase, 188–89, 204

Taiwan, 23, 24, 68, 95, 100, 110, 148, 149, 155
  China's dispute with, 177–78
  independence movement of, 175
Tajikistan, 174
Taj Mahal (hotel), 43
"tank man," 26, 33
tapped-out class (*yue guang zu*), 142
Target, 115
Tata, Jamsetji, 43, 57

Tata, J. R. D., 43, 51
Tata, Ratan, 50–51, 95
Tata Air Lines, 55
Tata Chemicals, 131
Tata Consultancy Services, 78, 95
Tata Group, 43, 131, 136, 222
  farm center network of, 131–32
  Voltas unit of, 50–51
Tata Steel, 43, 50, 57, 161, 223
TCS, 82
technology industry, 46–47, 53–54
telecommunications industry, 56
terrorism, 108, 129–30, 164, 175, 176, 204
Tetley Teas, 51
textile industry, 131
Thailand, 100, 114
Thite, Nalani, 86
Three Gorges Dam, 55
Tiananmen Square massacre, 26–27, 32–33, 153, 155, 168, 220
Tianjin, China, 111, 181
Tibet, 175
"T.I.C.," 63
Times of India, 56
Tomorrow Square, 144
Toshiba, 120
toy industry, 15–16
Toyota, 91, 100, 201
trans-border shipment, 97–98, 107–8
Trans Global Logistics, 98, 115
trona, 162
tsunami disaster of 2004, 172
24/7 Customer, 123
Tyco International, 235

UBS, 84, 120
unemployment, 85, 86, 90, 117, 127, 162, 191
Union Pacific Railroad, 84

United Auto Workers, 102
United Kingdom, *see* Great
  Britain
United Nations, 164, 165–66,
  168, 175
United States, 12–13, 15, 18, 37,
  42, 50, 57, 62, 64, 70, 73,
  74, 95, 104, 107–9, 110,
  116, 118, 131, 132, 182,
  185, 186
  advantages and resources of,
    204–5
  basic research in, 208–9
  budget deficit of, 206–7
  can-do spirit of, 204–5
  China investments by compa-
    nies of, 10, 60, 65–66
  China's currency rate contro-
    versy and, 195–96
  China's military challenge to,
    173–74
  China's trade deficit with, 67
  China-Taiwan dispute and,
    177–78
  China trade dependency of,
    198–200
  Chinese Nationalism and,
    149–50
  college graduates in, 84
  competitive challenge and,
    209–13
  current account deficit of, 235
  deteriorating infrastructure of,
    207–8
  diplomatic inconsistencies of,
    168–69
  economic unpreparedness of,
    190–91, 197
  education system of, 190,
    204–7, 208, 211, 219
  European aid of (1947–1953),
    219
  Europe's schism with, 164

  future economy of, 160
  GDP of, 145, 209
  housing market of, 198
  "impersonal services" and, 83
  Indian culture and, 122–23
  innovation in, 208–9
  interstate highway of, 28
  middle class of, 86, 193
  military budget of, 171, 232,
    233
  military hegemony of, 170–74
  nuclear aid to India by, 168,
    175–76
  offshoring practice and, 79,
    84–86
  oil conservation in, 163–64
  paradox of job losses and,
    191–92
  savings and loan crisis in, 68,
    224
  savings rate of, 141, 197, 207
  stressed financial foundations
    of, 206–8
  tsunami of 2004 and, 172
  unemployment rate of, 197
University of the Pacific, 36
untouchable caste (*dalits*), 129
UPS, 97, 104–5
U2 (band), 167
Uzbekistan, 174

Vajpayee, Atal Bihari, 9–10, 11,
  16, 52, 55
  in 2004 election, 134
Venezuela, 164, 165, 166, 175
Vicks VapoRub, 44
Vietnam, 83, 104, 107, 196
Volkswagen, 61

Wal-Mart, 11, 98, 159, 195, 200,
  201
  Chinese imports of, 102
  paradoxical success of, 191–92

Walter, Carl, 28–29
Washington Alliance of Technology Workers, 86
Washington State, 184
water pollution, 31, 180–81
Welch, Jack, 50–51
Wen Jiabao, 167
Whirlpool, 50
wind power, 181, 183–84
Wipro Technologies, 41, 49, 54, 78, 81, 82, 89
Woolworth's, 192
World Bank, 94, 107, 179, 180
World Health Organization, 179, 180
World Trade Organization (WTO), 63
Worldwatch Institute, 163
Wuxi, China, 104
Wyoming, 162

Xiaogang, China, 16–17, 19, 21, 35

xiao zi (little capitalists), 142
Xie, Andy, 60
Xie Xiaoyan, 171
Xie Zhenhua, 181
Xinhua (media outlet), 181
Xinjiang Province, 175

Yahoo, 84, 152
Yang, Robbie, 149
Yangtze River, 181
Yao Ming, 149
Yasukuni shrine, 177
Yeh, Ying, 141
Ye Lu, 139
yi zi er shi practice, 19
Y2K scare, 80
yue guang zu (tapped-out class), 142
yuppies (you pi), 142

Zhao Ziyang, 220
Zhu Rongji, 49, 222
Zweig, David, 22